A Pictorial History of the Automobile

by
Peter Roberts

Publishers   •   **GROSSET & DUNLAP**   •   New York
A FILMWAYS COMPANY

This book is for my nephews Paul Roberts and Stephen Manley.
Long may their interest in cars continue . . .

Contents

Acknowledgments

The author, editor, and publishers are deeply grateful to the following companies and other organizations which have helped compile this book by making available many old, historic, and sometimes rare photographs: Alfa Romeo, American Motors, Aston Martin, Automobile Association, Berliet, Bristol Cars, British Leyland, Chrysler (UK, F, and USA), Citroën, Daimler-Benz, Detroit Public Library, Fiat, Firestone, Ford (GB and USA), General Motors, Goodyear Tire, Jaguar Cars, Kodak, Lancia, Lotus Cars, Mercedes-Benz (GB), Motor Vehicle Manufacturers Association (USA), National Motor Museum, Opel, Peugeot, Punch, Renault, Rolls-Royce, Royal Automobile Club, Shell (Mex and BP), Skoda, Society of Motor Manufacturers, Vauxhall, Veteran Car Club of Great Britain, and Volvo . . .

. . . to the many friends and colleagues, including John Conde, R. P. Stowers, G. N. Georgano, James Bradley, James Wren, Tim Cullen, John Maciarz, Harry Calton, H. D. Shraerer, Karl-Heinz Scheuling, Alfred Woolf, Felix Schön, and Ronald Hall, who have spent time and energy in helping to locate illustrations, or who have supplied photographs from their collections; to Michael Worthington-Williams and Anthony Davis for their editorial contributions; and to Betty Athey for her able assistance in the production of this book . . .

. . . to the following contributors of private and club photographs:

A. B. Demaus	Santler, page 27
	Gobron-Brillie, page 134
	Vulcan, page 136
	Stevens-Duryea, page 147
	Castle Three, page 177
	Santler Rushabout, page 183
	A.C., page 209
A. Farrar of The Riley Motor Club	Riley, pages 27, 271
J. R. Davy and the Standard Register	Standard, pages 135, 147, 237, 272, 284
G. Lee and The Crossley Register	Crossley, page 156
D. E. A. Evans	Star, pages 159, 237
Howe B. Willis, the Issotta-Fraschini Owners Association	Isotta-Fraschini, page 190
Eugene E. Hustings	Kissel, page 204
G. N. Georgano	Walter, page 277
	Aero, page 285
	Tatra, page 294
	Skoda, page 298
A. Wood, Rapier Register	Lagonda, page 268
B. McKenzie, Railton Owners Club	Railton, page 283
P. Robertson	Alvis, page 280
R. W. May, The Allard Register	Allard, pages 290, 328, 344
The Austin Healey Club	Page 339
M. Worthington-Williams	Page 353
Roger Stower	Aston Martin, page 374

. . . and to The Automobile Association for furnishing the list of International Registration Letters.

International Registration Letters
established by international conventions and/or as notified to the United Nations

A	Austria	H	Hungary	RCB	Congo (Brazzaville)
ADN	Democratic Yemen (formerly Aden)*1	HK	Hong Kong*	RCH	Chile
		HKJ	Jordan	RH	Haiti
AFG	Afghanistan2			RI	Indonesia*
AL	Albania	I	Italy	RIM	Mauritania2
AND	Andorra	IL	Israel	RL	Lebanon
AUS	Australia*	IND	India*	RM	Malagasy Republic (formerly Madagascar)
		IR	Iran2		
B	Belgium	IRL	Ireland, Republic of*	RMM	Mali
BDS	Barbados*	IRQ	Iraq2	RNR	Zambia (formerly Northern Rhodesia)*1 5
BG	Bulgaria	IS	Iceland		
BH	British Honduras			ROK	Korea, Republic of
BR	Brazil	J	Japan*	RSM	San Marino
BRN	Bahrain	JA	Jamaica*	RSR	Rhodesia (formerly Southern Rhodesia)*1
BRU	Brunei*				
BS	Bahamas*	K	Khmer Republic (formerly Cambodia)	RU	Burundi2
BUR	Burma			RWA	Rwanda
		KWT	Kuwait2		
C	Cuba2			S	Sweden
CDN	Canada	L	Luxembourg	SD	Swaziland*
CH	Switzerland	LAO	Laos	SF	Finland
CI	Ivory Coast	LAR	Libya2	SGP	Singapore*
CL	Sri Lanka (formerly Ceylon)*1	LB	Liberia2	SME	Surinam (Dutch Guiana)*
		LS	Lesotho (formerly Basutoland)*	SN	Senegal
CO	Colombia2			SU	Union of Soviet Socialist Republics
CR	Costa Rica				
CS	Czechoslovakia	M	Malta*	SWA	South West Africa*2 4
CY	Cyprus*	MA	Morocco	SY	Seychelles*
		MAL	Malaysia*	SYR	Syria
D	Germany2	MC	Monaco		
DK	Denmark	MEX	Mexico	T	Thailand*
DOM	Dominican Republic	MS	Mauritius*	TG	Togo
DY	Dahomey	MW	Malawi (formerly Nyasaland)*	TN	Tunisia
DZ	Algeria			TR	Turkey
				TT	Trinidad and Tobago*
E	Spain (including African localities and provinces)	N	Norway	U	Uruguay
		NA	Netherlands Antilles	USA	United States of America
EAK	Kenya*	NIC	Nicaragua		
EAT	Tanzania (formerly Tanganyika)*1	NIG	Niger	V	Holy See (Vatican City)
		NL	Netherlands	VN	Vietnam, Republic of
EAU	Uganda*	NZ	New Zealand*		
EAZ	Tanzania (formerly Zanzibar)*1 3			WAG	Gambia
		P	Portugal (including Angola, Cape Verde Islands, Mozambique*, Portuguese Guinea, Portuguese Timor, São Tomé, and Príncipe)	WAL	Sierra Leone
EC	Ecuador			WAN	Nigeria
ET	Arab Republic of Egypt			WD	Dominica*2 } Windward Islands
				WG	Grenada* }
F	France (including overseas departments and territories)			WL	St. Lucia2
		PA	Panama2	WS	Western Samoa*
FJI	Fiji*	PAK	Pakistan*	WV	St Vincent (Windward Islands)*
FL	Liechtenstein2	PE	Peru		
		PI	Philippines	YU	Yugoslavia
GB	United Kingdom of Great Britain and Northern Ireland*	PL	Poland	YV	Venezuela
		PY	Paraguay		
GBA	Alderney* } Channel Islands			Z	See RNR
GBG	Guernsey* }	R	Romania	ZA	South Africa*
GBJ	Jersey* }	RA	Argentina	ZR	Zaire (formerly Congo Kinshasha)
GBM	Isle of Man*2	RB	Botswana (formerly Bechuanaland)*		
GBZ	Gibraltar				
GCA	Guatemala	RC	China, National Republic of (Formosa)		
GH	Ghana				
GR	Greece	RCA	Central African Republic		
GUY	Guyana*				

* In countries marked with an asterisk, the rule of the road is drive on the left; otherwise drive on the right.

Notes
1 Established under former country name
2 Not included in the United Nations' list of signs established according to the 1949 Convention on Road Traffic
3 The letters EAT are also used
4 The letters ZA are also used
5 The letter Z is also used

List of Abbreviations

A.A.A. — American Automobile Association

bhp — brake horse power

cc — cubic centimeters

cu in — cubic inches

cv — cheval vapeur

fwd — front wheel drive

G.P. — Grand Prix

ifs — independent front suspension

irs — independent rear suspension

NACC — National Automobile Chamber of Commerce (USA)

ohc — overhead camshaft

ohv — overhead valves

RAC — Royal Automobile Club (GB)

sv — side valve

T.T. — Tourist Trophy

Note: the abbreviation in parenthesis following a caption indicates the automobile's International Registration Letters. See the preceding page for list of abbreviations used.

DAWN OF THE AUTOMOBILE AGE: 1769-1885

From the ancient Greeks, through the time of Leonardo da Vinci, to the steam pioneers of the late eighteenth century, it had been the impossible dream of man to improve on the energies whipped out of a horse, ox, steer, or other beast of burden and by mechanical means to provide transport that either utilized forces in natural state, or a fuel that, when brought under control, would furnish a fleeter chariot than the next.

To hot air, falling weights, clockwork, wind power, passenger muscle, and gunpowder they applied their wits—Jesuit priests of the fifteenth century, physicists from Holland, noblemen of Switzerland, and engineers of Italy. All labored, with varying degrees of failure, to uncover a method of propelling a vehicle capable of carrying its inventor. But the names of Huygens; of Volta, who succeeded in igniting a gas mixure with an electric spark; of Frenchman Lebon; of Englishman Murdock; and of de Rivaz, who was granted patents as early as 1807 for a combustion engine for road vehicles, are set in the halls of history and fame as pioneers whose efforts edged us ever nearer the machine age. We must honor them for their work. Perhaps we must also forgive them, for they knew not what legacy they were leaving us.

Stationary steam engines were fairly commonly used for winches and pumps by the time the first genuine road vehicle was built in 1769 by Nicholas-Joseph Cugnot and offered as an innovation to the French army—"a carriage moved by the effect of steam produced by fire." That Cugnot built his wagon for the army is undoubted fact. The various reports of what happened after it started to rumble its dinosaur way down the Paris streets, on test, is now a confusion of legend, but it almost certainly demolished a garden wall en route.

Shortly afterward the clanking, steamy dawn of motoring moved to England and Cornwall, where engineer Richard Trevithick fabricated something between a mail coach and a railway locomotive. In 1801 (the year that Cugnot's machine was finally consigned to the Musée des Arts et Metiers in Paris, where it still resides) Trevithick took out a party of friends in his contraption. One described the journey thus: "We jumped up, as many as could, maybe seven or eight of us, when we see's that Captain Dick was agoing to turn on steam... 'twas a stiffish hill but she went off like a bird, and up the hill as fast as a man could walk." However, Britain's first motorist absent-mindedly left the boiler fire on one night, and the whole thing went up in smoke.

Thence to the steam-bus companies that first used Britain's improved post-Napoleonic War roads, setting up a network of relatively fast transport by around 1830. By 1835 they were being forced out of business, as stagecoach and railway companies put on parliamentary and private pressure that caused the tolls for steam business to be levied at something like twelve times those for horse-drawn vehicles. In France steam was also being developed, but without the crippling legislation that England stamped on its first "automobile" ventures.

Stationary engines using coal (town) gas had been in regular use since 1861, at first operating somewhat feebly without a compression stroke. Efficiency was vastly raised in 1876 when German engineer Otto built in a fourth stroke for squeezing the mixture before ignition, giving us the conventional four-cycle unit. At the Gasmotoren-Fabrik Deutz in Germany, then beginning to produce the new Otto four-cycle engine, thirty-eight-year-old Gottlieb Daimler was chief engineer.

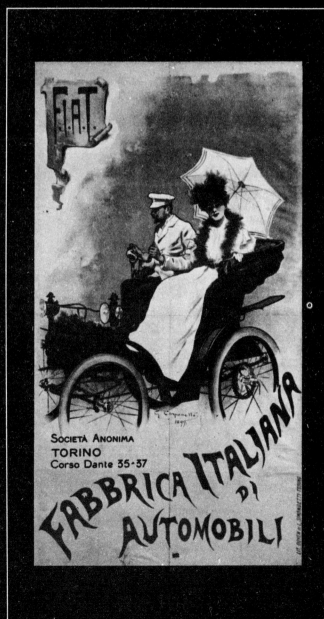

SOCIETÀ ANONIMA
TORINO
Corso Dante 35-37

FABBRICA ITALIANA DI AUTOMOBILI

Although a primitive form of steam power can be traced back to the ancient Greeks, Frenchman Nicholas Cugnot's 1769 steam tractor is generally accepted as the first mechanically propelled road vehicle. Commissioned by the army, the heavy tractor was designed to tow field guns. Cugnot's "improved" vehicle of two years later caused the world's first motor accident when it ran into a wall.

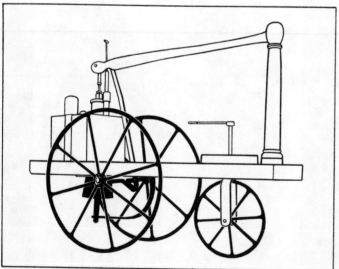

In England James Watt had been making stationary steam engines. His assistant, Will Murdock, built a miniature steamer and tried it out in 1784. It hissed and bubbled down the road in the evening gloom and almost frightened the local vicar to an early death.

The next step toward a practical road vehicle was taken by Cornishman Richard Trevithick. His high-wheeled steam coach may have looked more like a locomotive than a carriage, but it worked. Trevithick drove it from Cornwall to London in 1802, where he displayed it to an unenthusiastic public. It burned to a shell when he forgot to extinguish the boiler fire one night.

THE NEW STEAM CARRIAGE.

During the 1820s, road-building work in Britain encouraged steam-coach companies to be formed, and numbers of routes were covered by the large steamers of the time. In the 1830s and 1840s, the heyday of steam coaches, regular passenger-carrying routes networked England. One of the operators, Sir Goldsworthy Gurney, produced this formidable vehicle, which was said to be able to travel at 8 to 10 mph.

After the large steam-driven coaches were legislated off the roads of Britain, smaller steam cars began to appear, usually operating in defiance of the law. A partnership of engineers, Catley and Ayres, produced this three-wheeler wagonette around 1870.

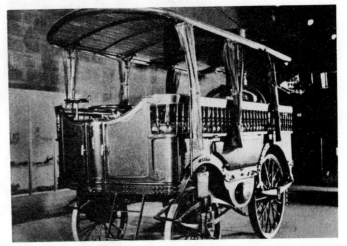

Amédée Bollée, bell founder of France, made this steam masterpiece in 1873 and called it "L'Obeissante," the obedient one. A tall, twelve-passenger bus, it was so impressive that the Minister of Works allowed it to use the highway provided Bollée gave three days advance warnings of his journeys.

The Comte de Dion met Georges Bouton in the early 1880s after buying a miniature steam engine that had fascinated him. He had learned that it was manufactured by a company making toy engines and working models for showcases, owned by Bouton and his brother-in-law. Together de Dion and Bouton made steam cars, some of them highly successful. This is one of the larger, built in 1885.

This Grenville steam carriage had a single cylinder when first made in 1875, but, as this was found to be unsatisfactory, a 2-cylinder unit was employed. The single front wheel turned on a vertically pivoted shaft, and the rear axle was driven by exposed gears. A top speed of 15 mph was claimed, but, as a contemporary report said: ". . . much depends on the efficiency of the stoker . . ."

One of the smaller de Dion, Bouton et Trepardoux vehicles (Trepardoux was Bouton's brother-in-law and made the boilers)—a steam tricycle with a single rear driving wheel, a spade steering handle, and a boiler over the front assembly so that the driver could keep his eye on it.

The Years of Promise:
1886-1899

Karl Benz was the complete automobile engineer and a practical businessman. He had worked on an engine designed to be an integral part of the total design of a road vehicle. Gottlieb Daimler was an equally skilled engineer, but had directed his efforts to an engine of universal application. He installed his first engine in a motorcycle, then a carriage. The following year, 1886, a small, self-propelled riverboat could be seen on the Neckar, and later a Daimler-engined airship made a maiden flight of four kilometers (2½ miles).

By means of a license to build Daimler engines, a death in the family, and a subsequent marriage, the French company of Panhard and Levassor became the first gasoline-engined automobile manufacturer in France — closely followed by Armand Peugeot, who built a car around the same power unit. By 1892 both companies were selling their products, and by 1894—the year of the first motor-sport event—motoring was established in France as a fashionable method of taking one's morning constitution in the Bois.

Benz had been on the French scene even earlier. One of his early models had been bought by Emile Roger, Benz' representative for stationary two-cycle engines in France (and who, curiously, kept it at the works of Panhard and Levassor), and in 1888 he started to sell, then assemble, Benz cars in France, under the name of Roger-Benz.

It took very little longer for American engineers to catch the fever, although for more practical reasons than the leisured European motoring set. Reliable transport over the vast reaches of the American continent was desperately needed, and "could transform life both social and commercial, if only the roads could be improved to accommodate the new vehicles," as one writer put it in 1897. The roads were not improved, but by 1900 no less than 8,000 private cars used them.

Britain needed a sort of gentlemanly revolution to get its automotive industry off the ground. An Act of Parliament that restricted speeds to 4 mph demanded that a pedestrian with a red flag should precede all vehicles, reducing their use to merely another way of saving boot leather. The Act was repealed in 1896 because of popular pressure in Parliament, but until that date it had delayed any serious participation in the infant industry that was to change the face of the world.

And so to the twentieth century. The years of the dreamers were over; man could now travel under a power many times superior to that of the horse— although, as often as not, he was less certain of reaching his destination. Mechanical layout was already that of the modern car—the 1891 Panhard had pioneered this—and the motor car actually worked. By the end of the nineteenth century the motor men were beginning to think not simply in terms of making the thing go, but of making it go well—there and back again.

1896 BELLO

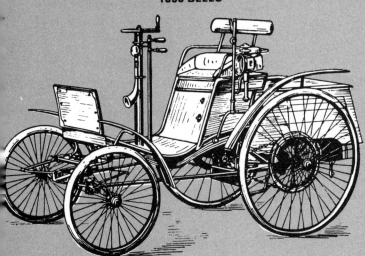

1896 BENZ MERTE

The Years of Promise: 1886-1899

The fathers of the automobile are legion, but two men are recognized as the first to build practical gasoline-driven cars: Karl Benz and Gottlieb Daimler. This is the first Benz Motorwagen, built in 1885 and patented on January 29, 1886. Its four-stroke, 1-cylinder engine produced 0.8 hp at 250 rpm. (D)

In 1886 Daimler also built, in some secrecy, the world's first motorboat, which was powered by his vertical, single-cylinder engine. At first he disguised it with insulators and draped it with wires to suggest electrical power.

Within an hour's drive in a modern car from the Benz workshop, Daimler had made a primitive motocycle, and in 1885 he was building a four-wheel vehicle based on a carriage body. In April 1886 his motor carriage was successfully tried out on public roads near Cannstatt, Germany. (D)

The historic workshop at Bad Cannstatt in which Swabian Gottlieb Daimler built his first "single-track" vehicle and his 1886 horseless carriage.

Karl Benz, grand old man of the automobile. The photograph shows Benz in his first car during a celebration in 1925 in which a vast motorcade of vehicles drove past his house in his honor. He died on April 4, 1929.

Benz envisaged a motor vehicle in its entirety; Daimler was an engine man whose dream was to propel various kinds of transport mechanically. This is part of his airship, built in 1888 and successfully piloted on a maiden flight of 2½ miles.

A Devon farmer's son, Edward Butler, drew up plans and took out a patent for "the mechanical propulsion of bicycles" in 1884 and produced his first machine in 1888, which he drove at 12 mph. It had a four-stroke engine with double rotary valves and an advanced jet-spray carburetor, many years ahead of its time. Unhappily, this machine was never commercially developed. (GB)

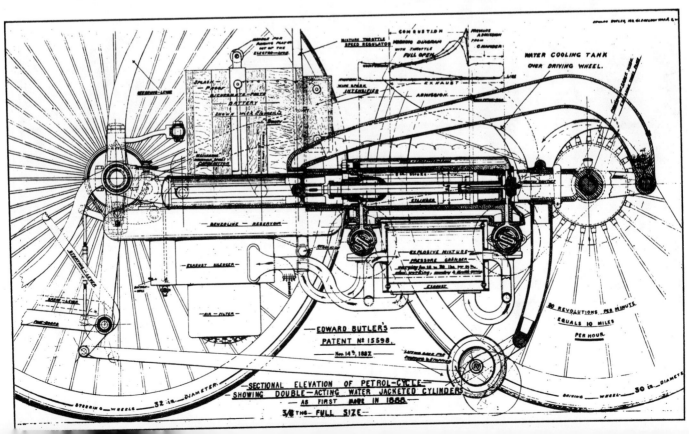

For many years this vehicle was accepted as the oldest surviving motor vehicle and was assumed to have been built in 1875. Recently, however, it was re-dated, after new evidence came to light in Austria, the country of its builder, Siegfried Markus, and it is now known to have been made no earlier than 1888. (A)

By 1889 Daimler had installed a twin-cylinder V engine into his new wire-wheel car, a light two-seater that broke away from the carriage tradition and showed a strong bicycle influence in its steel-tube frame—through which the cooling water circulated. (D)

Early Benz publicity material entitled *A Complete Substitute for Carriage with Horses*. Said an editorial in the *Scientific American* of January 5, 1889: "This motor is driven by gas which it generates from benzine or analogous material.... The motor ... is placed in the rear of the three-wheeled carriage over the main axle, and the benzine ... is carried in a closed copper receptacle secured under the seat from which it passes drop by drop to the generator...." (D)

René Panhard and Emile Levassor were partners in a woodwork machinery business. When Levassor married the widow of the only Daimler engine licensee in France, the stage was set for automobile production in that country. This dos-à-dos (back-to-back) was engineer Levassor's first attempt, made in 1890. Panhard is on the extreme left. (F)

In June 1891 the second Panhard-Levassor car was ready. "With Levassor conducting, the vehicle was driven," says a contemporary report, "as far as Etretat ... and home again without much trouble. His average was 10 km/h sometimes touching 17 km/h in spite of petrol that did no good to the sparking plugs." This was the first car to use a front-mounted engine, a new layout which set the classic pattern for over eighty years. (F)

Meanwhile, French bicycle-maker Armand Peugeot had seen Panhard's Daimler V-2 engine and had installed it in a machine of his own design. By 1891 it was sufficiently practical to follow a cycle race from Paris to Brest, on the west coast of France, and back. His quadricycle-type car averaged about 10 mph and was outpaced by most of the cyclists. However, this trip made history as the longest journey undertaken by a car at that date. (F)

By 1888 Benz had received favorable reports in the European and American press, but not one German buyer had come forward. When Emile Roger started to assemble Benz cars in France, business began to boom, and by 1891 the Patent-Motor-Wagen side of the Benz company (stationary engines were still the mainstay of the firm) had been given fresh impetus. This is an 1891 product. (D)

Second-generation Panhard-Levassor. Seen here on his 1892 car are René Panhard and his children. This car had four forward speeds, selected from an exposed-to-air transmission. (F)

French automobile pioneer René Panhard. The layout of the early Panhard-Levassors—vertical front engine, followed by transmission, and driven rear wheels— soon became famous as "The Panhard System." Levassor's epithet, "C'est brusque et brutal, mais ca marche!" ("It's rough and brutish, but it goes!") became equally famous in the annals of motor history.

In Armand Peugeot's first year of production five cars were made. The following year this Victoria was produced by Les Fils de Peugeot Frères, as the new company was called. This elegant vehicle had four seats, a twin-cylinder power unit of 1,282-cc capacity, a leather cone clutch, and a claimed top speed of 30 km/h (18½ mph), which, if true, put it in a class of its own. Eighteen of these were made at the factory in Beaulieu-Valentigney. (F)

Traditional setting in the Schwartzwald for an 1892 4-hp Daimler two-seater. That year Daimler began to install his twin-cylinder, in-line power unit in his cars, the more efficient engine finally supplanting his V-twin. (D)

The Years of Promise: 1886-1899

Meanwhile, back in Mannheim, Germany, Karl Benz was manufacturing a Viktoria, his first four-wheel model. He did not name it in honor of the British Queen, but in celebration of his victory over basic steering problems associated with four-wheel vehicles. His patent states that it was a "steering mechanism for a car with steering circles set at a tangent to the wheels"—kingpin steering, earlier developed by Georg Lanckensperger, coachbuilder to the royal court of Bavaria. (D)

Two years later, in 1893, from the Viktoria emerged the Benz Velo—the world's first standard production car, the first "small" car, and a step toward the goal of many later manufacturers—a "people's car." With a top speed of 12 mph, the Velo soon became the best-known of the Benz cars. It proved to be a stimulus for other car manufacturers throughout the world. (D)

A family picnic in the woods. Karl Benz (light suit) and his family are on the left; Baron von Liebig and his family are on the right. The cars are Viktorias. (D)

18

In 1894 a French newspaper, *Le Petit Journal*, organized the first motor-sport event in automobile history. The contest, a trial of reliability from Paris to Rouen, was designed to encourage the use of automobiles as a means of arriving at a destination, as well as to promote the joys of traveling. Over twenty entrants left the starting line, and the prize was divided between a Peugeot and a Panhard as the most economic and reliable vehicles to take part. This is a Peugeot break (or braker) posing for an admiring crowd before the start of the 79-mile marathon. (F)

Three competitors in the Paris-Rouen Reliability Trial of 1894, as seen by a contemporary artist. Maurice La Blant's steam bus with seats for nine (this large vehicle spent much of its time during the event picking up drivers of disabled cars); No. 15, the neat two-seater Peugeot; and a Panhard four-seater with "four-poster" draperies. (F)

Competitor No. 4 in the Paris to Rouen event, the de Dion steam tractor, with passenger trailer. It arrived first at Rouen but was dropped to second place, as it needed a crew of two. Said the announcement in *Le Petit Journal:* "SECOND PRIZE (2000 Francs) awarded to Messrs De Dion, Bouton et Cie, for their interesting steam tractor which draws a carriage like a horse and develops (though with a powerful engine it must be admitted) a speed absolutely beyond comparison, especially uphill." (F)

Karl Benz, 1844–1929.

An 1894 belt-driven Daimler vis-a-vis (face-to-face seating) was one of the first automobiles imported into Britain. Belt-drive advantages were chiefly quietness of running and flexibility when starting or when changing speeds. In 1896 Frederick Simms, an English friend of Daimler, gave the Prince of Wales, later King Edward VII of England, his first ride in a belt-driven Daimler, a ride that was to stimulate the first real interest in motoring in Britain. Engine: 2 cylinder, 25 km/h (15½ mph). (D)

Patent-Motor-Wagen Benz „Omnibus".

A hotel bus from the Benz catalog of 1895. (D)

A Daimler-engined Panhard delivery truck of 1895 in the streets of Paris—*a voiture de livraison* steered by a tiller . . . (F)

Gottlieb Daimler,
1834–1900.

. . . and a smart two-seater of the same year. Emile Levassor, Panhard's partner, won, unofficially, the great Paris-Bordeaux Race of 1895 in a similar car. Steering wheels were first seen in Panhards that year. (F)

The Wolseley Sheep Shearing Company of Birmingham, England, for some years had a general manager by the name of Herbert Austin, who by 1895 had built this "improved" Léon Bollée-type three-wheeler, a four-stroke flat-twin. At left is Austin in the driving seat. Austin went on to manufacture his own cars in 1906. (GB)

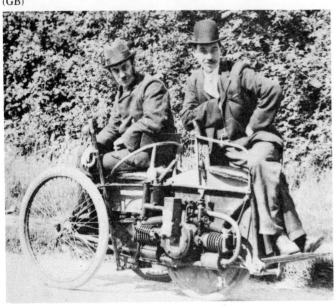

The genuine article, an 1895 Léon Bolée. Bolée suffered from a cardiac disorder and had been told not to ride his pedal bicycle. He decided to motorize it, and this 1-cylinder, horizontal-engined "voiturette" (Bollée's own name for it) was the result. Léon was the son of Amédée Bollée, the bell maker of Le Mans, and builder of the steam car "L'Obeissante" in 1873. (F)

John Henry Knight of Surrey, England, had built steam cars during the late 1860s and by 1895 had made this gasoline-engined car. With its single-cylinder, water-cooled unit it could run at around 9 mph— and the owner was fined by the police for doing exactly that speed on the highway near Farnham, Surrey, in 1896. (GB)

Vis-à-vis Peugeot, 1895–1896. Four-seater with twin-cylinder horizontal engine, capacity 1,056-cc, three forward gears and reverse, speed up to 30 km/h (18½ mph), pneumatic tires, and *consommation* of 18 liters (4½ gallons) to 100 kilometers (62 miles). Les Fils de Peugeot made eighty-seven of these at their Audincourt factory. (F)

America's first practical gasoline-engined automobile, a 4-hp, 1-cylinder high-wheeler made by brothers Charles and Frank Duryea, was first seen in operation on September 21, 1893, in Springfield, Massachusetts. This is the second car built by the Duryea brothers and was photographed during the first American motor race, from Chicago to Evanston on Thanksgiving Day, 1895. Frank Duryea is at the tiller, with umpire Arthur W. White in the derby. (USA)

Almost as soon as the first motor-sport event was over, enthusiastic Frenchmen drew up plans for a second, the 1895 Paris-Bordeaux-Paris race—a real race this time, over the staggering distance of 732 miles. Here a Daimler trundles past a knot of rustic spectators during the long trek. (D)

This car was the prototype Lanchester of 1895-1896, the first commercially successful four-wheeled gasoline car to be made in Great Britain. It was first fitted with tiller steering, but was later converted to steering-wheel control. Said an editor of F. W. Lanchester: "In my view he is the only engineer in the early history of motoring, all the others were just mechanics." Somewhat harsh on the rest perhaps, but "Dr. Fred," as Lanchester was often called, built a sophisticated vehicle without reference to horse-drawn-carriage design or stationary-engine tradition. (GB)

"1895: I constructed a first small car with two seats in tandem, which succeeded in travelling from Lyons to Villefranche and back." So read the notes of Marius Berliet, motor manufacturer of Lyons. This is Berliet No. 1, a quadricycle with a rear horizontal engine and back-seat controls. (F)

In 1896 Edward J. Pennington, a smart young entrepreneur from Chicago, managed, by making greatly exaggerated claims for his design, to sell patents to the newly formed British Motor Syndicate, which was then emulating the American lawyer Selden by buying up almost every patent in sight. The engine was a 2-cylinder, 2-hp 1,868-cc unit, and the passengers sat on bicycle-type seats fastened to the skeletal vehicle. Pennington is at the handlebars. (USA)

A Darracq three-wheeled motorcar of 1896—more like a wheelchair than the real thing. Former bicycle-maker Alexandre Darracq had turned to light cars after selling his French company. After some financial gymnastics, he began to make self-propelled vehicles—motorcycles, tri-cars, and quadricycles. This one shows a strong cycle influence. Darracq also tried his hand, unsuccessfully, at making and selling an electric car. (F)

Lutzmann, 1896: London to Brighton commemoration run. Thought by many to have been denied his rightful place in automotive history, Lutzmann was one of the first German designer-builders after Benz and Daimler: his first models were shown at the 1897 exhibition at Berlin. Here is the 1896 vis-a-vis, driven by a water-cooled, 1-cylinder, horizontal unit of 4 hp, with chain drive. A fine and airy horseless vehicle for the carriage trade of eighty years ago. (D)

Modern motoring as seen by the satirical British magazine *Punch*, 1899.

The belt-driven Daimler arrives in Britain in 1896. This is the vehicle in which England's future king was taken for a spin—and swung the smart social set, who followed his every whim, into the automotive age. (D)

The great Henry Ford in his first car, finished in June 1896—a lightweight, weighing only 500 lbs. Henry had made his first steam engine at fifteen, and in 1893 he began his career as a builder of automobiles when he began to construct a 1-cylinder engine, which sputtered into life on the small kitchen table of his home in Detroit. From it he developed a twin-cylinder engine suitable for fitting in a frame suspended on four bicycle wheels. The vehicle could travel up to 20 mph. (USA)

In the memorandum of the first Olds Motor Vehicle Company directors meeting, August 21, 1897, the company's general manager, Ransom Eli Olds, was instructed "to build one carriage in as nearly perfect a manner as possible and complete it at the earliest possible moment"—a somewhat conflicting order. Oldsmobile has the distinction of being the oldest automobile manufacturer in the United States.

The first gasoline car built by Ransom Eli Olds was this 1-cylinder, 6-hp horseless carriage of 1896, before his new company had been formed. R. E. Olds is at the tiller. (USA)

One of the last of the old-style Daimlers, a Motor Droschke of 1897. From this year Daimler began to develop his Phoenix car, which had a 1.5-liter, vertical, twin-cylinder engine mounted in the front of the vehicle. (D)

This controversial car built by Charles Santler of Malvern Link, Worcestershire, England, was made, so Santler claimed, between 1887 and 1889. However, available evidence puts the date nearer to 1897. It had several features in common with the Benz of the late nineteenth century, with whom Santler is reputed to have worked. Seen here as "discovered" at Newland, near Malvern, in 1909. (GB)

The first Riley car was a one-off voiturette made as an experimental model; belt-driven, single-cylinder. (GB)

The 1898 Benz "Ideal" shown here had a dummy hood that merely covered the water tank. It also had a full-length chassis frame, but still used the streetcar-type steering wheel. A single-cylinder, 1.05-liter engine developed 4.5 hp at 750 rpm and could make a top speed of no less than 40 km/h (24½ mph). (D)

Englishman Charles Jarrott, already a racing cyclist of repute and destined to become a pioneer competition driver in the early twentieth century, is seen at the driving position (rear) on this 3-hp Bollée voiturette in May 1897 before setting off on a Coventry-Birmingham run with the newly formed Motor Car Club. (F)

In the Bois de Boulogne, Paris, July 4, 1898: the flower parade after the Paris Motor Show. Gottlieb Daimler had begun to build trucks two years earlier and this was his 5,000-kg, 10-hp model. Daimler himself is seated on the extreme left. (D)

Automobiles M. Berliet first built rear-engined cars in small numbers. Company records tell us that . . . "The first motors were made feverishly: extremely rustic. The castings were as brittle as a biscuit . . ." A modest 2-cylinder, 1.2-liter unit was used in this, the second model from the Berliet works in Lyons. (F)

Enter a new name in the automotive industry—Adam Opel. The Opel family had been making sewing machines in Russelsheim since 1862, later turning to bicycles. In 1897 Opel's sons acquired production rights of the Lutzmann after seeing a demonstration of the engineer's machine, and in 1898 the first Opel-Lutz- mann (with a great deal of help from the latter) rolled out of the works. Its single-cylinder engine could propel the carriage at a surprising 19 mph and, it was whispered, could bowl it along at 30 on level ground. (D)

A spin in the park, German style. A Daimler Taxame- ter (taxi) posing in the diffused sunshine of Berlin's Grunewald in the spring of 1898. Daimler had set up his own flourishing "Motor Carriage Hire Depot" at Stuttgart, using mainly belt-driven six-seaters from the Daimler stables. (D)

The father of this family is testing the controls of one of the first Wintons, an 1898 two-seater with a single-cylinder engine housed under the driving seat. The previous year Cleveland-born Alex Winton had built an experimental car and had recorded a very creditable 33.7 mph on a 1-mile run. (USA)

Two pretty, young Victorians in a tricycle driven by the British Lawson Motor Wheel. The motor drove the front wheel only, and the assembly could be fitted as a third (motored) wheel to various types of two-wheeled, horse-drawn vehicles. (GB)

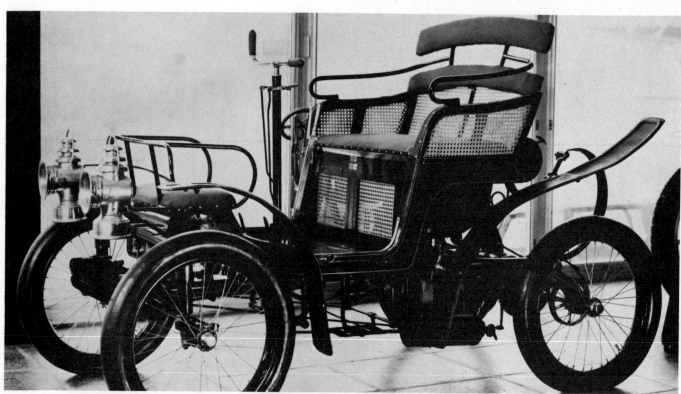

The Eisenach Company of Wartburg, Germany, started in 1898 by building a Decauville under license. The first Wartburgwagen had a 2-cylinder, water-cooled (or air-cooled), rear-mounted engine of 765 cc, developing 5 hp at 1,000 rpm—and the minimum of bodywork. Its reputed top speed was 40 km/h (24½ mph), and it proved highly marketable in Germany at the end of the nineteenth century. (D)

A competing Peugeot in the Marseilles to Nice race of 1898, a distance of 236 km (146 miles). This car, piloted by I. Koechlin, a well-known early competition driver, averaged about 32 mph. This was the start of the town-to-town racing age which saw marathons such as the Paris-Marseilles race, and introduced international events when, later in 1898, the big race of the year went from Paris to Amsterdam and back across the Dutch frontier. (F)

Strictly for town travel—another Peugeot of 1898. This Type 25 was a sort of three-quarter coupe, elegant in style and, say the records, made from 1898 to 1902. The records also state that precisely two were made. Twin-cylinder motor, 6–7 hp. (F)

The first world speed record was established on December 18, 1898, by French Comte Gaston de Chasseloup-Laubat in this exposed carriage, an electrically propelled Jeantaud. The Parisian company had made electric cars since 1893, although an experimental car had been built as early as 1881. The 1898 record of 39.24 mph, set over a single kilometer (½ mile) at Achères, was at once challenged and beaten by Camille Jenatzy, who had built an electric car to his own design. It was recovered a few weeks later with an average speed of 43.69 mph. (F)

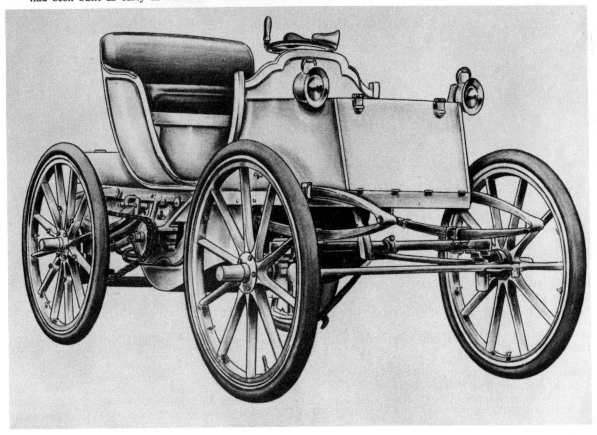

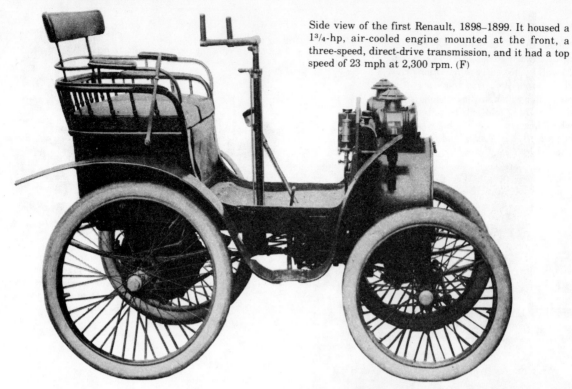

Side view of the first Renault, 1898–1899. It housed a 1³/₄-hp, air-cooled engine mounted at the front, a three-speed, direct-drive transmission, and it had a top speed of 23 mph at 2,300 rpm. (F)

In 1899—the first F.I.A.T. (Fabbrica Italiana Automobili Torino) is seen on the roads of Italy. This was a 3¹/₂-hp, 2-cylinder, rear-engined, 679-cc, chain-driven vis-à-vis typical of the period. Here Count Roberto Biscaretti di Ruffia, one of the founders of the automotive colossus, takes his family out for a ride in the last year of the nineteenth century. (I)

At the 1896 motor show in Britain, Humber displayed their newest product, the Pennington. They later made cars of their own design. Says a brochure of the day: "Horses work for a few hours only, motors keep on incessantly. Horses shy and take fright, motors cannot. Horses tire and go more slowly, motors run full speed day and night. Horses fall down and run lame, motors never slip anywhere!" and so on, listing so-called motor virtues that could usually be disproved within a half-mile trip. The picture shows an 1899 Humber, a quadricycle powered by a 2¹/₂-hp de Dion unit—with front-wheel drive and rear-wheel steering! (GB)

Garden-shed tinkerer Louis Renault made a small car based on a de Dion tricycle—and took a dozen orders from friends after its first test on Christmas Eve, 1898. Renault, called variously by his contemporaries a poet, a dunce, and a genius, then made his first "production" model and started a business that became the largest of its type in France. Here are the three stages of twenty-two-year-old Renault's first car. On the right is the 1899 car; in the center is Renault at the wheel of the prototype; and on the left is the earlier, modified de Dion. (F)

Daimler's patents were bought by F. R. Simms of Britain, and in 1896 a British Daimler was first made, although others were imported until 1900. The first British Daimler of 1899 was this 12-hp, 3-liter vehicle, seen here with Edward Prince of Wales in the passenger seat. In 1900 the heir to the throne bought a Daimler, thus establishing a long-lasting link between the British royal family and the Daimler company. (GB)

Renault's—and the world's—first attempt at a sedan (saloon) car. Sit-up-and-beg style it may have been, but it was the first car to have permanent built-on weather protection. Renault had made sixty voiturettes and one sedan by the time his company was six months old. (F)

The Columbia Electric Vehicle was an amalgamation of two pioneer firms, and the company was formed on one foundation—that the electric vehicle was superior to its competitors. Buses and taxicabs were made, some until 1906. This early model, circa 1899, was a hire or chauffeured vehicle, and its rear-high driving position indicates that it was a derivative of a hansom cab. In Britain the cars were marketed under the City & Suburban banner, and one was sold to Queen Alexandra, wife of King Edward VII, for use in her garden. (USA)

Steam power fared somewhat better than electricity as motive power in that it was used well into the twenties and even survived into the thirties, in the shape of the sophisticated Doble. The Stanley Brothers of Newton, Massachusetts, made their first steamers in 1897. They were an instant success, and the company sold over 200 in its first year. This is an 1899 Stanley Steamer of the type that climbed Mount Washington, New Hampshire, in August of that year. The manufacturing rights of this car had been bought by the Locomobile Co. (USA)

1899 Sunbeam. John Marston, a japanning- and tin-plate-factory owner, moved into bicycle-making in the 1880s and built his first car in 1899 (a belt-drive, 4-hp, single-vertical-cylinder prototype)—made, it is thought, entirely in the bicycle factory at Wolverhampton, England. (GB)

Automobile Club Show, 1899. Held in the Old Deer Park, Richmond, near London, this was one of the first Automobile Shows in England, during which part of the entertainment was a zigzag post race and a backwards race. Exhibitors included an Automotette, a de Dion, an Orient Express, a Vallée racing car, and no less than fifty-three other vehicles. The lady is in a Léon Bollée, followed by a golfer in a (de Dion-Bouton?) tricycle.

Turn-of-the-century French chic. This 1899 Decauville, one of the lightest cars of its day, was called a voiturelle—a rather spindly, tubular-framed four-wheeler with a rear-mounted, 2-cylinder engine (two coupled single-cylinder units) of a total of 3½ hp and a surprisingly advanced type of independent front suspension. (F)

The 1899 Canstatt-Daimler—cockpit view showing controls. (D)

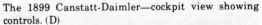

One of the first cars designed for competition, this Cannstatt-Daimler appeared in 1899. It had a 5-liter, four-cylinder power unit and could achieve a creditable 50 mph. Emil Jellinek, Daimler's representative in Nice, had suggested that a competition car be built, but this one proved to have a dangerously high center of gravity. Jellinek advised a lower line and other modifications. The result was the first Mercedes. (D)

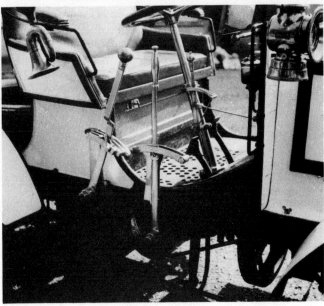

The last year of the nineteenth century — and the woman driver arrives. Here a fashionable female conducts an 1899 M.M.C. (The Motor Manufacturing Company Limited, of Coventry), the firm that succeeded British entrepreneur Harry Lawson's Great Horseless Carriage Co. (GB)

During the years that have been called the Edwardian Age by the British and the Belle Epoque by the French, motoring in Europe was almost exclusively for the wealthy, although it was somewhat more democratically enjoyed in the United States. Despite the production of light and relatively inexpensive cars from manufacturers such as Renault, Fiat, Austin, and Ford, the significant automobiles made during this time of high social contrasts were the craftsman-fabricated Rolls-Royces, Mercedes, Napiers, Alfas, Mercers, and Lanchesters — cars that were destined to become coveted treasures of the present day.

The long, golden summer of the Edwardian Age that ended so abruptly in August 1914 saw the acceptance of motoring as a sport, as an alternative to hunting, as a new venture for women, and as viable transport. The leisurely days of Edward VII saw the decline of the electric car, the losing battle fought by the eminently sensible steam car, the rise and fall of the gargantuan racing car, and the appearance of the astonishingly advanced Mercedes. These years saw the British Lion opening an eye to observe the infant motor industry bounding ahead in Europe and America — and giving chase. They saw, too, the Italian automotive industry giant, Fiat, begin its rapid growth into the largest industry of any kind in Italy.

The last vintage years before the first world war swept away established traditions and saw the beginnings of the mass motoring age when Ford, by 1914 well into his seventh year of the Model T, was making a quarter of a million automobiles a year, twice the number of cars on the roads of Britain at that time. America was already mobile, and, where America led, the rest followed — although it took most of the rest of the world until 1920 to pick up the threads of peacetime production once more.

In Europe the car was still regarded with some distrust and awe by the man-in-the-street up to the first war, but the automobile had by this time settled into both its role in society and its mechanical layout. Most of the technical advances in suspension, engine design, electrics, and so on that were to influence motor design to this day were already fact. Later advances were to be mainly those that stemmed from improved materials or further refinements of existing systems.

1900-1918

THE EDWARDIANS

The Benz 20–30-hp racing car of 1900. Benz still maintained that "a car which can attain a speed of over 60 km/h [37 mph] will soon rattle itself to pieces," even though his cars had been successful in several events. This car won the first international track race at Frankfurt in 1900 over a 30-mile course. (D)

Just before the Mercedes debut, this Daimler was produced at Cannstatt—designed by Gottlieb's son Paul. A small, 1.4-liter, 6.7-hp model, it was noteworthy for its honeycomb radiator at the front of the hood, with a fan behind it, similar to modern layout. (D)

A 1900 Daimler Wagonette from the Coventry factory in the Midlands. By 1901 the factory was in full production and the company had even opened a service station in London. This 4-hp vehicle was introduced in 1898 and was made for several years. (GB)

Lineup at the start of the 1900 Thousand Mile Trial organized by the Automobile Club of Great Britain and Ireland, now the Royal Automobile Club. Brainchild of newspaper proprietor Lord Northcliffe (what would the story of the automobile be without newspaper magnates?), the event helped to overcome much prejudice against the car.

A de Dion-Bouton voiturette returns home from the famous 1000 Miles Trial held in England, a demonstration of reliability that introduced the automobile to many in Britain to whom it had previously been only a legend. This vehicle is a 3½-hp, but by 1902 the car housed a 6-hp unit. (F)

With the same basic layout as the 1899 car, this 1900 1,082-cc, 2-cylinder, 6-hp F.I.A.T. was to develop by 1901 into the 10-hp (in this case a double-phaeton design, but with the mechanics unchanged), a heavier and roomier model. (I)

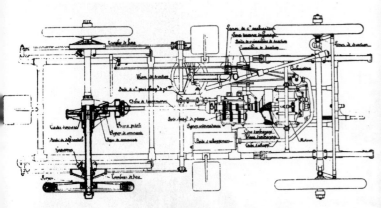

Working drawing of Louis Renault's light car, 1900-1901. In 1900 the de Dion engine with which most Renaults were equipped was increased from 1³/₄ to 3¹/₂ hp. By the end of the year the company had made 179 cars, and the 750-mile Paris-Toulouse race, in which Marcel Renault won the voiturette class, had produced no less than 350 orders. (F)

The Motor Manufacturing Company produced its first front-engined car in 1900. This 6-hp, twin-cylinder car made a marathon trip in 1953 from Scotland's John o' Groats to England's Land's End in ten days—on solid tires. (GB)

Mixed well into the columns of mid-twentieth century traffic is this French veteran Georges Richard, whose change of company names at least five times, and early offerings of bought-in vehicles, tends to make its history confusing. The products were later called Richard-Braziers (Brazier was a designer) and subsequently just Braziers. This is a 9-hp dogcart with a 2-cylinder motor. (F)

By 1901 Benz cars had engines at the front end and a longer driving belt. Although Benz had updated his designs, they were challenged by the advanced new Daimler product, the Mercedes, and sales began to drop. Benz Spider 1901; 60 km/h (37 mph) top speed. (D)

Marius Berliet of Lyons, France, started in a tiny workshop and had made just six cars in 1899. By 1901 his tandem model and later rear-engine cars had developed into considerably more ambitious vehicles (front-engined, chain-driven) after he took over another local company. Both 2- and 4-cylinder front-engined vehicles were produced from 1901. (F)

Made in the U.S.A., this little Columbia electric car (with batteries weighing the best part of a ton) was sold in Britain under the name of City & Suburban. Queen Alexandra, wife of pioneer motorist King Edward VII, bought one for use in her garden at Sandringham House. In New York Columbias were everywhere just after the turn of the century—they were the city's first taxis. (USA)

A de Dion-Bouton vis-à-vis at speed—around 20 mph—now with a power unit of 4½ hp. Easy to drive, the little "Ding Dongs," as the British called them, were popular with pioneer women drivers. The picture was taken during a veteran car rally in the north of England. (F)

The F.I.A.T. company was already diversifying by 1901, and this 8 hp, the last to be designed by the original company engineer, was the first to have a front vertical (2-cylinder) engine. No less than eight of these cars competed in the first Tour of Italy (an event that covered 1,000 miles), all of which finished the course. (I)

The first 4-cylinder F.I.A.T. appeared in 1901, and the end of that year saw this improved version, with honeycomb radiator and body by Alessio. The 12-hp, 3.7-liter unit developed 16 bhp, giving a maximum of 43 mph. One of the ladies is the Princess Laetitia Bonaparte, says the original caption—it does not indicate which one. (I)

A French *automobile à vapeur*, the Gardner-Serpollet. Steam had a strong following at this time, and Serpollet was one of the more advanced in the field. By 1901 his company had the financial support of American F. Gardner, and three models were offered to the public. One of Serpollet's steamers (with Serpollet at the wheel) broke the world speed record at 75.06 in 1902 at Nice, France. (F)

With its 5.9-liter engine and a power output of 35-hp at 8,000 rpm, the first Mercedes was the first car to have mechanically operated inlet valves, resulting in considerably increased engine efficiency. Its 4 cylinders were cast in pairs (each pair fed by a jet carburetor), and engine speed could be regulated by a hand lever within a range of 300 to 1,000 rpm by altering spring tension on a governor. These and other advances put the car far ahead of others on the market of the day. (D)

Nice Week, 1901. In the spring of 1901 the first Mercedes racing car won the steep Le Turbie (a village on the mountainside above Monte Carlo) hill-climb at an incredible average of 31.9 mph—a difficult feat to perform even today. Mercedes cars won almost every event that week, prompting a Frenchman to write: "Nous sommes entrés dans L'ère Mercedes" ("We have entered the Mercedes era"). (D)

A Mors at the start of a local race. The starter looks as though he is about to drop the flag—a newspaper—for the "off." By 1902 Mors was fielding 60-hp cars. One was entered in the Paris-Vienna event of that year and driven by Fournier, the idol of continental racing fans. (F)

The girl whose name started it all, Mercedes Jellinek. Daughter of Daimler's South of France representative, diplomat Emile Jellinek, hers was the name chosen for the new cars produced by the German company in 1901—preferable in France, it was thought, for the somewhat Teutonic-sounding Daimler.

The curved-dash Oldsmobile, a lightweight, motorized buggy with the single-cylinder engine that gave "one chug per telegraph pole," was inexpensive and looked enough like a horsed vehicle to allay the fears of a timorous public. Over 15,000 were made. (USA)

Sporting drivers Charles Jarrott and Selwyn Edge pose in a Panhard, circa 1901. Jarrott drove a Panhard in the Paris-Berlin race of that year. S. F. Edge had a similar career in competition from 1899 to 1904 and could claim the first British victory in a foreign event, the 1902 Gordon Bennett Cup. (F)

Louis Renault, aged twenty-two, before the start of the 1901 Paris to Bordeaux race. This 1-liter, 8-hp Renault had won the voiturette section of the Paris-Berlin event, the first major capital-to-capital race of the year, averaging 36.3 mph. (F)

Charles Santler, a Worcestershire engineer, made several claims to fame during his life, including having built the first car in the world and having been the part-designer of Karl Benz' first automobile. The first car from the Santler Company was based on Benz' principles, and this example, a 6 hp made in 1901–1902 and registered in 1904 is one of the earliest single-cylinder, front-engined cars from the Malvern, Worcestershire, stable. Charles Santler is at the wheel; his mechanics are grouped statuesquely around, and one seems to be testing the strength of the radiator. (GB)

Son of a French blacksmith, Leon Serpollet had patented an instantaneously vaporizing flash boiler in 1888 and a few years later changed his fuel from coke to paraffin. His early efforts at streamlining (his "Easter Egg," the car in which he created a speed record at Nice at over 75 mph was an example of early airflow design) mark him as a pioneer in this field. By 1900 he could name the Prince of Wales and the Shah of Persia among his customers, and, if he had not died in 1907, steam cars could have developed more quickly. (F)

This incredible Sunbeam Mabley was the first of its make put into serious production, a series which, perhaps deservedly, did not last long. The diamond-pattern wheel layout—hopefully designed to prevent skidding—necessitated the driver (at the rear) and passenger to sit facing opposite ways to each other, as on a love seat. Powered by a belt-driven 2½-hp de Dion single-cylinder. (GB)

Another angle of the odd Sunbeam Mabley, showing the curious roadwheel pattern and east-west seating arrangement. This lopsided, open-air machine included oil lamps. The spade grip seen on the left steered front and rear wheels—at opposite and equal angles, presumably. (GB)

The Sports Motor Car Company of North London imported several makes of continental cars, renaming them Mayfair. This voiturette could be a Belgian Linon or a Vivinus, with a single-cylinder de Dion engine of 4½ hp. The grandson of the driver still runs a business in North London. (GB)

Chain drive (primary and final) had been fitted to Wolseleys by 1901, and tillers had given way to steering wheels. There were 5-hp and 10-hp twin-cylinder models, and a racing 4-cylinder could be made to a customer's specifications. A steely-eyed Herbert Austin is seen at the wheel of this Wolseley, a 1903 tonneau. (GB)

The 1902–1903 Cadillac Model A; 1-cylinder, 5 × 5 in, 9.7 hp. The two-passenger car included patent leather fenders; brass lamps, horn, etc. were extra. Said the magazine *Horseless Age* of the new Cadillac: "The vehicle is of the runabout type, but is probably somewhat heavier and stronger than the average representative of this type." (USA)

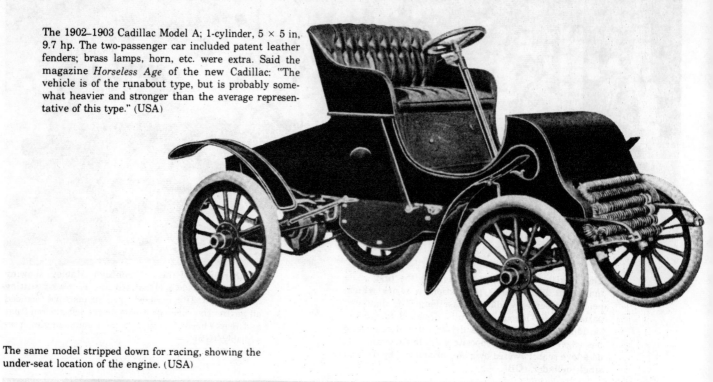

The same model stripped down for racing, showing the under-seat location of the engine. (USA)

In this home-built steamer designer and builder George Cannon set up several class records during 1902-1903. He called his machine the "Flyer," and its layout was unconventional, to say the least. The man in front steered, and the one at the rear attended to all other controls — not a very different arrangement from the mid-nineteenth-century steam buses used in England. (USA)

Artist's impression of the Mors World Land Speed Record car in which American Willis K. Vanderbilt established a new record at 76.08 mph on August 5, 1902, in which French driver Fournier notched it up to 76.60 in November of that year, and in which Frenchman Augieres took the record away from Fournier twelve days later with a speed of 77.13 mph. (F)

The first light 12-hp Napier, with Charles Jarrott at the wheel and Montague Napier as passenger during a London to Oxford run. This finely engineered touring two-seater created a large demand for Napier cars from the former "carriage trade." (GB)

This drawing of the 30-hp Napier driven by S. F. Edge in the Gordon Bennett section of the Paris to Vienna race (he won the event) shows an incident that, claimed Edge, never happened. The caption says, "The Englishman Edge driving a Napier skidded into a brook. Tyrolean peasants push the heavy car back on to the road." If they had, Edge would have been disqualified. (GB)

An Oldsmobile, now further refined, with spoked wheels and a seat at the back over the engine (and a small bicycle bell fitted on the tiller). (USA)

From a modern German film — the Opel Darracq. Darracq mechanics and Opel coachwork; 1 cylinder, water-cooled, battery ignition, three forward speeds and reverse, top speed 45 km/h (28 mph). (D)

The first of the completely German Opels was this 10–12-hp tonneau, housing a 1.8-liter, 2-cylinder engine with automatic lubrication, a steering column shift, and, the very last word, shaft drive. (D)

This massive Panhard was entered in the Paris-Vienna race of 1902, one of thirteen of that model. At the wheel is British driver Charles Jarrott, trundling the vehicle up to a control point en route. (F)

The Peugeot archives list this one as built from 1898 to 1902. Seen here driven by opera singer Harold Scott Russell, this vis-à-vis had a 2-cylinder, horizontal motor developing 10–12 hp. Just twenty models were made at the Audincourt plant. (F)

This Peugeot was imported from France to Britain—sold to an owner who crashed it and then disposed of it as "quite uncontrollable." It was "rediscovered" in 1935, restored, and still takes its present owner to rallies in various parts of Europe. This Bébé is a single-cylinder, 5-hp two-seater. On the right is automotive writer and editor Peter Roberts. (F)

During a break from work, George Eastman (of Kodak) rides with a friend in a Stanley Steamer, the product of two brothers who were formerly photographic plate makers. During 1902—but after this model was made—a noncondensing engine was produced, with a front-mounted boiler. Speed of starting, always a problem with early steamers, must have been fairly good on these cars, as evidenced by the fact that Stanleys were bought by fire and police forces in the U.S.A. (USA)

The year of Renault's greatest success was 1902, and the event was the Paris-Vienna race. Against 117 competitors Louis' brother, Marcel Renault, arrived first at the finishing line in Vienna—so early that officials at first hardly believed that he was in fact a competitor in the race. The Renault car, powered by a 3,770-cc, 4-cylinder, 14-hp engine, had beaten the giant 13-liter Panhards. Here, astonished Viennese officials gather around the winning Renault. (F)

An Edwardian couple pose (allowing their chauffeur a look-in) with their brand-new 1902–1903 Wolseley 10 hp. At a weight of almost one ton, the 2,605-cc engine made the overall performance somewhat leisurely. (GB)

One of the first cars built by Scotsman David Buick, a Detroit plumber and engineer. The 2-cylinder, valve-in-head (ohv) motor was under the seat, capacity 2.6 liters. Just sixteen were made before William C. Durant took over production and began dramatically raising the price. (USA)

A Benz racing car at speed in the tragic Paris to Madrid race of 1903. This event saw racing speeds of up to 80 mph. It caused carnage, killing drivers and spectators, and was stopped. (D)

The 1,610-cc, single-cylinder Cadillac Model A was so successful that, although a 4-cylinder car was made from 1906, the "one-lunger" was produced until 1909. Cadillac cars went through a test of considerable severity in England in 1908 when three Model K's were dismantled, the parts mixed up, and the cars reassembled and track-tested. They all worked perfectly. Here, a Model A is driven again by F. S. Bennett, the man who organized the test. (USA)

With the ubiquitous Charles Jarrott at the wheel, this French De Dietrich is about to start on one of the many early town-to-town rallies held in Britain during the first five years of the century. By 1902 the company was producing cars designed by Turcat and Méry (who also made cars under their own names) in four sizes—8, 12, 16, and 24 hp. This is a 4-cylinder (cast in pairs) model, probably the 16, with cone clutch, chain drive, automatic inlet valves, and ignition geared magneto — "the sweetest and most regular of ignitions," it was claimed. (F)

The engine compartment of a 1903 de Dion-Bouton displays its lonely single cylinder and attendant inlet and exhaust pipes. Bore 90 mm, stroke 110 mm, coil ignition. (F)

With the single-cylinder engine mounted in front, the de Dion-Bouton now began to look more conventional. It had a 698-cc capacity, two-speed transmission, and a true de Dion rear axle (a "dead" axle, separate from the two final driving shafts). Writer Peter Roberts is in the driving seat. (F)

The most weather protection Edwardians could expect is illustrated by this 16/24-hp F.I.A.T. tonneau of 1903 with its canvas hood. With an engine of just over 4 liters, this automobile, highly sophisticated for its day (although armored wood frames were still used in construction), could accommodate up to six passengers and cruise at 35 mph. Pressed-steel frames were introduced a year later. (I)

Model A Ford, with the optional-extra tonneau fixed on the back. (USA)

The Model A was introduced in the year of the Ford Motor Company's incorporation and sold on July 22 of that year. It was bought by Dr. Phennig of Chicago, much to the relief of the stockholders, who were nervously watching a bank balance that had dwindled considerably. The Model A could be had with a detachable tonneau that clamped to the back of the vehicle, increasing passenger capacity to four. A leather top, with side glass portholes, was also available. The car housed a flat-twin engine mounted under the floor and was described (by the company) as "so simple a boy of 15 can run it." Here Henry Ford rides again and doffs his hat to an earlier form of conveyance. (USA)

A famous Ford "special," the record-breaking 999, a gearless, clutchless, bodyless flatbed machine—with Barney Oldfield at the tiller. Henry Ford (standing) took over for the historic mile run over a frozen Lake St. Clair in 1904, setting up a land speed record of 91.37 mph. (USA)

The Gladiator Company was founded by Alexandre Darracq to produce bicycles and was sold to a British group of manufacturers in 1896. This model was powered by a 2-cylinder Aster unit developing 10-hp. The Mercedes-style hood (this company was not the only one to cash in on the Mercedes fashion) over the finned-tube cooler had just been adopted. (F)

Georges Richard Landaulette; 2-cylinders, 10-hp. Seen in England during the 1960s. (F)

A 60-hp, 9-liter, 4-cylinder Mercedes, based on the Simplex design. Developed from the 35 hp, this model was a sedan made for a large family (or perhaps a hotel limousine). (D)

The oldest Humber still running, this trim "Humberette" light car houses a 5½-hp motor (rotating counter-clockwise) of 612 cc, trembler coil ignition, and its original Longuemare carburetor. Designed by Louis Coatalen. (GB)

Willie Maybach, engineer and right-hand man to Gottlieb Daimler, and associated with him since 1865, continued with the company after Daimler's death, developing the Mercedes, but left in 1907 after conflicts with Daimler's successors. Here (in light suit) he is seen in an 18/22-hp Mercedes Simplex of 1903. (D)

The name Mercedes had been seen in the lists of motorsport winners for two years, and 1903 was also crowded with victories for the Daimler company. Here Camille Jenatzy is pictured at the wheel of the 60-hp Mercedes *rennwagen* that he drove to success in the Gordon Bennett race of that year, held near Dublin, Ireland, over a course of 327 miles. Jenatzy's average speed was 42.2 mph. (D)

A 16-hp, 4-cylinder Napier chugs along a quiet English country lane. The first 6-cylinder Napier appeared at the end of 1903. (GB)

Meet the Opel boys, the "Five Russellsheimers"—looking a little like a vaudeville act. Carl, Wilhelm, Fritz, Ludwig, and young Adam—all active at one time in the Opel company.

A Pope-Hartford, seen at a modern rally. In 1903 Colonel Albert Pope's small car was a single-cylinder car of conventional design, popular then and widely remembered now. This car has a surprisingly firm place in American auto "folklore" for one that existed from only 1903 to 1914. (USA)

Marcel Renault at speed in the 6.3-liter, 30-hp Renault during the 1903 Paris-Madrid race. Several cars went out of control (speeds were up to 85 mph on the rough roads of the French countryside) during the early stages, killing drivers, mechanics, and spectators. The race was stopped after the first leg, but not before Marcel Renault had run off the road and been fatally injured. (F)

Louis Renault, in another twin-cylinder Renault *voiture legère*, hears of his brother's tragic accident in the Paris-Madrid race from his other brother, Fernand. (F)

The Standard Motor Company was formed early in 1903 with R. W. Maudslay as managing director. His aim was to produce "a car to be composed purely of those components whose principles have been tried and tested . . ." a sensible philosophy in times when many infant manufacturers were building highly impractical machines in the first euphoric enthusiasm of motor design. This is the first Standard car, from Coventry, England. The single-cylinder, 6-hp unit is mounted low down between chassis members. (GB)

The first Vauxhall was seen on the roads of Britain in 1903. A light car with chain drive and tiller steering, it proved to be a popular vehicle with its forty owners— the entire number of cars made in that year. Powered by a single-cylinder unit, horizontally mounted; coil spring suspension, two forward speeds, no reverse. (GB)

The White Sewing Machine Co. of Cleveland produced this reliable 2-cylinder, 10-hp steamer—looking almost indistinguishable from a gasoline-fueled car. The 1903 White was the first of the line to have a front engine and a steering wheel. The three White brothers, Windsor, Rollin, and Walter, had made the transition from sewing machines to automobiles when they bought a steam vehicle for study, producing their own in 1900. (USA)

From a motor-show catalog. The 1903 Gobron-Brillie claimed to be the "first petrol-driven car with an engine absolutely without vibration" and used an opposed piston layout, with two pistons per cylinder. (F)

The British company with the improbable name of Alldays & Onions Pneumatic Engineering Limited first made quadricycles in 1898, then progressed to this shaft-driven, single-cylinder, 7-hp three-seater, seen here nearly seventy years after its year of production, with London's Big Ben and the Houses of Parliament in the background. (GB)

This is the 10/12-hp Beeston Humber tourer made in Humber's No. 2 factory at Beeston in Nottinghamshire (the other factory was at Coventry, the cradle of the British automotive industry), where the more expensive Humbers were produced. (GB)

This 1904 Buick was noticeably more advanced than the earlier car, although the catalog listed "horn, lamps, tool-box with sufficient tool equipment, *mats and rubber aprons to go under the car*." However, the 2-cylinder engine proved to be a winner and was continued almost unchanged until 1910 in some Buick products. (USA)

This English Daimler, an elegant 28-hp landaulet, was one of the first models to have the familiar fluted radiator and the three-section hood characteristic of Daimlers until recent years. The chauffeur's weather protection was unusual for the period in all but the most expensive vehicles. (GB)

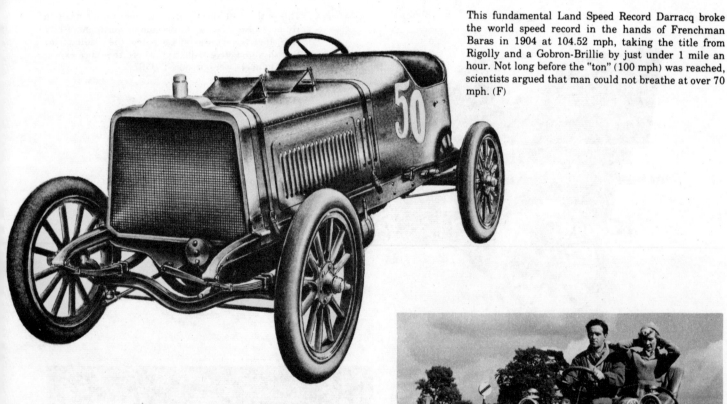

This fundamental Land Speed Record Darracq broke the world speed record in the hands of Frenchman Baras in 1904 at 104.52 mph, taking the title from Rigolly and a Gobron-Brillie by just under 1 mile an hour. Not long before the "ton" (100 mph) was reached, scientists argued that man could not breathe at over 70 mph. (F)

Genevieve herself, star of the 1952 comedy film about veteran cars. The other stars were John Gregson and Dinah Sheridan, seen on the Darracq's high seats. A French car of middle quality, the Darracq housed a twin-cylinder unit of 2¼ liters, had three forward speeds and reverse, and a reliable cruising speed of about 20 mph. (F)

Three months after opening for business, F.I.A.T. had entered motor sport and won a race, the prelude to several years of competition activities. Here Vincenzo Lancia, then a F.I.A.T. employee and later to build his own cars, drives a 75-hp, 14-liter, 4-cylinder Corso (racer) during Brescia week in 1904. He won the Coppa Florio at the high average of 72 mph. (I)

Made by Fahreugfabrik Eisenach, at Eisenach, Germany (where today's Wartburgs are made), this Dixi was "the last word," a free translation of its name. A 4-cylinder engine (in two separately cast blocks) developed 20 hp at 1,200 rpm. A stylish car, made by one of the earliest manufacturers in Europe. (D)

The Compagnie Parisienne des Voitures Electriques produced this streetcar-like vehicle, an electric in the tradition of the coaching era, and called it a Krieger. It had two electric motors—one driving each front wheel, giving a form of power-assisted steering. It also had four-wheel brakes—forward-looking mechanics in an ancient shell. Its speed was 15 mph and it ran 50 miles to each battery charge, claimed the makers. This is the brougham. (F)

Founded in Staines near London by American Wilbur Gunn, who had earlier made a steam launch and motorcycles, the Lagonda Motor Company started producing twin-cylinder tri-cars in 1904. Gunn was a stickler for precision and insisted that all parts except the carburetor (even the nuts and bolts) be made in his factory, and he produced some very reliable early Lagonda vehicles. (GB)

The first Maxwell, a flat-twin-cylinder two-seater. The company brought out two models in 1904; the smaller, a roadster, had a 2-cylinder, 8-hp unit and planetary transmission. In its first full year the company, formed by sheet-metal maker Benjamin Briscoe and mechanic J. D. Maxwell, made no less than 540 vehicles, pushing production up to 8,000 by 1908. (USA)

A two-seater Minerva (with a seat for a nonpaying passenger at the back); 2 cylinders, 5 hp, and very wet when it rained. By the De Jong brothers, Belgium. (B)

Seen in London—a heavy 4-cylinder, 24/32-hp 1904 Mors Roi des Belges, a large luxury car named after the King of the Belgians who, it was rumored, ordered the lavish and elegantly styled vehicle at the wishes of his mistress. (F)

Colonel Mark Mayhew and his 100-hp Napier racing car in 1904. Said a pioneer lady driver, Mrs. Edward Kennard, after a ride in the car: "I held a strap in my hand, sat in the mechanic's seat and kept my feet firmly pressed against a specially constructed footboard to maintain my balance. The speed was terrific and the pressure of air seemed to force my head right back. Rounding the corners was an experience not to be forgotten." (GB)

The Gordon Bennett Opel *rennwagen;* Fritz Opel at the wheel. Both Fritz and Henrich Opel drove in races in the 1900s and were highly successful in racing and trials. This Darracq-based 100 hp held a brief world record at 168.20 km/h (105.1 mph) in 1904. By then Opel was one of the leading German manufacturers. (D)

Clearly influenced by cycle and motorcycle design, the Riley sequence of forecars between 1903 and 1907 developed from handlebar-steered motor-tricycles, using a tiny 517-cc engine, to more sophisticated vehicles with padded seats, a water-cooled power unit, and a steering wheel. (GB)

On April 1, 1904, Henry Royce finished his first car at his Cooke Street works in Manchester. This is one of Royce's original 1.8-liter, 2-cylinder models, with Charles Rolls at the wheel and the Duke of Connaught beside him. Rolls and Royce came together later in the year. (GB)

The first four-wheeled Singer, a 15-hp, two-seater, 3-cylinder voiturette, was built in 1904 and sold in 1905. Unlike contemporary practice, it was offered complete with pneumatic tires, a spare wheel, and (so-called) all-weather equipment. Made in Coventry, England. (GB)

This Sunbeam was more conventional than its predecessor, the diamond-shaped Sunbeam Mabley. Using a 12-hp, 2.4-cc, 4-cylinder engine based on a French Berliet design, the first of these cars were built largely in France so that the designer could absorb French construction technique, which was then several years ahead of that of the British. (GB)

Tony Huber. This short-lived product (1902–1906) was made by a French company whose main purpose was manufacturing engines. This is an 8-hp, 2-cylinder model, one of four types produced by the firm. (F)

From the Austin archives comes this drawing of a Vanden Plas (a coachbuilding company with Belgian ancestry), signed 1904. Although the vehicle has a number of early Austin coachwork features, and the "official" caption states that it was the first Vanden Plas design executed for Austin (the company was to become a subsidiary of Austin in 1960), the Austin Motor Company was not formed until 1906. Possibly Herbert Austin had been planning well ahead. (GB)

A Vauxhall variant, circa 1904. It is reminiscent of a hansom cab, with the driver sitting high up behind the passengers, where the coachman had always perched. It need hardly be recorded that this curious vehicle was not a roaring success. (GB)

More than 100 different makes of steam car had been manufactured in America by the time the sophisticated Doble died in 1932, and this 1904 White was one of the most popular. It was highly successful in the Glidden Tours (first held in 1905; 870 miles from New York to the White Mountains and back) and had achieved a "perfect" score in the 650-mile reliability trials held in Britain. The company sold steam cars until 1911, although by 1909 a gasoline car had been built to replace the famous steamers. (USA)

Karl Benz answered the Mercedes *coup* of 1901 by developing his engines and designs, and he quickly recovered from the losses caused by the opposition. During 1903–1906 Benz produced a variety of cars— the 16/20-, 24-, 29/32-, 40-, 24/45-, and the 28/52-hp models. This Benz 40-hp tourer was entered in several sporting contests during those years. (D)

In 1905 F.I.A.T. absorbed the Ansaldi works, thus giving birth to the F.I.A.T.-Ansaldi models of 1905-1906. In 1906 the company was renamed Brevetti-Fiat (Brevetti in this context means patent), and this was the name used to describe the first cars made by the company. This is a 15/20, 3-liter cabriolet with a 37-mph claimed maximum speed. (I)

Model B Cadillac Surrey, with dummy hood; a single-cylinder, 9.7 hp. Later in 1905 Cadillac brought out the company's first 4-cylinder model D, using a 30-hp unit. Despite the necessity of sacrificing some production of the highly successful single-cylinder cars, Cadillac was convinced that multi-cylinder vehicles represented the future and had put its money into them. (USA)

This Cam voiturette was made by J. J. Cam, seen here at the wheel, in his small works at Charles St., Worcester, the home of several pioneer motor companies. The light four-seater with the strange look of a de Dion-Bouton in the hood line seems far too fragile to support the three healthy Edwardians in this, the only known surviving photograph of the miniscule car. Cam had earlier produced a number of motor tricycles and had designed what was contemporarily called "a novel carburetor." (GB)

F.I.A.T. entered its 100-hp racing car in the classic hill-climb, Mont Ventoux. Driven by Alessandro Cagno, it achieved the fastest time of the day, covering the 21 km (13 miles) in 19 minutes, 30 seconds—a new record. At over 16 liters, this F.I.A.T. Corsa had the largest engine made by the company up to this time. Its top speed was 100 mph. (I)

The 110-hp F.I.A.T. "Gordon Bennett" racing car was directly derived from the 100-hp of the same year, using the same massive 16,286-cc engine, but adding another 10-hp. It competed in the last Gordon Bennett Trophy and the Vanderbilt Cup that year. (I)

By 1905 Ford US was offering the Model C and this Model B tourer, the first of the company's 4-cylinder cars. Both the C and B had two-speed planetary transmission. (USA)

The Model C Ford, a direct derivative of the Model A, complete with under-floor, single-cylinder power pack, was designed with a dummy hood to give the car the current front-engined look demanded by an increasing number of buyers. (USA)

This 4-cylinder, 10/12-hp Humber was made at Coventry, England. (Humbers were also made at Beeston, Nottingham) and was a development of the earlier 8/10 hp. The front passenger seat swings forward to allow entry to the rear. (GB)

A light runabout with a 4-cylinder, air-cooled engine rated at 12 hp, the Franklin weighed 1,250 pounds. It is seen here crossing a ford over a country road. (USA)

British textile manufacturers near Manchester at the turn of the century, Horsfall & Bickham Limited found that their employees had made a crude car in their spare time. It worked, and the directors decided to produce it commercially. By 1905 it had gained a reputation for solidly built reliability. This is a 1905 10/12-hp, 3-cylinder Horbick Minor. (GB)

Shown to the public in 1906, this Model A Voiturette by Bohemian (now Czechoslovakian) motorcycle company Laurin & Klement (now Skoda) was produced to bridge the gap between the inexpensive motorcycle and the more costly conventional car. With a water-cooled V-2 unit of 7 hp, shaft drive, three forward speeds and reverse, and a top speed of 45 km/h (28 mph), the little two-seater found a ready response on home and foreign markets. (CS)

The Vanderbilt Cup races eventually had to be abandoned as spectators became uncontrollable. However, in its heyday the event was the greatest thing in motor sports—there was even a Broadway musical named after it. Here Joe Tracey makes dust on a bend in the Long Island circuit during the 1905 eliminating trials. The 90-hp Locomobile car took third place in the race. (USA)

From the Suddeutsche Automobil-Fabrik at Gaggenau came this little Liliput 1-cylinder "Volksautomobil" (a "People's Car" a generation before the first Volkswagen appeared) of 1.4 liters, 4 hp, and 30 km/h (18½ mph). The company was bought by Benz in 1908. (D)

Maxwell light car, circa 1905. A year or two later, Maxwells boasted three-point suspension, *unit construction,* multi-disk clutch, therm-syphon cooling, and "indestructible" metal bodies. (USA)

The Edwardians: 1900-1918

A 4-cylinder Mercedes Simplex tourer with studded rear tires. Just visible is the three-pointed Mercedes star *motif* of the time, a trademark taken from a star drawn by Gottlieb Daimler on a postcard to his wife. (D)

Based on the Mercedes "Simplex" car of 1902 (the designation refers to an improved version of the Mercedes engine), this is the Kettenwagen 4-cylinder, 35-hp (35PS is the normal German usage, the letters standing for *Pferde Starke* — horse power), chain-driven, laundaulet-type car. (D)

By 1905 the curved-dash Oldsmobile was undoubtedly the best-known small car in the United States. However, R. E. Olds was always ready for publicity, and when a Public Roads official had, for good reasons of his own, suggested a transcontinental race by curved-dash Oldsmobiles from New York to Portland, Oregon, over 4,000 miles of poor roads, the company readily agreed. This is the start of the event, May 8, 1905. (USA)

One of the unscheduled stops on "wet, sticky and treacherous roads," as the contestants described the first part of the trip. When the tires gave trouble during an earlier race, the drivers had simply filled them with oats! (USA)

Old Steady and Old Scout stop for fuel in Omaha while a White steamer looks on. Gasoline became dearer as the cars trekked west, says the story—twice as expensive in Wyoming and Idaho as in Ohio—and the competitors had to search for it or arrange with stage-coach drivers to have tins left at preselected places. Forty-four days after starting, Old Scout arrived in Portland. The car is still in running condition today. (USA)

A double-phaeton Opel built during the German company's "marriage" to the Darracq system, when Opel used the French chassis to support its home-produced bodies. This one housed a 4-cylinder, 16/18-hp, water-cooled unit with a claimed top speed of 60 km/h (37 mph). (D)

Bicycle backgrounds encouraged the manufacture of tri-cars, as well as quadricycles like this French *2-places* Peugeot, with the passenger seat "nearest the accident." It was propelled by a one-lung unit claimed to develop 7 hp with a *vitesse maximum* of 30 km/h (18½ mph). (F)

The 1905 60-hp Vanderbilt Cup Pope-Toledo racer with Bert Dinley at the high wheel. The Pope empire embraced Pope-Hartford (the town in Connecticut where they were made), Pope-Toledo, Pope-Tribune, Pope-Waverly (at this time), and several other models. (USA)

One of the finest motoring photographs preserved from early days, this scene illustrates the pioneering spirit necessary to travel away from home on American byways. This twin-cylinder Rambler Surrey Type 1 was photographed by the owner (reading the signpost), using an automatic delayed-action lens timer. Total Rambler sales in 1905: 3,807. (USA)

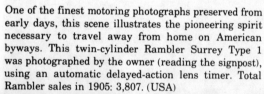

The Honorable Charles Stewart Rolls, son of Lord Llangattock, kicked against Edwardian convention and studied mechanics and applied science at Cambridge—and he became a car salesman before joining Royce in manufacture. His interest in flying led to his early death in 1910.

DEA EX MACHINÂ. THE GODDESS OUT OF THE CAR.

"But what is this? What thing of sea or land ?
Female of sex it seems,
That so bedecked, ornate, and gay,
Comes this way, sailing
Like a stately ship.
 *   *   *   *   *   *
An amber scent of odoriferous perfume
Her harbinger."—MILTON, *Samson Agonistes.*

How the British magazine *Punch* saw motoring at the turn of the century.

Although the company was not formed until 1906, the name of Rolls-Royce was used for the cars from Christmas 1904, when engineer Royce and aristocrat Rolls met and made a working agreement. This car, one of the earliest Rolls-Royce products, is a 10 hp, probably built in 1905 (and with the now familiar R-R radiator shape), and owned by Colonel Ruston, one of the original shareholders. (GB)

The spring of 1905 began to show the result of another year of Henry Royce's continual quest for mechanical perfection: a 15-hp, 3-cylinder model and a 20-hp, 4-cylinder car completed, and a 6-cylinder, 30-hp well on the way. This is the 15-hp Rolls-Royce, of which it is thought only three were made. (GB)

The first automobile built by Rover was a light 8 hp. The story is familiar — from bicycles to cars in the early part of the century. This car, said the brochure, had an engine with "4½ in. × 5 in. bore, stroke, heavy inside flywheels running on special ball-bearings; solid crankshaft; solid cams operating both inlet and exhaust. Tank (petrol) forms dashboard; carries sufficient petrol for 160 miles." The four-seater is shown; the two-seater version of the 8 hp had appeared in 1904. (GB)

This was the second (6-hp) model from the Rover factory, following the 8 hp (which was to be driven from London to Turkey in 1906 by a Dr. Jefferson), and sold in 1905. It had two brake pedals, the right one acting on the rear wheels and the left one on a drum on the prop shaft. The body was "nicely upholstered and roomy." (GB)

Late in 1905 the first Standard Six—a 6-cylinder engine ($3^1/_8 \times 4''$ bore and stroke) of 18/20 hp was fitted in this relatively low-slung touring car. A Standard car was exported from Britain to Canada in 1905 and caused headlines in the press of that country. (GB)

The small but distinguished Dutch automotive industry has produced several interesting cars, perhaps the most famous of which is the Spyker. This is the 1905 car (pretending to be a 1904 model in the film Genevieve, in which it takes part in the London-Brighton Run which has an upper limit of 1904), housing a 4-cylinder, 2,546-cc engine. This company was one of the first in Europe to show a 6-cylinder model (1902) and four-wheel drive. (NL)

In the center of the meet, a 1905 Stearns packed to the running board with six passengers. F. B. Stearns was one of the earliest pioneers on the American automotive scene, presenting his first motored buggy in 1898.

In the picture is a 4-cylinder, 40-hp car showing some European influence, notably in the up-market Mercedes-type radiator. A single female driver can be seen on the extreme left. (USA)

When Vauxhall moved from their Thames-side iron-works to Luton in the Bedfordshire countryside, this was the first car to be built—a 9-hp, 3-cylinder model, with chain drive. This one has been equipped with a windshield (more like a picture window), one of the earliest conversions for weather protection. (GB)

This was the era of the gymnastic publicity stunt. Automobiles had long since evolved from the experimental stage into a period of serious development, and now, to capture public imagination in the fast-growing buyers' market, something dramatic was needed. This White steamer, seen here in precarious balance, was described as "running noiselessly without odor, smoke or vibration, as simple to operate as an electric with a radius of operation as great as the higher-priced gasoline machines." Quite a claim. (USA)

Although the company did not begin production until 1911 with a 4-cylinder, 5/12PS Wanderermobil, this 2-cylinder prototype had been completed in 1905 by Wanderer Werke AG at Schönau in Germany. Motor production sprung from the familiar bicycle ancestry which had been born when Adolf Jaenicke and Johann Baptist Winklhefer formed the *Chemnitzer Velociped-Depot* in 1885. (D)

THE BRITISH NAVY IN DIFFICULTIES.

Sailor. "AHOY THERE! GET OUT YOUR COLLISION MATS! CAN'T YOU SEE HE'S GOING TO RAM?"

Punch, 1905. Britain's satirical magazine had commented on current affairs since the previous century. Now, in the automobile, it had material rich in allegorical possibilities. *Punch* made full use of the opportunities — and still does.

The car for 1906 in the United States was undoubtedly this Model H Cadillac, a 4-cylinder, 300-cu. in., 30-hp limousine. The company had made its reputation on single-cylinder models, which sold concurrently with the larger fours, Models D, H, and L. Cars were being produced at an aggregate rate of 600 a day in Detroit plants by 1906. (USA)

CADILLAC SINGLE CYLINDER MOTOR

NO better evidence of the unparalleled success of the Cadillac Single Cylinder Motor can be afforded than the fact that we shall continue its use for 1906. As it stands today, it is in all essential features the same as used in the first Cadillac built. If there is any other motor of which a similar statement can be truthfully made we do not know of it. It was years in advance of the times and up to the present, nothing has been made to equal it, much less excel. It has been imitated but the imitations lack its power and reliability, either because their makers cannot solve the secrets, can not successfully apply the principles, or are not disposed to incur the necessary expense. Recent examinations of several of our motors which have seen three years of

active service, have shown them to be practically as good as when new and in some respects even better than new, developing slightly more power than when they first left the factory. With proper general care and lubrication there is no reason why they will not remain serviceable for many years to come. But even granting that through neglect and abuse the replacement of some parts become necessary, it can be done at less expense and with less trouble than on any motor we know of. For example, suppose that through lack of attention to lubrication the piston or cylinder becomes badly cut. These are the most expensive parts liable to be affected by such negligence but the price of a new cylinder is only $4.50 and the piston only $3.50. The main bearings of the crank shaft are perhaps the most susceptible to wear from lack of lubrication. In the Cadillac motor, these bearings consist of the highest grade of babbit facing backed by a finished bronze bushing. If replacement should become necessary it may be done in a few moments, it being not even essential to remove the crank shaft.

The cheap method, the one usually adopted, is to cast the babbit into the frame of the motor. With such construction, when renewal is necessary, the motor must almost invariably be sent

Eulogy from the makers of Cadillac cars. (USA)

This Model K Cadillac runabout was a single-cylinder, 10-hp lightweight. "Capable of meeting every reasonable requirement," ran the ads, "Can be relied upon for service every day of the year; will climb any hill that any automobile will climb, will travel as fast as anyone ought to ride." (USA)

This F.I.A.T. (the company still used capital letters; the word Fiat was introduced in 1907) was a logical development of the earlier 24/32 hp made from 1903 to 1905 and had the same 4-cylinder 7,363-cc power unit, which could take the car up to 53 mph and climb a 1-in-5-gradient, a considerably more lively performance than many of its contemporaries. (I)

The Model K represented Ford's leap into the luxury market and was Ford's first 6-cylinder product, a 6-liter vehicle. It had transmission troubles and caused Ford to abandon manufacturing 6-cylinder cars for over thirty years. In fact, the Model K sold so badly that Ford had to allow a twenty-percent discount to dealers instead of the normal ten. (USA)

From the original Horch company at Koln-Ehrenfeld came this 4-cylinder 18/22PS, 2,725-cc car, winner of the 1906 Herkomer Trial. It sold well and was the foundation for several other models from the Horch stable. (D)

An early export drive to Japan is evident from this picture of a Type B from the Prague and Pilsen pioneers Laurin & Klement. This, their second model, was based on the V-Twin Type A but put out a higher horsepower than the 7-hp original. Work started on a 4-cylinder and in-line 8-cylinder products during 1906. (CS)

In 1906 Mercedes cars were fitted with 6-cylinder engines for the first time, developing 120 hp, and experience with the 93-mph racing version of this unit soon led to road cars capable of 70 hp. Cylinders cast in pairs, four-speed transmissions, steel chassis frames, and double-cone clutches were some of the features. (D)

The senior French firm of Panhard & Levassor had achieved a high reputation early in the field of motoring and had continued to make high-quality vehicles. This 1906 machine is a chain-driven Double Phaeton. (F)

Despite the Italian overtones, this Piccolo was a German car made by Ruppe & Son. Until 1906 the 704-cc, 2-cylinder engine sat out in the open air in front of the car. Later models enclosed it in a hood. This little

"strip cartoon" was probably part of an advertising campaign showing how the man with the car gets the girl. Things haven't changed much. (D)

A 1906 Pope-Toledo under reconstruction at Pontiac, Michigan, in modern times. This model was the best of several that were made by the various units of the Pope group of companies; a 4-cylinder, 35/40-hp Type 12. (USA)

Artist's impression of the 1906 Renault 90-hp racing car at speed at the first French Grand Prix, held at Le Mans that year. Tar had been laid on the 65-mile Sarthe circuit, but temperatures were so high that it melted and temporarily blinded several of the drivers. François Szisz—also partly blinded—won with this Renault at an average speed of 62.8 mph in a total two-part time of 12 hours, 46 minutes, 26 seconds. (F)

This beautifully restored Rapid twelve-passenger "tourister" may have been used for local "outings" or by a large American family. It has an under-floor, double, horizontally opposed, water-cooled, 24-hp unit, with bore and stroke of 5 × 5 in; chain drive, two forward speeds and reverse, weight 3,050 lbs. The company, basically truck manufacturers, became part of General Motors in 1908. (USA)

The Edwardians: 1900-1918

A single-cylinder Reo comes home to Lansing after taking part in a record run. Early Reo cars had a dummy hood that concealed the gas and water tanks and the radiator. (USA)

The original Rolls-Royce Silver Ghost was built by Henry Royce during 1906. Its aluminum-painted touring body gave rise to the apt name, which was used until 1925. The 40/50-hp side-valve car had a 6-cylinder, 7-liter engine, and a phenomenal degree of silence was achieved by having a special expansion chamber to each cylinder. In 1907 the car was driven for over 14,000 miles nonstop. When it was examined after the run, it was found to need very few replacements. This car (illustrated) has now traveled over half a million miles—and has no intention of retiring yet. (GB)

This 8 hp was basically similar to the original Rover 8-hp, single-cylinder model produced for 1904—but by this time the "special Rover cable steering" (wire-and-bobbin) had been replaced by rack-and-pinion. Rover now sold a range of cars, from the 6 hp to a 20 hp that was to win the 1907 International Tourist Trophy Race. (GB)

A factory shot of the first car to come from the Sunbeam Motor Car Company at Wolverhampton, England. Sunbeams had been manufactured for about six years, but with the designing of this 16/20 4-cylinder with chain drive and high-tension magneto, John Marston Limited decided to set up an exclusive motor-manufacturing enterprise. (GB)

In addition to a small 30 hp, Thomas of Buffalo, New York, offered a 40, 50, and 60 hp. This is the 4-cylinder, 50-hp Thomas, somewhat less than pristine after a summer A.A.A. run. (USA)

An experimental prototype showing the distinctive Vauxhall flutes on the hood for the first time. This was also the first Vauxhall to have a "live" axle and a 4-cylinder engine. Its 3.3 liters developed 18 hp. (GB)

After the disastrous San Francisco earthquake of April 1906, motor vehicles were employed to speed rescue operations and transport anti-looting troops through-out the area. Here a White steamer picks its way through the rubble. (USA)

In January 1906, just before the first Austin was seen on the roads of Britain, Herbert Austin (at the wheel) announced that his cars would be "the embodiment of all the best features in modern automobile construction." Ambitious, perhaps, but his earliest production models were not experimental machines, but fully fledged cars. Opened in 1906, the Austin factory had produced no less than seventeen different models by 1908. This is an 18/24 hp of 1907. (GB)

A Benz wins the Herkomer Trials of 1907. Fritz Erle is the driver seen making smoke on the 8-liter, 60-hp car—the favorite vehicle of Prince Henry of Prussia, a pioneer motoring fan who organized his own sporting events. (D)

Alanson P. Brush designed single-cylinder light cars and built them from 1907 until the company became part of U.S. Motors, a group that disappeared in 1913. Brush also designed the first (2-cylinder) Oakland in 1907 for that company's organizer, Edward M. Murphy, a buggy builder of Pontiac, Michigan. This picture shows the advanced front suspension of the Brush. (USA)

The third production model, the 1907 Buick "D," built in Flint, Michigan, had an engine of 255 sq. in. and was one of the first of Buick's 4-cylinder units, with sliding gear transmission. The engine, upper and lower crankcase, clutch and transmission housings were cast aluminum. (USA)

Bold front from a small French car. This brass radiator heads a single-cylinder, 8-hp de Dion-Bouton; the back seats could be swung out to facilitate rear passengers' entry. (F)

What looks like a development of the Model 10 Buick runabout does a hill-climb that few would believe possible from the picture. (USA)

This British Daimler has architecture rather more perpendicular than most; one of the highly successful line of poppet-valve, chain-driven models that were built by the company between 1902 and 1909. The fluted radiator, long the most visible mark of the Daimler, had been used since 1904. (GB)

The first Daimler vehicle, 1885. A 'single track'
machine of one cylinder and one-half horsepower. (D)

Karl Benz built this three-wheeler, his first machine,
in 1885 and patented it in January 1886. (D)

Gottlieb Daimler's first 'motorwagen', 1886. Four wheels and 1.1 horsepower. (D)

Peugeot vis-à-vis, 1892. (F)

Opel Luzmann, 1898. Single-cylinder, 19 mph. (D)

Benz Landaulet-coupé, 1899. Straight out of the carriage era. (D)

Cannstatt Daimler 1899. (D)

Daring De-Dion publicity, 1899. (F)

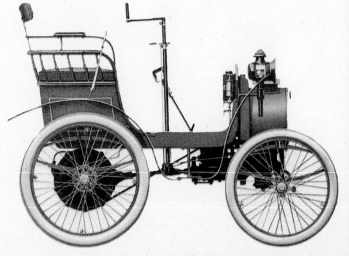

Renault single-cylinder voiturette, 1899. (F)

One of the most significant of early Fiats, the 130-hp Grand Prix de France car was designed by lawyer Carlo Cavalli, who had become technical director of the company. To meet the French competition requirement of a maximum fuel consumption of 30 liters to 100 km (9.4 mpg), the Grand Prix car was developed with this performance in view. Its massive $16\frac{1}{4}$-liter engine gave a top speed of 100 mph. Here an artist (Carlo Biscaretti) shows Nazarro at the wheel during the Grand Prix. (I)

At a Java Motor Club meeting this Fiat 28/40 (long-chassis model) is used as a platform for a super-family group. Built from 1906-1907, the car had a 4-cylinder unit of over 7 liters, with a top speed of 53 mph and, says the over-modest brochure, a seating capacity of 4 to 6. Exactly 557 cars of this model were made. (I)

A lineup of Model D Franklin cabs at a New York depot. By 1907 their air-cooled engines were 4- or 6-cylinder units with shaft drive located under the circular hood. Four models were offered: a runabout, a light tourer, a tourer (all with 4 cylinders), and a tourer six. (USA)

Quite a drive for "Four Ladies in a Haynes," as the sign says. From Chicago to New York may not be much of a safari today, but in 1907 road conditions over the journey of around 700 miles must have held many fearful hazards. Model 5, 4-cylinder, 30-hp, five-seater. (USA)

Louis Coatalen was in his mid-twenties when he designed the first car for William Hillman in 1907, a 4-cylinder, 25 hp built for the Tourist Trophy of that year. It was not until 1912 that the company, still producing in comparatively small numbers, turned to the light car, a 9-hp model, that set the pattern of Hillmans for many years. At the wheel is Louis Coatalen. (GB)

In 1907 the Tourist Trophy, run by the R.A.C. at the Isle of Man since 1905, mounted a Heavy Touring Car race, run concurrently with the T.T. The winner was this Humber, seen here with the obligatory 8-foot-high screen to simulate the frontal area of the normal closed car. (GB)

On June 11, 1907, five cars left Peking in China to "race" to Paris, 10,000 miles away. The winner was this huge 4-cylinder, 40-hp Itala, driven by Prince Borghese. After sixty days of unspeakable trials and privations, crossing deserts and swamps, rivers and mountains, to say nothing of the wasteland of Siberia, the victorious Italian car arrived in Paris, to be joined there three weeks later by two competing de Dions and a Dutch Spyker. (I)

The Peking-to-Paris marathon; the Itala cleverly used the bed of the Trans-Siberian railway part of the way, since the surface was considerably better than the local roads. The greatest danger on this section of the route was being the target of potshots from the bandit population of the region. (I)

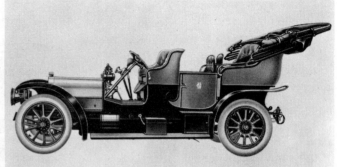

The first Lancia left the small factory in Turin in September 1907—via a doorway that had to be hastily widened with a pick to allow the new vehicle through! Vincenzo Lancia's car was a 4-cylinder side-valve developing 14 hp at 1,450 rpm—a high engine speed in days when gasoline motors rarely exceeded 1,000 rpm. The first production model, shown here, was originally called the 18–24 hp, then renamed "Alfa." (I)

Type E, 4-cylinder, 4½-liter, 24-hp Laurin-Klement—stylish enough to belong to a European monarch of prewar days. Laurin & Klement was yet another company to have a try at the 1907 Royal Automobile Club's Non-stop Run between London and Holyhead in North Wales, a distance of 265 miles to be negotiated without one single engine stop—which the two Bohemian cars succeeded in doing. Bohemia became part of Czechoslovakia after World War I, and in 1925 Laurin & Klement was taken over by an arms firm, and the product became known as Skoda. (CS)

Britain's Brooklands Motor Course, the world's first genuine permanent race track, was opened in 1907. In June, a month before the first race took place, Selwyn Edge took a stripped-down 6-cylinder Napier and drove it single-handed for 24 hours around the course at 65.91 mph. Edge's Napier is on the left; the other two cars, also Napiers, are pacers. (GB)

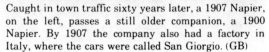

Caught in town traffic sixty years later, a 1907 Napier, on the left, passes a still older companion, a 1900 Napier. By 1907 the company also had a factory in Italy, where the cars were called San Giorgio. (GB)

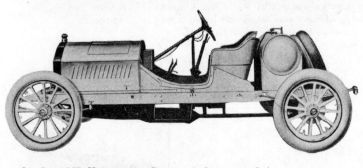

In the 1907 Kaiserpreis, Germany's big race of the year, Opels driven by brothers Carl Joerns and Michel Opel came in third and fourth, and Carl received the award for "the best German car" from the Emperor. The car used a 4-cylinder, 8-liter, side-valve unit developing 80 hp. (D)

When Ransom Eli Olds left the company that bore his name in 1904, he had founded the Reo Motor Car Co. The move was prompted by the disagreement between Olds and Sam Smith, his partner, who owned the bulk of the shares. Olds wanted to stay with a cheaper car—Smith wanted to make a bigger, more expensive model. This is a single-cylinder tourer, with dummy hood, chain drive, 8 hp. (USA)

The 8-liter Kaiserpreis Opel in action during the race — on its way to win the "Besten Deutschen Wagen" award, June 14, 1907. (D)

This Rambler Model 24 was one of the first 4-cylinder cars made by the Kenosha, Wisconsin, company. This picture, taken in 1907 in front of the old Marietta Country Club, Marietta, Ohio, gives a glimpse of the female fashion (and shape!) of the period. (USA)

The French Grand Prix team Renaults line up before the start of the 1907 race. François Szisz, winner of the previous year's Grand Prix (the French event was the only G.P. at that time) is on the extreme left. Renault had used the new quick-detachable wheel rims on their 13-liter cars in the 1906 G.P., and little was changed for the following year's race. (F)

Riley's first vehicle had been tri-cars, which were made until about 1907. The 2-cylinder, 60 degree V unit of just over one liter that had been used in the later three-wheelers was also used in the company's first four-wheelers. This is possibly the earliest four-wheel Riley in existence today and in 1907 was the latest word in sporting models, with quarter-elliptic suspension, direct steering, wire-spoked wheels, and three-speed transmission. (GB)

Rolls-Royce managing director Claude Johnson proudly demonstrated the car's ability to climb the infamous Cat and Fiddle Hill near Buxton in Derby. Here, an early meeting of pioneer motorists—all Rolls-Royce owners—takes place outside the old public house on the summit. (GB)

Over half a century later they do it again. It can be seen that at least one car, registration number AX201 (Silver Ghost), is present at both meetings. (GB)

Winner of the 1907 International Tourist Trophy, the 20-hp Rover. This race, Britain's oldest, and one of the earliest to be run regularly, was first held in 1905. The Rover Touring Car that won the 1907 event at the Isle of Man—by then attracting a large international entry—won against automobiles considerably better-known—Darracq, Metallurgique, Berliet, Humber, and sixteen others—in 8 hours, 23 minutes, 17 seconds, an average of 28 mph. Several close contenders ran out of fuel just before the finish. (GB)

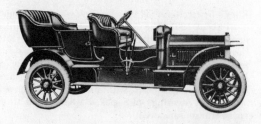

The Rover Company made the most of the T.T. publicity by offering the winning model immediately after its victory. (GB)

Country drive. Taking a steer to market must have been just as hazardous as the cartoonist suggests, in days when rustic folk may never have seen a car at close quarters.

Despite rocky finances, the Standard Motor Company produced an impressive 30-hp, 6-cylinder car in 1906. This is a 1907 Roi des Belges version. (GB)

Looking identical to a dozen other limousines of the Edwardian period, this Wolseley Cavallos was a 40/50 hp, used mainly for town travel. By 1907 the company was making vertical-engined fours to the designs of engineer J. D. Siddeley. Herbert Austin had left after a disagreement; he had wanted to continue fitting horizontal units. (GB)

This is the side-valve, 4-cylinder, chain-drive, 16-20 Sunbeam introduced in 1906. It had completed the reliability run from Land's End to John o' Groats and back again without an engine-stop, to prove its qualities, and had become a popular car in Britain. It was designed by Sunbeam's chief engineer, Albert Shaw, who also drove it in the long-distance run. (GB)

One of the very few cars made in Scotland, the Argyll Brougham, a 16/20-hp, 4-cylinder cab, was used as a "station car" for some years. Its extraordinary control system (a long, tortuous path of control linkages) made it a somewhat troublesome vehicle to maintain. (GB)

Obviously taken at a time when women's lib first showed its colors in Britain under the suffragette banner, this early Austin illustrates the Edwardian brand of female militancy. Also illustrated is Herbert Austin's early Landaulet, a 4-cylinder model that preceded his great early luxury car, the 50-hp, 6-cylinder landaulet of 1913. Austin also made Gladiators during 1908-1909 for Frenchman Clement; in fact, they were Austins in all but nameplate. (GB)

Three special Austin racers were built in 1908 and entered for the 1908 French Grand Prix. Herbert Austin used his design experience of building racing Wolseleys a few years earlier, and, although the cars did not distinguish themselves in the race, they were the only British entries to finish. The two-seater cars used a 100-hp, 6-cylinder unit of 9,677 cc, were shaft-driven and had four-speed transmissions. (GB)

Produced from 1908 to 1912 and extremely modern in appearance for its day, with near-torpedo bodywork, this Benz was a modest 4-cylinder family car of 10/18 hp. (At this time the first figure represented the power developed at 1,000 rpm and the second figure was the power developed at the maximum engine speed, although the definition changed in later years.) (D)

Marius Berliet had been making automobiles since 1895, had made a modest excursion into motor racing, won a few classes, and in 1908 was victorious in the Targa Bologna. This Type C2 double phaeton was produced in the year that Berliet first offered compressed-air starting on his larger 6-cylinder car. (F)

The French Grand Prix of 1908 saw Benz racing cars in second and third places. French driver Victor Hemery, who took second place, was plagued with tire trouble (it was not unusual for all four tires to be punctured more than once during a long race) and suffered an injury to his eye which slowed him down. Here his Benz gets a new set of spares. (D)

This Model F Buick was on the road at the time Buick became a charter member of General Motors. By 1908 the American gas buggy had become a full-fledged motor car — including running boards. Engine: 2 cylinder, 159 cu. in., 22-hp. (USA)

One of the most noticeable features of this Delaunay Belleville, its fat, round hood (reminder of an earlier boiler-making background), housing a 4- or 6-cylinder engine, was continued until the 1920s. Several makes of the first decades of the century copied this style, no doubt hoping for some sales spin-off from the motoring public's respect for the Delaunay Belleville, which was considered by many to be a finer car than the Rolls-Royce in the late Edwardian period. (F)

Rural scene in Bloomfield, Connecticut—horse-owner's dog chases motorist. Produced between 1903 and 1912, the car chugging through the greenery was a 4-cylinder, 36-hp Corbin. (USA)

A British company well established in the oil-engine business, Crossley Brothers Limited, chose to enter the automotive field and in 1904 offered a 4-cylinder, 22-hp, chain-driven model. A year later the company had produced a T-engined, 40-hp car, built on conventional continental lines both in engineering and coach work. The picture show Charles Jarrott, racing driver extraordinary and sometime member of the company marketing the cars, driving the 40-hp Crossley into Folkestone docks for one of the first cross-Channel car trips from England to France. (GB)

The 18,146-cc Fiat SB4 racer, called "Mephistopheles" by most, was brought to England by Nazarro in 1908 to be matched against a British Napier at the new Brooklands track. It won the challenge, lapping the circuit at an average speed of 119.9 mph. After World War I its owner blew up the engine, which was later replaced by an enormous Fiat airship unit of 21,714 cc. Its new owner, Ernest Eldridge, broke the world speed record in the car in 1924 at a speed of 146.01 mph. (I)

Automobilwerk Eisenach, today in the German Democratic Republic, was the site of much pioneer automotive work, under the name of Wartburg from 1898, then as Dixi. This Dixi coupe limousine was very much in the coach-work mode of the day, a time when all luxury cars seemed to look exactly alike. Weather protection for passengers was just taking over from the fresh-air attitudes of the early part of the decade. Made from 1907 to 1910. (D)

Another Model T — coupe version. There the similarity with Ford ends, although early Model A Cadillacs were very similar to Fords of the same years, no doubt owing to Henry Leland's association with Henry Ford before forming the Cadillac Motor Company at Detroit. This model housed a single-cylinder, 10-hp, 98-cu. in. unit — one of the last one-lung Caddies to be produced. (USA)

In October 1908 the first Model T Ford, "Homely as a burro and friendly as a pair of shoes," was delivered to the first buyer. An unprecedented total of 10,000 were sold in the first year, and by mid-1927, when the Model T was discontinued, close to 15½ million had been delivered. Propelled by a 20-hp, 2.9-liter, 4-cylinder unit, the Model T weighed 1,200 pounds, had a ground clearance of 10½ inches (necessary for all but town roads), and pedal-operated planetary transmission with two forward speeds. It was capable of 45 mph and 20 mpg. The use of vanadium steel wherever possible allowed a light, strong construction and gave the car a go-anywhere reputation—a claim vindicated in 1909 when a Model T was driven 4,100 miles from New York to Seattle in appalling weather conditions over roads so poor that some had almost ceased to exist. (USA)

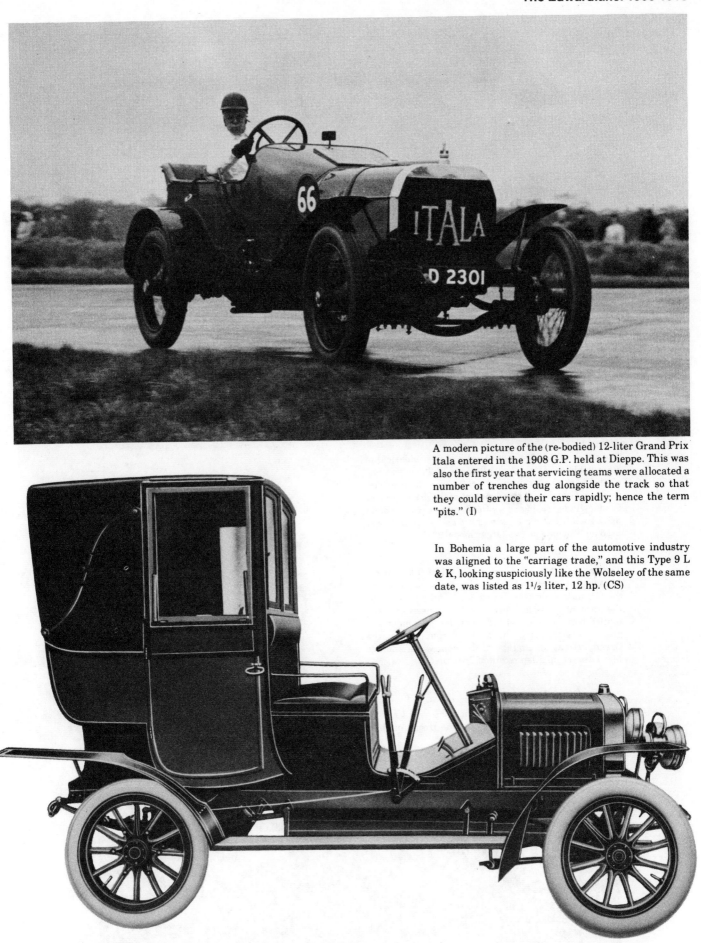

A modern picture of the (re-bodied) 12-liter Grand Prix Itala entered in the 1908 G.P. held at Dieppe. This was also the first year that servicing teams were allocated a number of trenches dug alongside the track so that they could service their cars rapidly; hence the term "pits." (I)

In Bohemia a large part of the automotive industry was aligned to the "carriage trade," and this Type 9 L & K, looking suspiciously like the Wolseley of the same date, was listed as 1½ liter, 12 hp. (CS)

The shape of this Mercedes is also almost identical to other vehicles of its class. This car, a 10/20 hp, was one of the first shaft-driven vehicles from the Daimler works in Germany, a development of the drive used for the 6-cylinder racing cars of two years earlier. Chain drive soon became a back number and after 1908 was used on only one or two larger models. (D)

The winning Mercedes, driven by Christian Lautenschlager, one of the 1908 *Grosser Preis von Frankreich,* as the Germans called the French G.P. This car, built for the race and using a long stroke to overcome the limited-bore regulations (155 mm for 4-cylinder engines), developed 135 bhp at 1,400 rpm. It won the Grand Prix at an average of 69 mph, while another Mercedes set up a lap record of 78.6 mph. (D)

Salutes all around for Czar Nicholas and Czarina Alexandra of Russia as they visit the troops in their Mercedes. (D)

In 1908 the Paris newspaper *Le Matin*, sponsors of the first motor competition, the Paris-Rouen Trial of 1894, and organizers of the Peking to Paris race in 1907, now offered a trophy for a race from New York to Paris, a distance of 13,000 (driving) miles. One of the entrants was this French Motobloc made by the Bordeaux company. The race was won by an American 60-hp Thomas Flyer. (F)

Built by Napier, the 4-cylinder Hutton was so called because Napier at that time was promoting its 6-cylinder cars and extolling their superiority over 4-cylinder models. It was specially built for the 1908 T.T. to the order of racing driver J. E. Hutton, who also planned to break class records with it at Brooklands.

Indeed, the 26-hp, 5.8-liter engine took the car to several records: the ten-lap Brooklands, the flying 1/2 mile, and its main claim to fame—it won the race for which it had been made, the 1908 Isle of Man Tourist Trophy. Both front and rear views of this rakish racer are seen here. (GB)

The Oldsmobile Model M Toy Tourer, more stylish and luxurious than its predecessors, appeared during the same year the company became part of General Motors. Only 1,000 of these 3½-liter, 4-cylinder cars were made. In 1908 one of these cars completed the 1,669 miles of the Glidden Tour with a "perfect" score. (USA)

Another version of the Model M—titled rather grandiloquently the "Palace Touring." A beautifully bodied car by Oldsmobile, this and other contemporary models were designed, as the company stated, "on French lines," which simply meant that the engine had been moved to the front from what was charmingly called the "engine room" under the body of the car. (USA)

This was also the year of the Oldsmobile Model Z, unveiled in Madison Square Garden in 1908, a year after another engineering "first" had been recorded by Oldsmobile—the use of nickel plating. This was a 6-cylinder vehicle—the company's first—and, at 8 liters, it was the first of the company's really large automobiles. (USA)

This is the elegant 10/18-PS "Doppel Phaeton" from Opel—with a 4-cylinder, water-cooled engine; timed valves; magneto ignition; dredge lubrication; three forward speeds and reverse; gate-type gearshift; and a top speed of 60 km/h (37 mph). It was a popular buy in Germany. (D)

After entering giant 18-liter cars in the first Grand Prix in 1906 and 15.5-liter cars in the 1907 G.P., racing Panhards were less monstrous for the 1908 G.P., when the literage had shrunk to a mere 12.8. However, the cars did not distinguish themselves, and the day of the giant Panhard racing vehicle (and those of others such as Fiat, whose faith had been pinned on "the more liters the more successes") was over, particularly as Grand Prix racing virtually died for three years. Top speed, according to Panhard-Levassor records, was 155 km/h (96 mph) — and the horsepower was 120. (F)

How an artist saw Carl Joerns Opel in the car entered for the Grand Prix of 1908. New for the race, it was a 4-cylinder, 12-liter juggernaut that took Carl Joerns to sixth place in the event held on a road circuit outside Dieppe and won by Christian Lautenschlager in a Mercedes. (D)

Archetypical of all subsequent taxicab styles in London, the Unic was a 4-cylinder, 14-hp produced for two decades and seen in the streets of Britain's capital until after World War II. So many were used in London that Edwardians coined the phrase, "It's unpatriotic to take a taxi!" (F)

Disguised as a brougham (style terms were almost impossible to sort out in this transitional time when carriage body-style names were used for motored transport), this Sunbeam was in fact an open tourer with a detachable top. Chain-driven, with a 4-cylinder engine developing 20 hp. A magazine of mid-Edwardian times rightly said of the coach work: "It cannot be called graceful, the abrupt square form that rises suddenly behind the front seats . . . nor can the owner of such a vehicle take the wheel himself without looking as if he were a coachman." (GB)

With its bicycle background, the Rambler was first built as an American light runabout, but by 1905–1906 it had developed into a sturdy 2-cylinder car of conventional design. In 1907 a 4-cylinder model was introduced, of which this Model 37 is the two-seater. Here, Rambler dealer Harry Vail nails up one of the signs purchased by the company in the interests of the motoring public in Wisconsin and Illinois in 1908. (USA)

A cheaper car sold by Studebaker, the E. M. F. (and its sister car the Flanders) was built by the Everitt-Metzger-Flanders Co. at Detroit. The car was driven by a conventional 2.7 liter 4-cylinder unit throughout its production from 1908 to 1912. Picture taken at a rally in the 1950s. (USA)

By 1908 Herbert Austin, mainspring of the Wolseley company in its formative years, had left to organize his own firm, and a young designer, J. D. Siddeley, had been producing vertical-cylinder engines for Wolseley, now with a large range of vehicles in production and experience in racing. This is a landaulet coupe, with the chauffeur out in the cold. (GB)

This 20-hp, 4-cylinder Vauxhall began a long series of sporting successes for the British company. In the R.A.C. and the Scottish Reliability Trials of 1908 it became the first car in the world to complete 2,000 miles without an involuntary stop of any kind. Designed by engineer Laurennce Pomeroy, it formed the basis for all sporting Vauxhalls that followed. (GB)

Posing for the cameras before the start of the New York to Paris race of 1908, the occupants of this Italian Zust are dressed for inclement weather and then some. The trek took them across the United States, Russia, and Europe in the worst of weather conditions. An American Thomas won, taking 168 days, followed by a German Protos and the Zust. (I)

The first Austin Seven was sold some thirteen years before the famous model of 1922. A single-cylinder, open two-seater, this early "Baby" Austin was an attempt to produce a really low-cost, low-powered automobile for the new motoring public. However, this was not a genuine Austin—Swift of Coventry made most of it and also sold an almost identical car under their own name. (GB)

Called a Park Phaeton, this 6-cylinder car shows its carriage background strongly, with the back end looking almost as though it had been grafted on. During this period Austin made a number of "town" cars and a large range of other styles, including 10-, 15—24-, 40- and 50-hp vehicles. (GB)

The 1908 Benz Grand Prix car appeared in cowled and
streamlined form as the now legendary "Blitzen-Benz"
(Lightning Benz) in 1909, with an engine of 21.5 liters
and a claimed 200 hp. It captured the world speed record at 125.95 mph in 1909; in the hands of American
Barney Oldfield in 1910 it clocked a flying-start mile
record of 131.7 mph at Daytona. Driven by another
American, Bob Burman, the car gained further world-
class record successes. (D)

The "Blitzen-Benz" power unit — a claimed 200 hp at
1,600 rpm; 4 cylinders. (D)

A new 14/30-hp Benz was produced in 1909 on the basis of earlier engine designs and recent knowledge gained through racing. The car had its 4 cylinders cast in one block, a bore and stroke of 90 × 140 mm, and developed 35 hp at 1,500 rpm. This is the phaeton-landaulet version made from 1909 to 1913. The two photographs show the development that took place during those years. (D)

The Model 30 Cadillac first made its appearance in 1908. This is the fashionable roadster of 1909. The car was undoubtedly a masterpiece of quality: its four separately cast cylinders were copper-jacketed and, said the brochure, the car was "truly a marvel for noiselessness and smoothness in action . . . with a power of 28.9 hp." Over 5,900 were made in 1909 (and were relatively inexpensive in standard form), and a total of 66,939 were sold by the end of 1914. Cadillac became part of General Motors in 1909. (USA)

The first Hudson advertisement was seen on June 19, 1909, and the first Hudson car was completed (in some haste, it could be imagined) by July 3. Seen here is one of the originals, the Model 20, a 4-cylinder, 20-hp vehicle with a top speed of just under 50 mph. That year the first mile of metaled (concrete) road was built in rural America — in Wayne County, Michigan — and a woman drove across the country from New York to San Francisco in fifty-three days. (USA)

A smart two-seater for the young set, this twin-cylinder Humber was part of the company's bid to capture part of the lighter car market. It was fitted with Dunlop tires, side and tail lamps, horn, roof (hood), and tool kit. (GB)

Twice-restored and now in superb condition, this 1909 Model L-D9 Kissel Kar shows little hint of its farm-machinery background. A 4-cylinder, 30-hp tourer, this well-made vehicle (a reputation for workmanship was held by the company throughout its life from 1903 to 1931) underwent stringent engine bench-testing before leaving the factory—and was rejected if the unit developed less than the stated horsepower. "Noiseless, fast and powerful . . . has shown immense reserve time and again in the severest hill-climb tests" ran the ads. (USA)

The Lion-Peugeot was a product of the Beaulieu-Valentigney factory, an old Peugeot works used by Robert Peugeot to build his own cars after a disagreement with the original company. By 1910 he was reunited with the family firm, and by 1913 Lion-Peugeot ceased to exist. This vehicle with the Disney look is a 9-cv (9-hp) cabriolet. (F)

H. A. Lozier and Company had begun by making steam trucks to a British design in 1896. Entering the passenger-vehicle field, they made a few experimental steam cars, but turned to internal-combustion-engined vehicles by 1905 when they showed their first model at Madison Square Garden. The model became one of the finest quality American cars as it developed; however, that did not save them from extinction in 1917. These two Loziers were photographed in the Bronx in 1909. (USA)

Fine cars at a price that would have excluded all but the rich. Hence this name-dropping by Napier in the advertisement for its latest 6-cylinder landaulet—an attempt to capture some of the Rolls-Royce trade. (GB)

The Mitchell Wagon Co. started making horse-drawn vehicles in 1834, entered the motor field in 1903 with the help of bicycle engineer John W. Bates, and stayed with the automotive industry for thirty years; then the company was liquidated and the buildings were sold to Nash. The Mitchell seen here at a tollgate in Pennsylvania around 1909 was a shaft-driven, water-cooled car of 35 hp. (USA)

The brothers Opel had long been participants in motor sports, and in 1909 the big event was the Prinz Heinrich-Fahrt (Prince Henry Trials). Wilhelm Opel won the event, and Opel cars also took third, fifth, sixth, and tenth places. The trials were an effort by Prince Henry of Prussia, a keen automobile enthusiast, to provide a form of motor competition that was *not* a race, and they were actually a type of rally. (D)

In 1909 members of the Automobile Association in Britain mounted an ambitious maneuver: to transport a battalion of Guards from London to Hastings on the south coast. This 30-hp, 6-cylinder Napier, seen on the commemoration run fifty years later, had a swept volume of 4,077 cc. (GB)

The "Doktorwagen" (doctor's car) style was offered especially to physicians to (as the advertisement said) "safeguard harassed country doctors from the hazards of the unsurfaced byways." It was a bright idea that caught on in several countries. Medical doctors were among the first to appreciate the speedy mobility of the car and were eager buyers in pioneer motoring days. This Opel model had a 4-cylinder, 1,029-cc engine. (D)

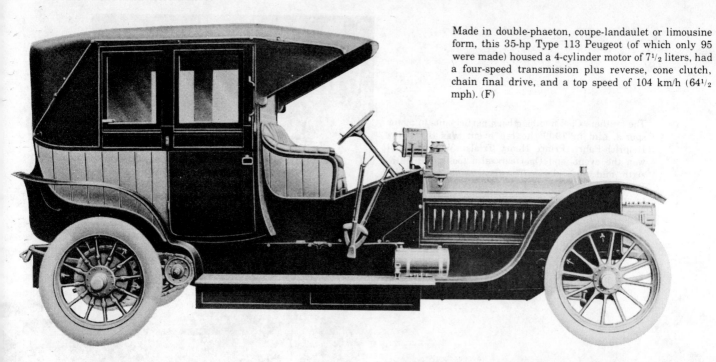

Made in double-phaeton, coupe-landaulet or limousine form, this 35-hp Type 113 Peugeot (of which only 95 were made) housed a 4-cylinder motor of 7½ liters, had a four-speed transmission plus reverse, cone clutch, chain final drive, and a top speed of 104 km/h (64½ mph). (F)

Carrying President Taft (left) is a 1909 4-cylinder Rambler. Its gas lighting was supplied by the brass carbide generator seen just behind the offside front wing, on the running board, and the throttle was a ring just under the rim of the steering wheel. In 1909 Rambler became the first company in the United States to offer a "fifth wheel" (or spare tire), thus simplifying tire-changing. (USA)

The New York 24-hour race has just started, and a 4-cylinder, 35-hp Renault, driven by Raffalovitch, leads another car around the oval circuit. The Renault driver stopped after the first lap and fitted mudguards to protect himself against flying stone and dirt. He had kept quiet about his intentions to use these and used them as a "secret weapon," hoping they would prove an effective aid to fast driving. They did, and he won the race. (F)

A popular feat for the day—find a steep hill, take your car and a photographer, and you have a publicity picture extolling its virtues. Here a Riley 10 hp negotiates a notorious hill at Bideford, Devon. Under the fashionable Edwardian round hood was a V-twin, water-cooled unit with a bore and stroke of 96 × 96 mm. (GB)

This extraordinary machine with the driverless appearance is a Rochet-Schneider cab-de-ville, a 4-cylinder, 80x120 mm, developing 16 hp. Somewhere inside the chambered-glass passenger compartment are the controls, no doubt. (F)

The Raffalovitch Renault at the pits before having mudguards fitted during the 24-hour 1,000-mile New York race. (F)

Stanley Steamers were simple to maintain, cheap to run, and could out-accelerate anything powered by any other fuel. By 1909 the Stanley had adopted its "traditional" shape, had an unexplodable boiler, high seating, reliable performance, and could travel over 50 miles on a single fill of water. However, no manufacturer could please everyone—some even complained that the Stanley was too quiet and consequently a danger to unwary pedestrians. This is the 10-hp touring version. (USA)

Clement Talbot Limited of Kensington, London, had imported French cars into Britain since 1903, but the company eventually (from 1906) made its own products in England. This is the 1909 Talbot 4T, with a 4-cylinder, 105 × 120 mm, side-valve engine, transmission brakes at the rear, and four-speed transmission. (GB)

Manufacturered in the same year as a new sporting two-seater Vauxhall, this model had a 4-cylinder, 16-hp power unit; the landaulet body with a large front window was designed to convey milady in comfort and to allow the populace to admire her through the glass. Top speed around 45 mph, with cruising in comfort at 30 mph, and a fuel consumption of about 30 mpg. (GB)

This 3-liter Vauxhall had been fitted with a long, narrow body and christened KN (cayenne pepper—hot stuff) by a Vauxhall wit. It put up some very fast speeds at Brooklands in England in 1909 and later recorded 100.08 mph over the kilometer, the first car of its type to reach the "ton." (GB)

The Edwardians: 1900-1918

This 18/24-hp Austin would have been considered a small car compared with some other Austin products of the day—the 40, 50, and the 6-cylinder 60 hp. This was not Herbert Austin's smallest car, however: the previous year he had introduced the first "Baby" Austin, a single-cylinder Seven. Early Austins were sound and reliable if somewhat conventional vehicles and were the solid foundation of the manufacturing empire that grew to maturity after World War I. (GB)

The "Blitzen-Benz," this time in the hands of Bob Burman at the 1910 American Grand Prix at Savannah. The car scored a second world-record title, with Barney Oldfield at the wheel at Daytona with a flying-start 1-mile speed of 131.72 mph. After this, records were not recognized unless a two-way run was made. (D)

The British Daimler company had adopted the "Silent Knight" engine in 1909 for all their cars. Knight, an Englishman who had emigrated to the United States, had built a sleeve-valve-engined car that had impressed Daimler's manager when he saw it on a visit to that country. The company's silent, smooth cars became a byword in the following years. (GB)

In 1910 Fiat started to revise its range considerably and produced a new series of models: Types 1, 2, 3, 4, 5, and 6, ranging from 1,846 cc to the Type 6's 9,017-cc power unit. This is a Type 4 (first series), housing a 4-cylinder, 5,699-cc engine, made from 1910 to 1912. Several styles of bodies were fitted, this being a rather old-fashioned (even for 1910) landaulet. (I)

The Model T Ford roadster, built from 1910 to 1915 and, according to contemporary advertisements, disguisable in many ways—"by means of a streamlined hood with radiator shell and crown fenders" said one ad, as if owners should be slightly ashamed of their front ends. Many accessories were also available from an early date: floor mats, topping outfits (fabric tops), seat covers and pads, side screens—even a radiator cap with "Baby Lincoln" on it! (USA)

A more conventional Model T of the time was this tourer for the family. With tires still bald, the tough T could cope with the roughest terrain—and out-of-town roads were all rough—but the puncture rate must have been high. By 1910 doors were part of the standard equipment on tourers, although the left front door was "for decoration only" for several years of production. Looks like Henry himself in the passenger seat. (USA)

Out for a Sunday afternoon rally in Detroit are these ladies with their parasols and their escorts, every single one in a 1910 4-cylinder Hudson "20" roadster. In 1910 Hudson ranked seventeenth among American makes in total registrations. (USA)

Laurin & Klement had been participants in motor sports since their formation in 1906, and in 1909 they had brought out this Type FCR racer, a big 4-cylinder (85 × 250 mm) vehicle that competed for several years and in 1910 and 1911 gained a number of major European successes. Between 1908 and 1911 L & K cars scored an impressive fifty-seven firsts, twenty-five seconds, and eleven thirds in motor-sport events. (CS)

The famous "Limited" was introduced by Oldsmobile in 1910. Its big 60-hp, 707-cu in power unit had 6 cylinders, and it was also a big car in other dimensions— needing two mounting steps to board! With a cruising speed of 65 mph, the "Limited" was, in its day, the ultimate in fast luxury motoring in America. It was immortalized in a painting depicting it racing a great New York Central express train. (USA)

1901 Pieper voiturette. (B)

Opel tonneau, 1902, with 2-cylinder engine. (D)

Lanchester 1903. Twin-cylinder, 12 hp. (GB)

Fiat Corsa, 1902. Four cylinders, 23 hp and a racing
speed of 60 mph. (I)

Touring Mercedes, 1903. (D)

A 1903 Clement Talbot at a recent London- Brighton
Commemoration Run. (GB)

Winton, 1903. (USA)

Aristocratic Edwardian; a 20-hp Thornycroft. (GB)

One of the most popular models of its time,
a 1903 de Dion Bouton. (F)

Daimler 'Detachable' 1905. The roof could
be removed. (GB)

Vauxhall, 1904. (GB)

Soon after this five-seater was offered to the American public, Packard, already noted for quality, produced a model in the new style — a "torpedo." Seen first at the 10th National Auto Show, the "torpedo" (in this case) was a high-sided, open car with a clean line from windshield to rear end, with the dashboard brought closer to the driver by means of a cowl, or scuttle. The police officer's familiar gesture needs no explanation. (USA)

Seen clearly is the radiator-behind-engine layout of the Renaults of 1910. This tiny 2-cylinder, 1.2-liter, 6.2-hp unit still takes the two-seater some 35 miles to the gallon. The car was built as an open voiturette and as a sedan. (F)

A Reo at the start of the 1910 A.A.A. Annual Tour. The Reo Motor Car Company of Lansing was, in addition to producing cars, busy introducing its Speed Wagon, a value-for-money delivery truck, in 1910. (USA)

The Edwardians: 1900-1918

Nautilus. A curious vehicle with a name evocative of the Jules Verne undersea story, this racing Sunbeam was fitted with a 4,256-cc, 4-cylinder (92 × 160 mm), overhead-valve engine with four valves per cylinder, operated by pushrods and rockers. The pointed nose unfortunately caused some overheating, and the car was not a great success. (GB)

A 1910 Riley sporting the fashionable cylindrical hood (also used by the Dutch Spyker and the aristocratic French Delaunay-Belleville). Since 1908 the British company had moved its engine from midships to the front, and Rileys now housed a 96 × 96 mm, water-cooled, V-twin unit of 10 hp with mechanical inlet valves, trembler coil ignition, cone clutch, and three-speed transmission. (GB)

The French manufacturers of this Sizaire-Naudin built some fine voiturettes from 1905 to 1910, and, in the hands of Naudin himself, one had won Sicilian Florio's race for small cars in 1906. This is the 12 hp of 1910, reputed to have been rediscovered in 1953 when a wall of an old house was demolished and the wooden chassis was found behind one of the panels. (F)

Designer Laurence Pomeroy at the wheel of the prototype Prince Henry Vauxhall, a car that was to become internationally famous in the sporting world, and the most distinguished vehicle ever made by the company. The 3-liter car took part in the Prinz-Heinrich Trials of 1910. (GB)

This odd car is a 4-cylinder, 15-hp Austin Town Carriage—an unusual venture, with the engine inside the cab and the passenger compartment in coaching tradition. (GB)

A Type A19 Berliet. By 1911 shaft drive and four-speed transmissions were used on all cars from the Lyons factory—and this 4.4-liter vehicle was on offer to the public. Considered very smart for its day (compare it with the picture of the 1911 Brush), it has the long, low line of a touring car of at least three years later, although its mechanics were uninspiring. (F)

The single-cylinder Brush Runabout was, the ad said, "Everyman's car" and, priced inexpensively, it was indeed value for money, with a tough wooden frame and helical suspension on all four wheels. Running costs were advertised at "less than a cent a mile." The driver of this two-seater typifies the hardy attitude in America toward motoring some seventy years ago. (USA)

Louis Chevrolet, who had come to America from Switzerland to sell wine pumps, entered motor sports, won several events, became a Buick team driver, and designed this experimental car in 1911 before forming, with W. C. Durant, the Chevrolet Motor Company of Michigan, which started production with the 4.9-liter T-head Classic 6 on November 3, 1911. (USA)

A street scene in Coventry, England—heart of the motor-industry region. Daimler made a wide range of cars from 1910 to 1914 (this is one of the middle range) and they were much used by British royalty. The single-studded tire and the large horn mounted centrally were characteristic features of the period. It seems hardly necessary to add that, sadly, this historic street has long since disappeared. (GB)

A French company from Luneville in Lorraine, De Dietrich is part of the fabric of motor history from its earliest days in 1897, when Baron de Turckheim obtained a license to build cars on the "systeme Amédée Bollée." He later built Belgian cars under license, following with the Turcat Méry. Ettore Bugatti also designed for the company. The name was changed to Lorraine-Dietrich in 1908. (F)

The Belgian Excelsior company introduced two new models in 1911, the 4½-liter, 6-cylinder 20/30 hp, and a smaller 14/20. The company enjoyed a high reputation for both their sporting and family cars before World War I, and during the early twenties the Brussels company offered a very fine 5,350-cc model, the Adex. (B)

The President of Chile rides in a Fiat Type 2 15–20 of 1911. The car, with a 2,612-cc engine, was made in various forms until 1920 and was the first car to be adopted by the Italian armed forces during that country's Libyan campaign. (I)

The transitional period between graceful phaeton, landaulet, and other coach-influenced bodies and the more slab-sided, tourer-torpedo designs seemed to have passed by this distinguished Delaunay-Belleville. This is the 6-cylinder Coupé-Ville. (F)

The elephantine Fiat S76 was an incredible one-off record-breaker. The monumental overhead-valve engine of 28,353 cc (it had a stroke of 9.67 in) produced some 300 hp at a loping 1,900 rpm. Built to take the World Land Speed Record away from Germany's "Blitzen-Benz," the S76 was sent to Britain's Brooklands to be tried out by Pietro Bordino; later, at Saltburn Sands, it reached 124 mph. It actually set up a world record in Belgium with French driver Duray at the wheel, but the recorded 137 mph was never confirmed because of suspect timing equipment. (I)

The Ford Model T "Torpedo" (looking very little like the new automobile shape) from the Highland Park factory, into which Henry Ford had moved from the Piquette plant in 1910. (USA)

The 40/50-hp Gobron-Brillie Landaulette (with small passenger in traditional boater hat). This French firm had produced cars since 1898 with the intention of offering cars that were free from the main discomfort of the day, vibration. The opposed-piston system (two pistons per cylinder) that was used certainly made for smoother running. The brochure explained, "As the pistons draw apart, a charge of gas is drawn into the cylinder through the inlet valve. This charge is compressed by the pistons coming together again and then fired, the impulse being transmitted to the crankshaft by the lower and upper connecting rods. On the next upward stroke the exhaust gases are disposed of through the exhaust valve in the usual way." (F)

The first "Indianapolis 500" was held on May 30, 1911, and won by a 6-cylinder Marmon Wasp driven by Ray Harroun, who had led the race for about 300 miles. He averaged 74.59 mph and covered the distance in 6 hours and 42 minutes. (USA)

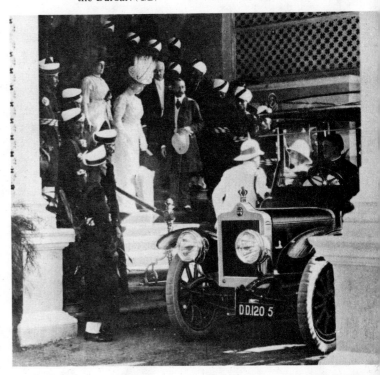

A glimpse of the front end of a 6-cylinder, 20-hp Standard Landaulette during the Delhi Durbar (India) celebrations of 1911. King George V and Queen Mary are on the steps. No less than seventy Standard cars were sent to India to convey various parties attending the Durbar. (GB)

A fire almost completely destroyed the Russellsheim Opel works in 1911, allowing the company to install a completely new and sophisticated plant. The difference between 1911 and 1912 products may be seen clearly by comparing the Puppchen with this 4-cylinder, 5/12, two-seater sedan with "inside steering." (D)

The Regal Company started life with a great sales gimmick—it took back all its first models after a year and replaced them with new 1908 Regals. Needless to say, the offer was not repeated in 1909. This Regal Underslung was unusual for 1911 in that part of its frame was designed to pass under the axles. This is the two-seater 18/20 hp, housing a 3.2-liter engine. (USA)

The mobile Czar of Russia again, visiting maneuvers of the Kaiser's army in Germany, this time with his daughters, one of whom is said to be the mysterious Anastasia. The car—a Mercedes "Knight." The company used Knight sleeve-valve engines in several models after the Daimler Company of Coventry had proved their worth in series of tests and had used them in the British production cars. (D)

A Prince Henry in action. First seen in 1910, the legendary 3-liter Vauxhall became available to the public at the 1911 Motor Show in London. Shortly afterward three were entered in a Swedish rally; one of them won the event. Fifty were built in 1912 on a 9-ft, 6-in wheelbase, after which the engine was enlarged to 4 liters and the size of the chassis was increased. The Prince Henry, built until 1914, made a name in record-breaking and racing and was the immediate ancestor of the company's famous 30/98. (GB)

The Lancashire Vulcan Motor & Engineering Company went into automobile production in 1902 (after making its name in commercial vehicles) with a single-cylinder light car. By 1911 the product had matured into this large 6-cylinder model. Both 2.4- and 3.6-liter engines were offered in 1911. (GB)

The Tipo Zero shown in 1912 and first sold in 1913 was conceived by Fiat as a popular car for the motoring masses and was intended to be produced in quantity. However, World War I interrupted production, and just 2,000 models were made between 1912 and 1915. The car could be considered the first small, inexpensive Fiat to be manufactured in a large single series. At first only one body, an open tourer, was offered. Engine: 1,846 cc, 4 cylinder, developing 19 bhp at 2,000 rpm. (I)

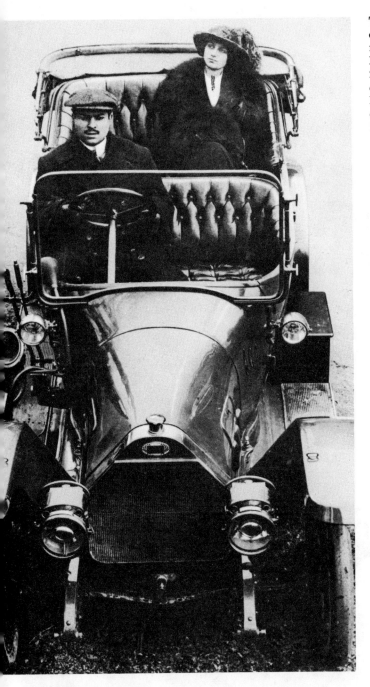

Made by Austro-Daimler from 1912 to 1914 and again from 1919 to 1920, this 4-cylinder, 6/25-PS personenauto, a light "Alpine" shaft-driven vehicle with two-wheel brakes, four-speed transmission, and magneto ignition, was a smart tourer from Vienna. The Austro-Daimler Company was formed in 1899 when Gottlieb Daimler built a works in Austria to produce Daimler cars. By 1906 the company became independent. (A)

The car (No. 20) in the smoke mist is the winner of this Grand Prix of America at Tacoma in 1912. Driven by Teddy Tezlaff, this Fiat S61 (4-cylinder, 10,087-cc) was made in Grand Touring form as early as 1908; the competition model developed from it was produced specifically for the North American market. (I)

The Edwardians: 1900-1918

The Model T, growing up into something approaching luxury — although Henry Ford would probably not have admitted that this was a landaulet. Its monoblock, 4-cylinder, side-valve unit still plugged along at around 45 mph maximum, and its transmission had changed little by 1912. The plant at Highland Park, Detroit, now covered sixty acres. (USA)

As the Franklin Company claimed, the most successful air-cooled car in the United States had "done away with the plumbing," a phrase that sold large numbers of Franklins before World War I. The case for air-cooling was strong in pioneer days—no radiator was necessary, there were no leaky hoses, no pump was used, and a considerable weight was saved. (USA)

One of the founders of the motor industry. August Horch, born in 1868, worked first with Benz, then on his own. By 1909 he had left the Horch works at Cologne-Ehrenfeld to produce cars that he named Audi. This Horch 25/55 PS model, a 4-cylinder, 6,395 cc, was a "special," made for German royalty. (D)

The designers of this L & K forgot that even a chauffeur can catch a chill. A Type RK Vierzlinder-schiebermotor (4-cylinder push-motor) from Prague. By 1912 L & K were losing interest in motor sports as, in the words of the company, "They had gained everything there is to gain in sport." (CS)

Made between 1912 and 1914, this small 13/25-hp, 6-cylinder Hillman from the Coventry factory was designed for the "sporting family." Its torpedo shape was very clean and modern for 1912 and looked somewhat similar to some of the contemporary Fiat range. (GB)

A Model 33 Hudson touring in India. Many of these were exported during this period—their ruggedness and dependability made them ideal for long journeys on unmade roads. During 1912 5,708 Hudsons were shipped overseas. (USA)

For a company that started life in Canada by making sleighs, the transfer to the automotive world seems unusual. However, the Ontario-based firm of McLaughlin produced this sturdy, high-sided vehicle using a 4-cylinder Buick engine and various other parts by agreement with W. C. Durant. The bodies were Canadian-built, and at first the wood-framed coach work was considerably different from the Buick product. About 1912 the company began to use the name of Buick coupled with its own, but the practice was discontinued after sales fell. (USA)

One of the last cars to be made before Opel's factory fire of 1911 was a 6/16-hp torpedo. By 1912 the revised car was seen in two-seater form with a jump seat and a 5/14-hp engine. It was, almost by popular acclaim, called the Puppchen (Dolly) because of its dainty appearance. This is a four-seated version. (D)

The writing on the windshield of this Maxwell says "Perfect Score, Winner Glidden Tour AAA 1911," and, if the terrain under the car in the picture is any indication of the type of ground covered in the 1911 event, it says much for the car. The scene is northern Mississippi, and the caption indicates that this is part of the 1912 Glidden Tour, which was indeed won by a Maxwell (this one?) after a varied trip over 1,272 miles through Detroit, Indianapolis, Louisville, Memphis, Baton Rouge, and New Orleans in twelve days. (USA)

The Model 28 40-hp, 4-cylinder Autocrat was a companion to the great Oldsmobile Limited. This was part of the company's comparatively short venture into the up-market zone. (USA)

One of the larger Renaults of the period, this 6-cylinder, 40-hp, "carriage-trade" open tourer with coach work by Gache, was the height of elegance on the boulevards and the Grand Tour. Renault layout continued to place the radiator behind the cylinder block until 1930. (F)

Designer Leslie Hounsfield built this prototype Trojan, a "people's car" for the cheaper market. It housed a two-stroke, 4-cylinder, 1,523-cc engine, produced a modest 10 hp, and had chain drive and solid tires. This and another prototype had the engine mounted vertically between the two seats. (GB)

Seen here at Pont D'Anseremme on the Circuit des Ardennes in Belgium is a 3-liter Type L3 Peugeot. In 1912 Peugeot 7.6 GP cars heralded the demise of the giants of earlier years. At 7.6 liters they were small by racing standards of the time—cars of 14 liters had been entered for the French Grand Prix. The Peugeot, reputedly designed by Swiss engineer Henry (before doubt was cast on his ability to do so) had twin overhead camshafts and four values per cylinder; stroke and bore were 110 × 200 mm, and the unit developed 135 bhp at 2,200 rpm. The car won the two major races of 1912. (F)

In the interest of mechanical silence numerous makers had sought to tame chattering valve gears and there were many bizarre attempts to emulate the noiseless Rolls-Royce and other high-quality cars. The Valveless was one that got through—with a two-stroke engine of 2 cylinders—and sold successfully until 1914. (GB)

A long-tailed racing version of the great Prince Henry, the car from which Vauxhall's early sports vehicles were developed. Works driver A. J. Hancock (who scored some notable successes in the sport) is at the wheel. (GB)

The introduction of the electric self-starter, plus electric lighting and ignition, in 1912 had confirmed Cadillac as one of the leaders in the U.S. automotive world. Women drivers who had previously found the starting handle an obstacle were now able to drive without the aid of a strong male arm. This 1913 Cadillac is the 48.7-hp Model 30, with torpedo body; production run—15,017. (USA)

A smaller edition of the big luxury 6-cylinder, 50-hp Austin Landaulette, this 10-hp, 1.6-liter Aylesford Cabriolet was elaborate enough for most. The year 1913 marked the excursion of the company into yet another field (Austin engines had already powered a motorboat) when a 20-hp, 2–3-ton truck was built and marketed. (GB)

Late in pre-World War I days Fiat, who had earlier offered only one type of body with the Tipo Zero, its new people's car, allowed coachbuilders to construct their own designs on Zero chassis. This Spyder (two-seater sports model) and a landaulet type were the most popular during 1913-1914. Engine: 1,846 cc, 4-cylinder, producing 19 bhp, maximum speed 39 mph. (I)

Called a drophead coupe by the makers, this little Hillman two-seater was a 9-hp, 4-cylinder, 1,357-cc runabout made in Coventry. Said the contemporary ad: "Nine — and Fine! Never was a better two-seater than this 9-hp Hillman at the price...on June 21st last the Hillman was FIRST in short handicap at Brooklands, attaining an average speed for three miles from a standing start of 60 miles an hour. And the Hillman is only 9-hp!" (GB)

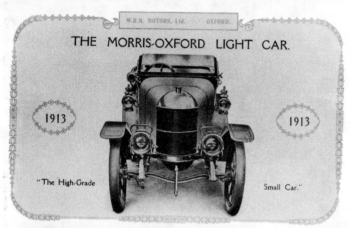

William Morris was Herbert Austin's main British competitor in the years between the wars. A former cycle-shop owner, he started the production of his own cars in 1913 with the Morris-Oxford light car, buying parts, including the 1-liter engine. Said the brochure of the time: "The consumption is from 50 to 55 miles to the gallon, and tyres and lubricating oil are upon an equally economical basis. Speeds range from 5 to 55 miles per hour on top gear on average roads." What more could you want? (GB)

Scottish singer-comedian Harry Lauder rides in a Model 37 Hudson phaeton. Early in 1913 the company introduced another series — the 57.8-hp Six-54 with a long wheelbase of 157 inches. (USA)

A classic American sporting car of pre-World War I days, the Mercer Raceabout was the envy of all who owned anything else. With its slow-revving, 5-liter, T engine (58 bhp at 1,700 rpm), it loped along at speeds much faster than passengers appreciated. The car had a top speed of about 75 mph (at just 2,000 rpm); the only disadvantage was that its brakes were not of similarly interesting specifications. The company called it "The most talked-about car in America," and it held that reputation for many years. (USA)

In 1913 Peugeot achieved great success at Indianapolis, where Jules Goux won the race at an average of 75.93 mph and also pushed up the world one-hour speed to 106.22 mph at Brooklands on this 5,600-cc so-called Henry-designed G.P. car. France's favorite driver, Georges Boillot, also won the French Grand Prix in a 5.6-liter, followed by Goux in a similar car. Seen here is Boillot before the start of the G.P. de L'A.C.F. (Grand Prix de L'Automobile Club de France, still the official title of the French Grand Prix). (F)

The Russellsheim company of Adam Opel had been scoring successes in races and events such as the Prinz-Heinrich Trials for several years when this 260-hp *rennwagen* was first seen on the grid, although it was later, after the war, that the 4-cylinder, 12-liter car recorded most of its triumphs. The engine was a water-cooled unit of 125 × 250 mm, with a single overhead camshaft. Top speed 228 km/h (141 mph). (D)

This pretty little "Bébé" Peugeot, made to Ettore Bugatti's designs, was a simple runabout seen in comparatively large numbers in France (3,095 were made at Beaulieu-Valentigney from 1913 to 1916). This is the early Type BP1, with an 855-cc, 4-cylinder motor of 6 hp, a two-speed transmission, and a *vitesse maximum* (top speed) of 35 mph. (F)

Curious coach work made by a German company for a big 35-hp Renault. In 1913 the Renault factory made the mechanics and chassis, preferring to "farm out" bodywork, which was still constructed mainly to individual clients' wishes. (F)

After building cars since 1892, Frank Duryea found he needed more capital and entered into an agreement with the Stevens Arms and Tool Co. The first Stevens-Duryea models came off the stocks in March 1902. Models H, L, R, S, U, X, XXX, Y (a big six that was made until 1912), and AA followed. By 1913 the Model C had arrived, a 6-cylinder car with a choice of two wheelbases (131 and 138 in). The picture shows the shorter. (USA)

For some years Newton & Bennett were agents for S.C.A.T. cars and handled the British sales of a 20/30-hp car called a Nazarro, designed by the racing driver of that name. For several years the company also made and sold the well-made, 4-cylinder Newton Bennett tourer seen here with racing driver Graham Hill at the wheel. (GB)

A 20-hp, 6-cylinder Standard Landaulette, with Lord and Lady Baden-Powell posing for the camera. "BP," as he was known throughout the world, was the founder of the Boy Scouts. In 1913 he married, and his wedding present was this Standard car; scouts purchased it with voluntary contributions which were limited to one penny each! (GB)

The Edwardians: 1900-1918

Bicycles, typewriters, motorcycles, aircraft, and cars, the German Adler Company from Frankfurt has at one time or another made the lot — starting in 1865 with cycles. One of the smallest Adlers, this 5/13-PS, 4-cylinder, Model K light car was one of the few designs to have seats arranged in tandem, similar to the Peugeot Quadrilette of 1923. In the years before World War I the company was prolific in its car production— almost 12,000 cars of thirty different models were made between 1910 and 1914. (D)

Hungarian François Szisz in one of three Aldas entered for the French Grand Prix of 1914. Winner of the 1906 Grand Prix, Szisz never had a look-in during the 1914 event. His highest place was seventeenth, and he retired after eleven laps, after he was hit by a passing car while changing a tire. (F)

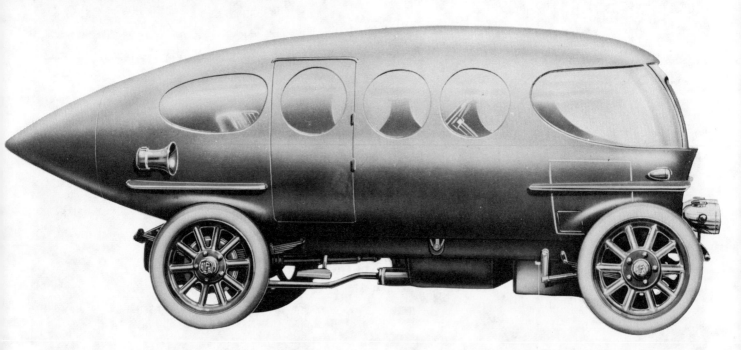

It is difficult to believe that this Alfa was designed in 1913 and built as early as 1914 (by Italian coach-work designer Castagna), but the proof is in the archives. An amazing essay into streamlining, this 4-cylinder, 40/60-hp, 6,082-cc six-seater looks more like an attempt at a spacecraft than a custom-built sedan for an important client, Count Ricotti. Top speed, 139 km/h (86 mph). (I)

Still steered by a tiller, the two-seater Baker Electric seen here at the Lars Anderson museum has a dummy hood (used to house batteries), as had several other contemporary makes. The Baker was one of the more popular electric cars in the United States prior to America's entry into World War I. The company ceased operating in 1916. (USA)

This was the breakthrough for Chevrolet; the Model H4 Baby Grand touring car and roadster Royal Mail sold well and established the company as a serious contender in the automotive market. This is a 1914 4-cylinder, overhead-valve model. (USA)

Six "B" models were introduced in 1914 (this is a B55, the first 6-cylinder model) by Buick at Flint, Michigan. Total production for the year was the highest to that date—32,889, from no less than twenty-eight plants. Torque tube drive and electric starting equipment, introduced the previous year, were now standard on all Buick cars. (USA)

Electric cars caught on in a big way in the days before World War I. Before 1912 the heavy labor of starting had been the main barrier to women who wished to drive, and the electric carriage solved the problem by requiring no cranking; it was also free of the noxious effluvia associated with the gasoline engine. Most electrics were extremely simple to drive, with lever steering, five forward gears, and a top speed of no more than 15 to 20 mph. The most serious disadvantage was (and still is) that they could not travel more than about 50 miles without elaborate arrangements for recharging the batteries. The Detroit Electric Company produced about 1,000 cars a year (this model has the Renault-shaped hood, characteristic of several electrics up to the late 1920s) during the period from 1907 to 1914, and the company survived until 1942. (USA)

Brothers Horace (left, rear) and John (right, rear) Dodge take delivery of the first car from the production department of the Dodge assembly plant in Hamtramck, Michigan. This 4-cylinder touring car was readily accepted by the public, as the Dodge company had already made its reputation by supplying transmissions, axles, steering gears, and other parts to Olds and Ford for several years. (USA)

Made in Belgium, this two-seater F.N. from the works of the *Fabrique Nationale d'Armes de Guerre* was the exception to the Belgian rule of manufacturing expensive automobiles for export, mainly to Great Britain. With a power unit of 1,245 cc, developing about 10 hp, it was the rival to a number of smaller cars on offer from Germany and elsewhere. (B)

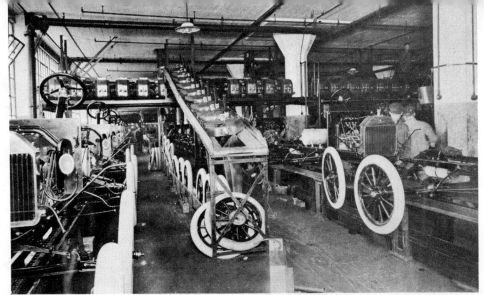

Assembly lines at the Ford Highland Park plant in 1914, showing the pioneer flow-line system that was to help drop the price of the Model T progressively. In 1914 the company made one-half of the nation's cars, using one-sixth of the nation's automotive labor force. (USA)

Here a victorious Dr. August Horch acknowledges the cheers as he brings his 14/35PS Audi to the finish line of the 1914 Austrian Alpine Trials. Horch had left his original company after a disagreement and had started to manufacture Audi cars (Latin for his own name) in 1910. The 14/35PS, called the *Alpensieger*, after its success in the 1913 and 1914 Alpine Trials, was produced until 1921. (D)

One of the earliest French pioneers, Hurtu made a small, single-cylinder vehicle for the first fourteen years of its life (1896–1929), then built cars with "dashboard radiators" behind the engine in Renault style, also using a hood shape that could be confused with earlier de Dion-Bouton products. By the end of the Edwardian era Hurtu was producing 4-cylinder, 10-hp automobiles. (F)

Several companies of international repute in America and Europe had changed to the Knight sleeve-valve engine, and others had developed new mechanics to compete with the Silent Knight engines. By 1913 Itala had made a successful rotary-valve engine, which was installed in road cars and some racing cars during this period. This is the large, 50–60-hp tourer. (I)

The 1914 Jeffery Allweather Four Model 93AW. This somewhat dated-looking "button-backed" coupe had an aluminum body and a 4-cylinder power unit. Jeffery cars were made for just four years, from 1914 to 1917, and were named after founder Thomas B. Jeffery, who built the first Rambler in 1897 and went on to head that company. (USA)

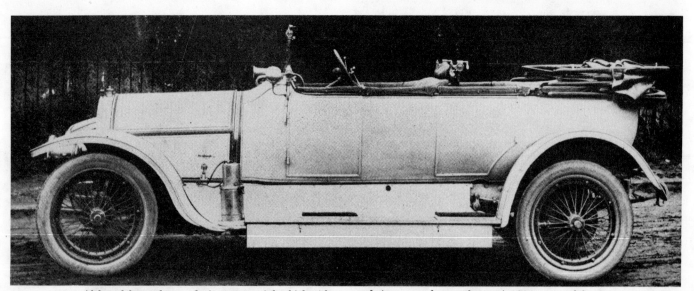

Although better known for its commercial vehicles (the company built its first steam wagon in 1835), Maudslay made several attempts at private transport. First producing cars in 1902 — a 3-cylinder 20 hp with overhead camshaft, Maudslay went on to make fours and sixes — and more threes. A 1914 one-model principle caused the larger cars to vanish, leaving only the 17 hp (Sweet Seventeen) first seen in 1910. Another branch of the Maudslay family formed the Standard Motor Company in 1903. (GB)

Forty-one cars of fourteen makes from six different countries took part in the French Grand Prix of 1914, the race that was to end an era of motor racing. Mercedes had entered five cars in the race and by team tactics (almost unknown at that time) won the race, taking the first three places. Here Christian Lautenschlager, the winner, drives his Mercedes through the downhill esses of the Lyons circuit. The cars, designed by Paul Daimler, had single overhead camshafts, 4¹/₂-liter engines, developing 115 bhp at 3,200 rpm. (D)

Action at the pits during the 1914 French Grand Prix—a change of tires for a G.P. Mercedes. The cars had rear brakes only, a strong cornering disadvantage when several others had braking on all four wheels. Wagner, seen here adjusting a control in the cockpit, took second place in the race. (D)

S.A. des Usines Renault had been building medium and large cars for some years, and this was one of the smartest—a 20CV, 4-cylinder sports torpedo with body by Labourdette. Also fashionable in 1914 was a single-studded, anti-slip tire, fitted here on the left front wheel. Later, Louis Renault was to build even larger cars for the luxury market. (F)

A three-seater, 1,145-cc, 5/15 PS, this little Wanderer was called the Puppchen (the first models appeared in 1911, nearly a year ahead of Opel's car of the same name). The Puppchen (Dolly) was made at the Wanderer Werke at Schonau bei Chemnitz. (D)

Although England's King had died in 1910, the end of the Edwardian era is generally accepted as August 1914, when Europe went to war. This photograph was taken in London's Regent Street in the summer of that year and shows a mixture of motor buses, taxis, private cars—and horse-drawn vehicles.

The Rolls-Royce Silver Ghost was made for nineteen years, from 1907 to 1926, first in Manchester, then in Derby from 1908. Late in 1920 a factory was opened in Springfield, Massachusetts, where Ghosts were made until 1926. Rolls-Royce reinforced its claim as "the best car in the world" in 1913 when a team of Silver Ghosts won the Austrian Alpine Rally with ease against the best Europe could muster. Shortly afterward, James Radley, one of the victorious Rolls-Royce drivers, reduced the London-Monte Carlo record (1,000 miles) from 33 to 26 hours in his 7.4-liter Silver Ghost Alpine Eagle, the car seen here. (GB)

This Simplex "semi-racing runabout" is one of the more distinguished American cars of its time and rightly famous in early racing in that country. In 1914 the company offered 38-, 50-, and 75-hp models of 4 cylinders, and a 6-cylinder 50-hp. One of the fastest cars in the country, the Simplex 50-hp (dating from 1912) was probably the last chain-driven car to be made in the U.S.A. (USA)

Another company to graduate to automobiles from sewing machines, Swift of Coventry followed through bicycles and motortricycles to cars—at first small ones. By 1914, however, after a period of offering a better-than-most cycle car, the company settled down to this 4-cylinder 10-hp, which was good enough to be continued in modified forms until 1931 when, sadly, the Swift company died. (GB)

In 1915 Cadillac became the first U.S. manufacturer to offer a V-8 water-cooled engine (discounting the 1909 Coyote and a brief Marmon venture) in a production car and also the first to use thermostatic control of cooling, thus setting the pattern for every quality carmaker in the United States. (USA)

Known familiarly as the RFC Crossley, many examples of this car saw service in the Royal Flying Corps during the war. With a 4-cylinder, 4.5-liter engine, it was the big brother of the 3-liter, 15-hp model which was also supplied to His Majesty's armed forces. Various types of bodies were mounted in this 20-hp chassis, from light tender trucks to ambulances. (GB)

This specially ordered 20-hp Daimler coupe looks older than its years—presumably because its British purchaser had conservative tastes. It housed the famous 4- cylinder Knight sleeve engine, however—modern for its day—had electric starter and lamps and detachable wire wheels. (GB)

Car and refugees pack the country roads of France during the Somme retreat. Taxis and private cars were used extensively to transport British and French troops back to new lines of defense. On the right is a Daimler; at left is a Vauxhall. (GB)

Model 3A Fiats assemble for troop-transport work. By 1915 this model, first seen in 1912, was fully equipped with electric lights and used a starter operating through a starter ring on the flywheel. With a maximum speed of about 50 mph and seating for five, this type of massed motor transport began to change the methods of war at both tactical and strategic levels. Engine: 4-cylinder, 4,396-cc, developing 40 bhp at 1,800 rpm. (I)

Now very much part of the motoring scene in America, the Model T Ford, long outstripping any other make, was enlarging the horizons of millions of people who previously had hardly ventured beyond the next town. This is a 1915 touring model, now in flush-sided form. Over 300,000 left the factory in 1915. (USA)

Behind Captain Eddie Rickenbacker, America's top World War I flying ace, seen here being greeted by a French general in Paris, is a 4.5-liter, high-compression-engined Hudson Super Six, the model (and engine) that finally established the company as a producer of quality engines. (USA)

At last, the closed car in Model T form. This is the Tudor (a later and slightly larger one was called the Fordor). This sedan still used the same tough 4-cylinder engine, pedal transmission, and two-speed transmission, but seems to accommodate at least five people. (USA)

Help for mother to descend from a 1915 Packard tourer. The previous September Cadillac had brought out a V-8 engine, and on January 1, 1915, Jesse Vincent, the man who took Packard into the upper bracket of the market, had begun to draft his 12-cylinder engine, the first to be offered to the public. Twelve months after the opposition's V-8 appeared, Vincent unveiled the 6.78-liter Twin-Six Packard. (USA)

Scania-Vabis, an amalgamation of two rival companies, Vagnfabriken and Scania, concentrated mainly on commercial-vehicle production. However, 485 cars were made between 1906 and 1924 — and precisely 4 between that date and 1929. This 1915 model was a 2,102-cc, 4-cylinder 30-hp with side valves, four forward speeds, and shaft drive. (S)

By 1913 the Star Engineering Co. had rationalized their range of cars to the 10/12-hp, 12/15-hp, 15.9-hp, and 20.1-hp models. The 10/12 and 12/15 models had bores and strokes of 80 × 120 mm, giving 2,409 cc from their enblock and biblock engines, and the 3,013-cc 15.9 had 80-mm bore × 150-mm stroke. The 15.9-and 20.1-models were the only Stars to be fitted with bullnose radiators, and it is rumored that these were adopted after Star had built a number of Knight of the Road cars with similar radiators. The car shown is a 1915 15.9-hp tourer. (GB)

During World War I, Vauxhall built nearly 2,000 staff cars for the British War Office, cars that saw grueling service in many theaters of war. This Vauxhall 25 carries General Allanby on his entry into Jerusalem in 1917. (GB)

The Edwardians: 1900-1918

Just one more summer to pick the flowers before the Americans join the "war to end wars" . . . this Hudson Six-40 Town Car, brand new in 1916, shows its elegance at fashionable Grosse Pointe. Even at this date the buyer could choose his colors: India blue, dark Brunswick green, light beige, or light Orriford Lake. (USA)

Another of the last American prewar productions. This seven-passenger touring car was the first to attempt a round-trip transcontinental trek. It was driven from San Francisco to New York in 5 days, 3 hours, and 31 minutes and was then conducted back almost as quickly. The picture shows the Hudson Super Six and crew at the end of their remarkably rapid journey. (USA)

With no extras to buy, this Maxwell (it housed a side-valve four) was more economical than most cars. The company from which the Chrysler giant was to grow in the middle of the next decade produced cars of this period on a strong economy basis, often listing the extras that purchasers would be forced to buy for other cars, showing that they alone could cost a third of the price of a Maxwell. (USA)

In 1916 Woodrow Wilson had three Pierce-Arrows in his garage at the White House—but none of them as sportive as the speedster shown here. Built on the lines of the Mercer and the Stutz, this model was a stark, twin bucket seat, uncompromisingly fast car. The great 66 with its 12.7-liter unit was discontinued in 1917—

thus the largest production car built in the United States to this date disappeared. The cars were often sold with two bodies, a closed one for winter use and an open one for fair weather. The respect that surviving Pierce-Arrow cars command says much for a company that once made bird cages. (USA)

Vauxhall 'semi-racer', 1909. (GB)

A two-seater 2½-liter Star, 1909. (GB)

First of the Alfas, the 24-hp Torpedo of 1910.
The company was called Alfa Romeo after
World War I. (I)

Model T Ford, 1910.

Rolls-Royce Roi-des-Belges, 1910.

Renault two-seater, 1910.

Opel 10/18 hp Double Phaeton, 1909. (D)

1908 Hutton, built by Napier for racing. (GB)

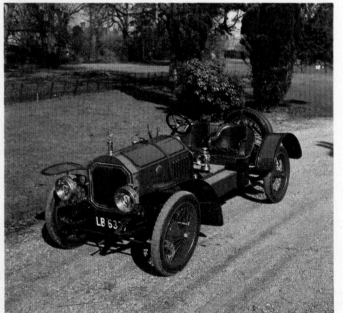

The famous Renault 'Taxi de la Marne', first made in 1906. Six hundred were used to rush French troops to the front in 1914. (F)

In 1917 electric lights and starter became standard equipment for Chevrolet, as well as the introduction of a closed tourer, the first closed body in the Chevrolet line. The first V-8 engine was fitted into the 1917 D-series—an overhead valve unit of 288 cu in. (USA)

Since Percy Pierce won the Glidden Tour in his Pierce-Arrow in 1905 and then went on to win three more before 1910, the model has been a respected piece of American engineering, and its antique value today is of the highest. This prestigious automobile was considered so well-known by the *cognocenti* that its name was not displayed on the radiator except for a single year, 1928. (USA)

During this period, while European motor manufacturers were still phrenetically making vehicles of war, America alone managed to produce cars that could be bought by the public. This Buick Model E4-34, a 27-hp two-seater, was one of the few specifically made for civilian use. (USA)

This distinguished Town Limousine, with its smooth V-8, 314-cu in power unit, developing a comfortable 60 bhp, was one of the most fashionable Cadillacs of its day and is not so unfashionable over half a century later. Over 20,000 of the Type 57 Cadillac in various body styles were made during 1918. (USA)

A Model 34 touring coupe from the Oakland Company at Pontiac, Michigan. This rather conservative vehicle, using a 6-cylinder Northway Power unit of 177 cu in, developing 41 bhp at 2,500 rpm, sold extremely well to the middle market, some 35,000 being produced and purchased during 1918. (USA)

A shooting party and a Studebaker, somewhere in California, circa 1918. A four and a six were made during the year, both with 353 cu in displacement, developing 50 hp. The model shown here still sported hickory wheels with demountable rims. The last Studebaker 4-cylinder motor was made in 1919. (USA)

Baker Rauch & Lang of Cleveland, Ohio, claimed to "banish the commonplace" with their upper-bracket product, the Owen Magnetic. This they did, if only because a standard 6-cylinder engine was used to generate electricity to power the drive (at around 33 hp) to the rear roadwheels, employing an electro-magnetic automatic-transmission system that had been developed in 1915. (USA)

World War I had shown too much of the world to many men, but it had also thrown off the shackles of Edwardian convention, bringing a wider appreciation of travel to many who previously had been content with an annual hay-cart ride to the local church social. Motoring had up to now been far beyond the pocket of the European man-in-the-street — although in America the story of the automobile had more earthy origins and had been associated more with hard work than with leisure.

Now everyone wanted to take the family for a spin on the weekend. The open road beckoned to a world that recognized the joys of real mobility for the first time. In the U.S.A. the car had left the experimental and development stage and by 1920 had become an established part of domestic, social, and, particularly, commercial travel. Production of passenger cars in 1920 totaled 1,905,560 — four times the number manufactured in 1914, the year Europe went to war — with an overall registration of 8 million on the roads of America. The middle-income earners of Europe were also ready to join the motoring fraternity that a decade earlier had been confined to those who could afford a chauffeur.

Less-expensive cars were run off the drawing boards and soon started to sell in large numbers. Established models such as Opel, Renault, Dodge, Ford, Morris, and Citroën began to flood their countries of origin, with overspills into neighboring markets.

Quick to seize a commercial opportunity, new companies grew as rapidly as field mushrooms, some producing motoring's worst joke of the period, cycle cars — crude, spindly caricatures of cars that nevertheless sold to those aspiring motorists who could afford nothing more elaborate.

During this period, popular makes were produced in numbers that would have been totally impossible a few years earlier — the classic example of this was of course the Ford T model, which ran to over 15 million before it finally ceased in 1927. Conversely, Ettore Bugatti, maker of fine and startlingly beautiful cars, produced less than 10,000 models over a period of 47 years. This was, paradoxically, also the age of the rare, hand-built auto, the super-luxury car with a production run of as few as a dozen.

During these vintage years, Rolls-Royce lorded it in Britain (and opened a factory in Springfield, Massachusetts); the fantastic Duesenberg set new records of performance and quality in the United States and Europe; Charles Kettering designed his 16-cylinder Cadillac; exotica such as the Hispano Suiza and the Isotta-Fraschini were written into motoring history; and Henry Ford—much to the astonishment of other manufacturers—announced a five-day week for his workers.

BRAVE NEW WORLD: 1919-1929

Engineer André Citroën had produced shells for France during World War I. By 1919 he had moved into motor manufacture and presented his first car, the Type A 10-cv torpedo designed by Jules Salmon. This 1.3-liter model, the first in Europe to be mass-produced and delivered complete, was available to the public from July 1919. Production started with a run of just 30 cars, but under the pressure of success 27,000 were made and sold by December 1920. Engine: 4-cylinder, effective output 18 bhp at 2,100 rpm. (F)

Plain but very much in the contemporary torpedo line, this Chevrolet presents a neat and attractive appearance for its day. After a couple of years of the overhead-valve V-8, in 1919 Chevrolet went back to 4-cylinder models — the new 490 and FB-4. This is the FB-4, with a unit of 223 cu. in. displacement. The company continued to make fours exclusively until 1929. (USA)

The Dodge Brothers sedan, introduced in March 1919 on a wheelbase of 114 inches, had a standard 4-cylinder, 35-hp engine of 212.3 cu. in., with a compression of 4 to 1. Here the 1919 car (right) is seen with a 1914 Dodge. (USA)

Natural California grandeur dwarfs this Hupmobile tourer on a visit to Yosemite Falls, although this publicity picture was obviously intended to link a natural phenomenon with a phenomenal automobile. This wooden-wheeled five-seater had a 4-cylinder, 17-hp engine of conventional design. (USA)

When the Humber factory resumed peacetime work in 1919, the 10-hp 1914 car, advanced for prewar days, was manufactured again. This is a 10-hp driven by Captain Sir John Alcock, with passenger Lieutenant Sir Arthur Whitten Brown, shortly after their epic first-ever nonstop flight over the Atlantic in a Vickers bomber. (GB)

With this car Fiat produced a model completely new in shape and mechanical design (to the plans of Fiat's technical director, who was a lawyer) after the standstill following the war. The engine was a 4-cylinder, 1½-liter, developing 35 bhp at 2,600 rpm, and the car had a modest top speed of 45 mph. An important model in the Fiat line, the 501 had overwhelming commercial success: 45,000 were sold by 1926. (I)

Originally makers of farm equipment at Hartford, Wisconsin, the Kissel Motor Company entered the automotive field in 1906 with a 4-cylinder car. Sixes and a V-12 were built later. Both the 1918 and 1919 models were built in the general form of the car seen here; early examples had a glass window in the scuttle (cowl) and the D radiator core; later 1919 models had a flat core. Cycle fenders and step plates with side-mounted spare wheels appeared on cars in the 1921 Auto Show. This is a Custom Silver Special four-passenger speedster. Pull-out seats on either side made up the complement; 6 cylinders, 26–33 hp (N.A.C.C. rating). (USA)

Vincenzo Lancia's company had already established its name for quality when the Theta, his outstanding car to date, was introduced in 1913. This 4-cylinder, 4,940-cc, 70-bhp Kappa was a development of that car, with innovations such as a variable steering-wheel rake, electric engine-starting controlled by a pedal, and a central gear lever instead of an outside one as in past Lancias. Top speed was around 75 mph. (I)

This picture shows the "All Year Gibraltar Body" offered from 1914 to 1920 by the Kissel Motor Company for the following styles: two-rear-door sedan; staggered-door sedan — left front and right rear; sedan, a close-coupled, four-passenger roadster-coupe type having two doors only; Victoria Touring/Town car. There was a complex selection of removable hardtops. (USA)

The Mercer Automobile Company made few cars, but made them to move fast, safely, and to last—a difficult combination. However, their market was not for penny-pinchers; the Mercer was a car for the elite and the sports fanatic. Raceabouts were still made in 1919, only a little less stark than they had been eight years earlier. However, the postwar public needed more practical transport at a practical price, and the company died in 1925. This is the 4-cylinder, 4,900-cc "22–70," circa 1919. (USA)

Like the Coventry firm of Humber, Singer had made a highly successful Ten immediately prior to the war—a two-seater with a channel-steel chassis, 4-cylinder power pack, and the transmission in unit with the back axle. After the war the company, not yet retooled after making wartime vehicles, continued with the popular Ten, now with complete electrics and some styling modifications. The 1,100-cc car sold well, although inflation pushed up the price, until the company had the bright idea of giving a free insurance policy with each Singer Ten sold. (GB)

In 1920 the Lyons company of Berliet confined passenger-car production to this model, the 15CV VB which had the stamp of an American car and indeed was called the "Fake Dodge" by many in France. The American company thought so, too, and took legal action. Four cylinders, 3.3 liters, three forward speeds. (F)

Now under the stewardship of businessman Nicola Romeo (whose name had been added to the radiator badge and to the company), Alfa-Romeo resumed production in 1920 with several modified prewar models, including the 4-cylinder, 4,084-cc 20/30 and the 6-cylinder G1 (1921). The sporting version of the 20/30-hp won its spurs in the hill-climb and racing field after the war, and 1920 saw the start of a long line of Alfa-Romeo successes. This is the four-seater berlina (limousine), which was fitted to several chassis. (I)

A Frontenac, with Gaston Chevrolet at the wheel after winning the 1920 Indianapolis 500 at 88.62 mph. The name Monroe-Frontenac was given to the cars raced in 1920 by Chevrolet—Monroe because he built them (seven identical 2,982-cc cars) at the Monroe works at Indianapolis, and Frontenac because that was the title of the corporation formed to make them. (USA)

This improbable De Lesseps merits a place in any pictorial history, if only because it illustrates the restless minds of automotive designers of the time. A Renault-based design by De Lesseps (70CV, 8-cylinder Aero-engine) for winter maneuvers. (F)

The incredibly rugged Dodge Four had for some time been the platform on which the company's prosperity was founded, and it continued to be so until 1927. With a slow-running unit (bore $3^7/_8 \times 4^1/_2$ in) pushing out about 25 hp (N.A.C.C. rating) and still with the back-to-front gear change, the car had one new feature in 1920—a slanting windshield. The wheels were still wooden, although the company had flirted with wire a couple of years earlier. Dodge brothers Horace and John died in 1920 within a few months of each other, both from pneumonia. (USA)

Outside St. Peter's Cathedral at the Vatican a lonely Fiat taxi looks like an overgrown matchbox. Designed specifically for hire work it had an 1,846-cc engine, developing 18 hp at 2,000 rpm—almost identical with that of the Tipo Zero, produced until 1915. Top speed 37 mph; maximum climbable gradient 15%, consumption 12 liters per 100 km (24 mpg). (I)

The Model T had by now been used for just about every sort of transport—down on the farm they had the tractor version, and the tourer was pressed into service as a power saw, milking machine, and so on. In 1920 the station wagon appeared—Ford's first venture into the multi-seater private car. (USA)

Opening for business in 1914, Guy Motors of Wolverhampton, England, was more concerned with commercial transport than with cars, but opted to make this one during 1919 (this is the 1920 Olympia Motor Show Guy in semi-polished aluminum). It was a genuine luxury car, with a V-8 unit, and it incorporated the first automatic chassis lubrication, operated by a cam on the steering lever every time the car was turned on extreme right lock—the forerunner of a system used in later commercial vehicles. (GB)

A Super Six touring limousine—the "official" Hudson used by Italian tenor Enrico Caruso during his Montreal appearance in 1920. First seen in 1916, the great Super Sixes were renowned for their sporting exploits and service reliability. (USA)

The prototype Leyland Eight Speed Model, designed by J. G. Parry-Thomas and first seen in 1920 was aimed at the postwar luxury market. It housed a 6,967-cc (later 7,300-cc) straight-eight unit with a single overhead camshaft, inclined valves, and hemispherical combustion chambers. Other advanced features were a torsion bar, a starter incorporated in the transmission and automatic lubrication. It had rear brakes only. Just sixteen were made, although the car was later developed for racing. (GB)

Looking most unlike a car from the house of Lanchester, this is a stylist's example of the panel-beater's art. The 6-cylinder "Forty" was first seen in 1919 (a quick turn-around after four years of making aero-engines) and was made for the next ten years. It housed a single ohc engine of just over 6 liters, giving 90 bhp. (GB)

The four-door sedan version of the 6-cylinder Oldsmobile Model 37B. Some 18,000 sixes were produced in 1920; other models included the 37A (6-cylinder, open), the 43A (4-cylinder, closed), 45B (V-8 open or closed), 46 (V-8 open or closed), and an "economy" truck. Oldsmobile completed a large expansion program during 1920, and Billy Durant left General Motors. (USA)

Russelsheim's 1920 offering, at a difficult time for German production, included this 8/25-PS Opel six-seater of 2,330 cc. Built in the torpedo style, it was a conventional model in all ways and was strongly reminiscent of prewar products. With outboard gear lever and hand brake, four speeds and reverse, the car had a top speed of 80 km/h (50 mph). (D)

At least Peugeot could not be accused, as others were, of using American styling in their immediate postwar passenger cars. This slim-line, 10-hp torpedo Type 163 (made from 1919 to 1924) sported a modest 1,437-cc motor, four forward speeds and one that marched the other way (as the brochure put it), and a maximum of 60 km/h (37 mph). (F)

For the Grandes Boulevards, this great 24CV 6-cylinder Renault limousine of 1920 was based on an improved prewar design and was part of a wide range of vehicles from 10 to 40 hp, and *camions* (trucks) from 1,000 kilos to 7 tons, as well as agricultural tractors and industrial motors. By 1920 Louis Renault had built the largest manufacturing empire in France. (F)

After making what was reputedly the largest production car in the United States (the 66 at nearly 13 liters), only Pierce-Arrow models 38 and 48 were offered by 1920, both with the steering wheel on the right-hand side (this was changed the following year). Although the car did not display its name, it could easily be identified by the headlight fairings, an early streamlining attempt introduced in 1913. (USA)

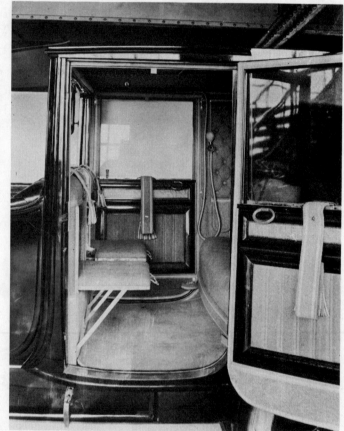

The interior of the luxury Renault of this period equaled in richness the brocade, walnut, and mother-of-pearl fittings of the *Belle Epoque* of prewar days. (F)

The last of the 1,100-cc Stellites made by a company owned by Wolseley of England was seen in 1920. Since 1913 this small 2-cylinder car had been on the market and was now almost indistinguishable from the small Wolseley. By this time the market had caught up with it, and small cars, mostly of continental make, proliferated. Rated at 9.5 hp, the engine was 1,100 cc. (GB)

First produced in 1913 (although only thirteen were made before the war), the 30/98 (no one knows why it was called this) was the Vauxhall car of the twenties. Developed directly from the earlier Prince Henry, the 4½-liter, 4-cylinder engine produced 100 bhp on the bench, and the car leaped to fame in sporting circles during early postwar years. In three seasons it scored an astonishing seventy-five racing wins and fifty-two second places, apart from numerous hill-climb victories. With the car came a guarantee that "with a single-seated body, the 30/98 Vauxhall will attain 100 mph on the track." In 1920 that was really sticking your neck out. (GB)

Parliamentarian Lord Lytton with daughters in his 1920–1921 Sunbeam tourer. This 24-hp model was one of a range of the refined and comfortable cars that bore little relation to the Sunbeam vehicles that were participating in Grand Prix racing. The conglomerate Sunbeam Talbot Darracq was formed in 1920. (GB)

Five minutes to midday in downtown Detroit. Bakers, Fords, Cadillacs, Packards, Dodges—and a horse—appear in this picture of America's automobile capital. By 1920 the car had taken over, and the "Roaring Twenties" began to wind up . . . and the bustling city of this photograph produced a total of 1,905,560 passenger cars this year.

Autocarriers, formed in 1911 (preceded by Autocars and Accessories Limited in 1908), had produced the successful 10-hp A.C. before the war, and this was the updated version, offered with a 1½-liter, lightweight, wet-liner, 4-cylinder Anzani engine or a choice of two sizes of 6-cylinder unit. The smaller A.C. was successful in reliability trials and other sporting events, and in the London to Edinburgh run six were entered and six gold medals were won. (GB)

The 20–30 ES Sport Alfa-Romeo made little impression on the sporting world in 1921, except that the 1921 "Grand Prix Gentlemen" race run at Brescia was won by a 20–30 ES Sport driven by a lady—and Ferrari took first place in the Grand St. Bernard hill-climb later in 1921. This one is well-stripped-down for racing. Engine: 4-cylinder, 4,250 cc. (I)

Following the 1920 VB — the "fake Dodge" — Marius Berliet produced his 16 CV VL in very much the same style, although this model represented a determined effort to recover from a severe reverse of his fortunes. Known as the Etoile Argent (Silver Star), the 3,308-cc, side-valve product sold reasonably well, allowing the company a further lease on life — until 1939. (F)

Possibly because of Bianchi's later close association with Fiat and Pirelli and the change of name to Autobianchi, this company, one of the oldest in the Italian automotive field to be active, is often overlooked in the history of motoring. Eduardo Bianchi went unspectacularly from bicycles to voiturettes and then to more ambitious vehicles of a steady, middle-of the-road character. This is a 1,692-cc, two-seater tourer with a rumble seat. (I)

This seven-passenger sedan Type 21-6-50 from Buick at Flint housed a 6-cylinder, 242-cu in unit and had a reinforced pressed-steel frame—one of seven types listed in 1921, ranging from a three-passenger roadster to this luxury product, of which 7,292 were made. (USA)

Some 350 of these Castle-Three 4-cylinder, water-cooled three-wheelers were produced by the Castle Motor Company of Kidderminster, Worcestershire. Designed by Stanley Goodwin, the first dozen or so used Dorman-type 4KL engines; later cars had the Belgian Peters units of 1,207 cc. The Castle-Three was one of the more elaborate, less spindly cycle cars of the period. (GB)

This B2 *Conduite Intérieure* (which merely means that the driver is inside with the passengers) Citroën was built between 1921 and 1925. First to be introduced was the "Luxury Open Tourer" with a 1,452-cc, 4-cylinder, side-valve engine rated by the French Treasury at 9 hp. Later forms of the B2 were the Clover Leaf, Caddy (with sports tendencies), Torpedo, and taxi (with the well-known wickerwork body). (F)

Not much of the Essex touring car can be seen here, but the ingenious trailer constructed by the owner (it could be lowered to the height of the car) was good publicity for its towing ability. The 4-cylinder, 2.9-liter, 55-bhp Essex, built for the lower-budget car market by Hudson, who had already made their name with the Super Six, was by 1921 a respected model currently enjoying sporting successes at Pikes Peak. Advertised colors were "a rich dark Valentine blue, with hood and fenders in black." (USA)

Fiat's great essay into the upper bracket was the SuperFiat, seen here in a town-carriage style called D'Orsay. The 6.8-liter, V-12 engine, the first and last 12-cylinder unit in the history of Fiat design, produced a powerful 90 bhp, and the six-passenger car's top speed was around 75 mph. The fact that only five were made is sufficient comment on the venture and the times. (I)

The 901–401 Corsa was a new postwar Grand Prix car from Fiat, first entered in the Parma-Poggio di Berceto event run on May 8, 1921. It finished first in the 3-liter class in its first race, at an average speed of 81 mph. The power unit developed 112 bhp at 4,000 rpm, and top speed was around 100 mph. (I)

It's a commercial vehicle—but this irresistible shot of a Model T at work would grace any pictorial history. Ford brought out its first truck in 1917, rated at one ton; the front end was basically a passenger car, but the frame was heavier and longer (and looks as though it needed to be!), and the rear suspension was stronger. (USA)

This Jordan cabriolet from the Cleveland company was typical of Edward Jordan's high standard. Powered by a 6-cylinder Continental unit rated at 25.5 hp, with three forward speeds and reverse, the model was offered either as a "Silhouette" five- or seven-passenger tourer, a Brougham, sedan, or "Playboy." Remembered as much for his advertising as for his cars, Jordan's *West of Laramie* ad was yet to appear and change the face of motor publicity in America. (USA)

The Lambda is universally recognized as Vincenzo Lancia's masterpiece. One of his engineers said at the time: "He intends to design a car that will carry the mechanical units without using the classical frame. The hull of a ship is quoted as a possible model. Sgr Lancia also tells us of his idea of replacing the rigid front axle by a suspension in which the movements of the wheels would be independent of each other" — in other words, unitary (or monocoque) construction and independent front suspension. This is the prototype. (I)

Laurin & Klement had established itself as the largest automobile producer in the Austro-Hungarian Empire as early as 1914, but now the formation of the Czechoslovak Republic reduced its home market, and the political instability of Europe stunted its export market, notably to Russia. During this period L & K produced 4-cylinder cars based on the most successful of the prewar range. The Type S was revived at 2,402 cc, and a Knight side-valve engine was produced for the Type MK (3,200 cc) and the MK6 (3,498 cc, 50 hp). (CS)

Seen at a modern meet is this big Sportif Series B Locomobile tourer from Bridgeport, Connecticut. In 1908 this model, in the shape of the 90-hp Locomobile, driven by George Robertson, had made its name by winning the Vanderbilt Cup in appalling weather conditions. The Sportif shown here was an N.A.C.C.-rated 48.6-hp six, with bore and stroke of 4½ × 5½ inches, and was classed, surprisingly, as a four-seater. (USA)

In 1911 T.B. Andre & Co. began making a Marlborough of moderate power from French component parts but intended for sale in Britain. The car then created was the direct ancestor of the model shown here, but by this time many parts were British-made. Engine: 4-cylinder, 1,327 cc, rated by the R.A.C. at 10.4 hp. (F)

The choice of color offered by Maxwell was little wider than Henry Ford's notorious restriction—black or blue-black for this five-seater, 4-cylinder, 21-hp, touring Maxwell. Wooden wheels still prevailed except for a few go-ahead manufacturers like Saxon, Elkart, Anderson, Cunningham, and Jackson (all now defunct), who now turned out blank-eyed disk wheels, which later became typical of the period. (USA)

The German Daimler company had begun experiments with a supercharger (kompressor) as early as 1915, and the results were turned to account when the war ended. Two Mercedes models, the 6/25 and the 2,610-cc 10/40/65 shown here, were first fitted with super-charged engines as standard-optional equipment. Both used two-bladed Roots-type blowers brought into use only when the accelerator pedal was almost fully depressed. (D)

An unfortunate conformation that never really captured the public imagination, the Peugeot Quadrilette seating was arranged in tandem, a layout more suited to horses and cyclists. Its track of 2 feet, 6 inches was just wide enough to turn it into a narrow, side-by-side two-seater in the later model. Type 161, 4 cylinder, 667 cc, three-speed transmission, top speed 55 to 60 mph. Predictably, only 3,500 were made. (F)

Out for a spin in the Bois, four visitors to Paris sit comfortably in the back of a 13.9-hp Renault taxi. Successor to the historic "Taxi de la Marne," this very basic 4-cylinder vehicle was produced in large numbers for the cities of France. The rear-mounted radiator was retained until 1928, although some attempt was made to disguise it before that date. (F)

This long-stroke, 10.8-hp Riley was the first 1½-liter postwar Riley offering, introduced in 1919. Its 1921 4-cylinder unit had inclined valves, detachable head, and aluminum pistons. (GB)

Engineer Edmund Rumpler designed this early aerodynamic car, presenting it to astonished visitors at the 1921 Berlin Motor Show. Built on an aircraft-type hull supported on pressed-steel bulkheads with a rear engine and the driver up ahead at the central wheel, the Rumpler car was unorthodox in every way. The engine itself was an extraordinary 2½-liter, W-formation, 6-cylinder unit. (D)

Thomas Santler is still something of a figure of mystery in the automotive world, claiming to have helped Benz in his early work and to have made a car in 1887, although little evidence of this has been found. However, the Santler "Rushabout" seen here certainly existed and was made at the Malvern works. Virtually a "Chinese copy" of the contemporary Morgan produced not 600 yards down the road, some twelve models were made. It was powered by a 10-hp M.A.B. engine. (GB)

The 3-liter, straight-8 Sunbeam (or Talbot-Darracqs, as they were called in some events) were not as successful as the cars of the same make that used half their engine size—cars that won everything in sight in 1921. The 3-liter cars took part in the French Grand Prix and the Indianapolis 500, taking fifth in both. (GB)

An artist's view of two Talbot-Darracqs in the 1921 French Grand Prix. The winner, Thomas (No. 22) is seen overtaking Lee Guiness, also in a Talbot-Darracq. This make was both French and English (Clement-Talbot of London) and had joined Sunbeam of Wolverhamptom. Buyers could choose one of three radiators with two or three different names on them, dependent on their national preferences! The 1½-liter, 4-cylinder cars from the S.T.D. combine won every race they entered during 1921 and 1922. (F)

By 1921 the Vulcan company had made a large range of cars and commercial vehicles on standard lines and this year were offering 12-, 16-, and 20–50-hp vehicles all with 4-cylinder engines. Later in the year this 3.6 "sports-tourer" was announced, with a new Howard sleeve-valve unit. (GB)

Wolseley had been given the contract for producing Hispano-Suiza aero-engines during World War I, and some of the technology had rubbed off on their postwar products, notably in their overhead camshaft power units—although they found that such sophistications did not appeal to some of the buying public. This, the 4-cylinder, ohc, 10-hp Wolseley Moth, lapped Brookland at a creditable 88 mph in 1921. (GB)

American level-crossing, circa 1921. Model T Fords at the barrier. (USA)

This revamped prewar 15.9-hp Arrol-Johnson was brought back into production after an ignominious failure of the Scottish company's "Victory" car of 1919, which broke down repeatedly while being used for a Royal tour of Britain's West Country. Engine: 4-cylinder side-valve, 2.9 liters, fixed ignition. A larger car was introduced in 1922. (GB)

The first real racing Aston Martin had been seen in 1921; the car seen here was made for the voiturette class and had a 1½-liter, 4-cylinder, 16-valve, twin-overhead-camshaft engine of extremely advanced design—doomed to mediocre performance from lack of development because of financial troubles. Two of them raced against the larger Grand Prix cars at Strasbourg in 1922. (GB)

"The sensation of the Sicilian Florio of 1922," said the original caption to this picture of The Austro Daimler "Sascha." Four of them in 1,100-cc form ran in the Targa in 1922 and one, driven by Alfred Neubauer (later Mercedes team manager), won its class, the first of forty-three wins out of fifty-one starts in 1922. On the right of the picture, in sporting cap, is the designer and company *generaldirektor*, Ferdinand Porsche. (A)

To the British, Herbert Austin is as Henry Ford to the Americans—the man who put the nation on wheels. Although he had built his first cars in 1896 while working for Wolseley and had manufactured cars under his own name since 1906, it is for the Austin Seven that most remember him—if only because this simple little vehicle was the first transport of thousands of young English motorists. Weighing just over 1,000 lbs, with an overall length of 8 feet, 9 inches and an engine of 696 cc (later 747 cc), the car was looked on by most with some amusement, and jokes about "buying one for each foot" were rife. However, it rapidly took the place of the unloved cycle car and made inroads on the motorcycle-and-sidecar brigade. It was built under license in Germany, France, Japan, and America. Here Herbert Austin (later Lord Austin) is seen in one of the first Sevens. (GB)

During the same year that the first car designed by Capt. W. O. Bentley of aero-engine repute was offered to the public (first seen at the 1919 Motor Show in London and on sale in 1921), a Bentley was raced. The following year, 1922, a Bentley, modified for racing, was entered in the Indianapolis 500; it was not fast enough to keep up with the action, although it finished the race. Engine: 4-cylinder, single-overhead camshaft, 3 liters. (GB)

Called the Tropfenwagen (Teardrop) this 90-hp, race-and-record Benz was designed by engineer Edmund Rumpler, who had already produced his own unorthodox car, the rear-mounted, 2-liter, twin-ohc Rumpler, the previous year. Its 6-cylinder engine, with curved radiator over the engine compartment, and its bomb-like shape made it the most arresting car of 1922, and it was the first German rear-engined car to race — eleven years before the Auto Union rear- or mid-engined cars. It was an influencing factor in the later rear-engined designs of Dr. Ferdinand Porsche. (D)

This picture of a stripped Tropfenwagen shows the curious conformation of the radiator, the engine, floating rear axle, and inboard brakes. Maximum speed is recorded as 160 km/h (99 mph). (D)

Brave New World: 1919-1929

Like many other British firms, the Birmingham Small Arms Company designed a small 10-hp car in an attempt to get in on the ground floor of the postwar light-car boom. This two-seater BSA, first seen in 1921, sported a 1,080-cc Hotchkiss V-twin unit developing 18 hp. (GB)

Introduced in 1922, the famous lemon-yellow, two-seater 5CV Citroën—easy to run and highly maneuverable. It met with swift success and was one of the continental vehicles that put an end to the postwar cycle-car reign. Inevitably, it was called the "Citron Citroën" for its color, and it was one of the first small cars to attract women buyers in large numbers. It was followed by the three-seater version, Clover Leaf. Engine: 856 cc, 11 hp. (F)

Indianapolis winner in 1922 was the Duesenberg-Miller driven by Jimmy Murphy, No. 1 driver for Duesenberg and victor of the 1921 French Grand Prix. Murphy put a Miller engine into a racing Duesenberg chassis for the 1922 500-mile race and broke several records during the event. The Miller unit was a two-year-old design, a straight-8, 3-liter with an ancestry of Peugeot, Ballot, and Duesenberg. (USA)

The Essex Coach produced by Hudson was designed to fill a gap in the market: "Until Essex brought out the Coach there was no closed car at a moderate price on a first-rate chassis," Hudson told its dealers late in 1922. "The success with which that car took the market naturally invited competition — and today we have many closed cars on the market that are selling at about the Essex or Hudson price." Fast work on the part of the other manufacturers. Engine: 2.9-liter, 55-hp. (USA)

Off to school by car-drawn toboggan-train, these children of rural Italy had it made with a smart if somewhat chilly Fiat 501 Spyder sport as their sleigh horse. The 1½-liter 501 was offered in several sporting forms; this is a version of the SS, sold with stark open bodywork as a two-seater. (*Spyder* or *spider* is still used in several European countries to denote an open two-seater sports model.) (I)

This four-passenger Hudson Super Six coupe is a backdrop to the modes of the day, as shown by these professional models. The 4-cylinder, 19-hp cars sold in quantity in half a dozen different forms all around the world in 1922. The company reported these cars were replacing the bullock cart in India and that a Japanese hotel proprietor had taken delivery of forty-two Hudsons. (USA)

Brave New World: 1919-1929

The old-established Milan company of Isotta Fraschini made cars that were the stuff of dreams in the twenties and thirties. Luxurious and exotic, the Tipo 8 was made from 1919 to 1924. Its relaxed 6-liter engine was not designed to beat the Blue Train to Nice (as many novels of the time had it) but was a deluxe carriage of great elegance. This one has a sports body by Sala. (I)

ISOTTA FRASCHINI—1922

The first production year for the legendary Lancia Lambda was 1923, but the car was shown in 1922 to a motoring public shocked by the production of a car without a frame, but who soon saw the sense in its rigid monocoque construction. The 2,120-cc engine in 4-cylinder, narrow-V formation produced 49 hp at 3,250 rpm, and over the eight years of its production the car was constantly modified and improved, the engine size increasing to 2,570 cc and the power to 69 bhp. Nine versions and 13,000 Lambda models were made. This is an example for the 4th Series. (I)

The Mors—large, luxurious, and French. The Mors had gained its laurels in the early days of racing, particularly in the tragic 1903 Paris-Madrid race. The car shown is the sports boat-tail Mors SSS (Sans Soupapes Silencieuse) with a 3,500-cc, 4-cylinder power unit. The car appealed in vintage years to a select few—too few, unhappily—and the distinguished company ceased making cars in 1927, although its name lived until just after World War II as a manufacturer of scooters. (F)

Called the Sportsman's Roadster, this rather square two-seater-plus-rumble was one of the last of the Oldsmobile fours. When the 6-cylinder Model 30 appeared on the market in 1923, the fours retired into history. The two different kinds of tread on the spare wheels would be frowned on by the discerning motorist today. (USA)

The Packard Twin-Six, as the name implies, was a big V-12 (at 60 degrees) cast in two blocks of six, and was the first ever to be made for the commercial market. Its 7 liters developed about 88 bhp (N.A.C.C. rating 43.2) which took it up to some 83-mph maximum. The Twin-Six was first seen in 1915, when it impressed the automotive world by its flexibility and smooth operation — moving up from 4 to 30 mph in top in a vibrationless 12 seconds. (USA)

The grim-visaged driver is conducting a Renault 3-seater, 8.3 Sports tourer built from 1922 to 1929. In 1922 a new Renault shape was seen—the "alligator" radiator gave place to a flush-line hood that concealed the cooling apparatus, although it was still at the back of the engine. This design was a direct challenge to Citroën's 5CV. A number of innovations were included, the most noteworthy of which was a removable cylinder head—the first used by Renault. (F)

One for the curio file — this 11.6-hp Standard from the Coventry company was presumably an attempt at streamlining, except that they appear to have gotten it back-to-front, producing a model that was as unique as the guarantee. (GB)

The former Austrian arms factory built this 4-cylinder, 2-liter Steyr for the 1922 Targa Florio, then run over four laps of the island's 268-mile "medium" circuit. It finished third, behind two French Ballots. (A)

Somewhat overshadowed by the famous Stutz Bearcat which had first captured the motoring world's imagination in 1914, touring models came in two sizes—the four- or five-passenger, close-coupled Series K; and the six- or seven-passenger Series K. This is the larger, N.A.C.C.-rated at 30.63 hp. (The N.A.C.C. calculated horsepower on the cylinder bore alone, similar to the British R.A.C. system.) (USA)

The new 2-liter Grand Prix formula hatched a 4-cylinder Sunbeam (four valves per cylinder) against the opposition of Fiat, Bugatti, Ballot, and Rolland-Pilain with sixes and eights. They were not highly successful in this form. However, the 350-hp Sunbeam, using a V-12 Sunbeam aero-engine of 18.322 liters, established a world speed record of 133.75 mph in 1922 to mark the year for the company. (GB)

The 25-hp Vauxhall had been used by the hundreds throughout World War I and had put up many challenging performances. This 23/60 was developed from the 25 and also shared many parts with the famous 30/98. The 4-cylinder engine was Vauxhall's first overhead-valve unit. (GB)

This Wills St. Clare housed a 4,350-cc V-8 engine (designed by Childe Harold Wills after he left Ford in 1919), a unit that owed much to the wartime Hispano-Suiza aero-engine. After an initial success, the highly sophisticated car (modestly-priced) suffered when the American public came to the conclusion that it was too elaborate in design and too expensive to maintain. This is the 65-hp Model A68 Roadster. (USA)

Hispano-Suiza Alfonso, 1912; named after the King of Spain. (E)

Renault on land and in the air, 1913. Louis Renault
had made his first aero-engine in 1907. (F)

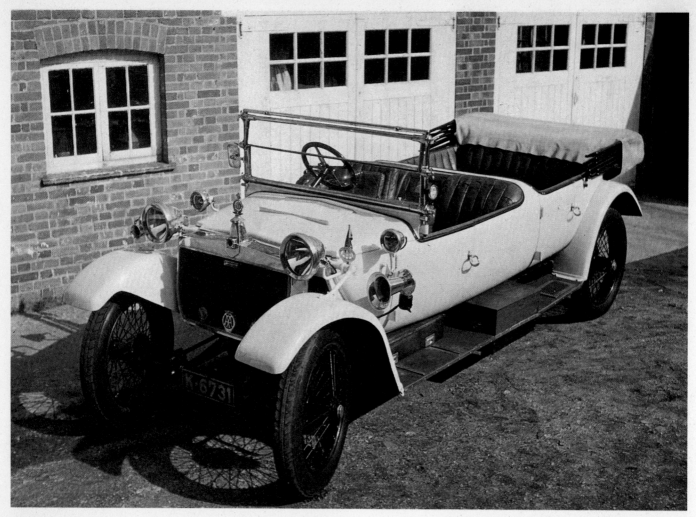

Touring elegance for Edwardians: a 6-cylinder, 38-hp
Lanchester of 1913. (GB)

1913 Morris, with 8.9 hp White and Poppe engine. (GB)

Vauxhall's advanced Prince Henry, 1911. (GB)

1911 Opel Torpedo; 4-cylinder, 1540 cc. (D)

Edwardian top brass. A 1912 N.A.G. raceabout. (D)

It has been said that the Ansaldo hovered between a sports car and a tourer, and the specifications bear this out: 4 cylinders, single overhead camshaft with inclined valves, plus aluminum pistons on the sports side of the scales, with a three-speed transmission using wide-spaced ratios and central ball change on the tourer side. The 4C shown here had a 1.7-liter unit with an output of 38 bhp. (I)

The 1½-liter Type 13 Bugatti was first seen in 1909 with two valves per cylinder operated by the single overhead camshaft, later with four (it became known as the "Brescia" after a 1—2—3—4 win at that venue in 1921), and continued as the Types 22 and 23, with longer wheelbase. The forerunner and template for most high-performance light sports cars that followed, the Bugatti was, and still is, one of the seven wonders of the automotive world—with steering, suspension, chassis design, transmission, and engine mechanics far ahead of its time in sheer accuracy and operation. (F)

This is the Chalmers, made by the Maxwell-Chalmers organization, a combine that had been formed immediately after World War I to consolidate sales and manufacture in the face of cash difficulties. The organization finally made way for Walter Chrysler's new car and company. Engine: 6-cylinder, 3¼ × 4¼ in, N.A.C.C.-rated at 25.35 hp. (USA)

This little 1.5-liter Aston Martin, nicknamed "Bunny," performed like a giant on the Brooklands track. In 1923 the car took the standing half-mile record at 62.76 mph, the standing kilometer at 66.54 mph, and the standing mile at an average of 74.12 mph. It also

climbed the Brooklands Test Hill in 9.14 seconds, establishing another record. Here the car is being refueled during a record run. Bunny had also taken ten world records and twenty-two class records in 1922. (GB)

Successor to the popular "490" series, the Chevrolet Superior introduced in 1923 became the model line for ten years, to be interrupted only by the ill-fated "Copper Cooled" Chevrolet that was also seen in 1923—an air-cooled car designed by the famous Charles Ketter-ing, but which was discontinued after just 759 were built. The Superior still used the 170-cu in, 4-cylinder engine and rode on wooden artillery wheels. Total emancipation from the prewar look did not take place until 1924. (USA)

Following the Type A, the 1½-liter B2 Citroën, built between 1921 and 1925, had a detachable cylinder head and engine-clutch-transmission unit. A multiplicity of bodies were offered in addition to the basic open tourer which had three seats and a boat-shaped back.

A souped-up "Caddy Sport" with high-performance tendencies and a skiff-type body was popular with the young bucks—and this Coupé de Ville with their mothers. (F)

Clyno had a background of motorcycle manufacture (they had supplied the British Army during the 1914–1918 war) before turning to cars in 1921. They hit the jackpot with an 11-hp light car of 1.4 liters—pleasant to handle, reliable, and from 1926, with four-wheel brakes as standard (unusual even then on light vehicles). Large-section tires were also an advance pioneered by the company. The powerful competition of the Morris finally put Clyno out of business. (GB)

The great breed of de Dion-Bouton began to decline in the 1920s. Many reasons have been put forward—poor performance, technical stagnation, and so on—but in fact the company failed (in 1932) because the cars were not glamorous and exciting enough to attract buyers away from the other classic automobiles, and they were not cheap enough to compete with Austin, Citroën, Ford, and the others at the other end of the market. This is a 1923 4-cylinder IW model, well-made but heavy. (F)

The Type GL 40/50 Delage (this one has bodywork by Graham-White), made during the company's five-year racing Program, benefited greatly from the success of the great French company's sporting activities. The

GL (Grande Luxe) used a sophisticated, 6-cylinder, overhead-camshaft unit of 5.9 liters and was one of the finest French vehicles of its day. (F)

Early established in the production of engines, Crossley first made cars in 1904. In October 1923 the company announced its 20/70 hp, with a high-lift camshaft jacking up the bhp so that 75 mph could be guaranteed. Recommended for "fast touring" by former British competition driver S. F. Edge, it also enjoyed numerous sporting wins at Brooklands and other events. (GB)

Says the brochure poetically: "Elegant styling is the keynote of this four-door Dodge Brothers Four sedan. Molded body panels and flowing fender lines combined with chrome wheelcovers make the expanded 116-inch wheelbase the fashion-plate of the auto industry. Equipped with the 4-cylinder 212.3-cu in engine, the car is the largest yet built by the Dodge Brothers. . .compression ration is 4 to 1 and the horsepower 35 at 2,000 rpm." (USA)

A Fiat 505 torpedo carries two veiled ladies of Algeria past a typical Moslem building—although why they are traveling on the sidewalk is anybody's guess. With a 2,300-cc engine, this was the "big sister" of Fiat's highly successful 501. It had a long production run—1919 to 1925—during which time it was improved considerably, particularly by the addition of front-wheel brakes. Maximum speed was about 50 mph. (I)

Made in Britain at Ford's Manchester works, this was a right-hand-drive Model T, a copy of the American model—as were all Manchester Fords, except one, until 1932, when a newly built factory in the south began to manufacture the tiny Ford 8. (GB)

On the left is the phaeton, and the right-hand car is the speedster—or is it the other way? The only apparent difference between these Hudsons is that the phaeton is a seven-passenger model and the smaller speedster carries only four. Both housed 30-hp, Super-Six power units made by the company for about fourteen years. These open tourers were favored by the gangsters of prohibition days, as their lack of pillars and other restrictions allowed a wide arc of fire from automatic weapons at a time when, as one writer said, "even the beer trucks had tail gunners." (USA)

Neat, sober, unspectacular, the Humber products were solid, reliable vehicles during these years. This one, the 8-hp, had a certain claim to special notice — it used overhead inlet and side-valve exhaust disposition. Front-wheel brakes were not yet available. (GB)

Ford had bought out the foundering Lincoln company in 1922 after it had manufactured just 3,407 cars. One of the first Ford-produced Lincolns was this four-passenger phaeton built on a 136-inch chassis with a 5.8-liter V-8 engine—another car much-loved by gangsters of the period. (USA)

Typical of the vast seven-passenger sedans of the day, this Locomobile had more than enough headroom for the tallest hat. This Model 48 (48-hp) had a long wheel-base of 142 inches, wooden wheels, and a 6-cylinder (cast in pairs) engine. Four-wheel brakes, foot-controlled head-lamp dippers, and powered windshield wipers were fitted as standard to a number of U.S. cars in 1923. (USA)

The Good Maxwell had appeared in 1921 when Walter Chrysler had reorganized the Maxwell Company and had re-named the car and improved its quality. He increased Maxwell sales, but associate company Chalmers had lost cash, and the organization was wound up after the new Chrysler had begun to attract most of the available buyers. Engine: 4-cylinder, bore $3^5/8 \times 4^1/2$ in, rated at 21 hp. (USA)

Common practice in the early Twenties was to offer a slightly tuned version of the family car for those whose pockets were somewhat deeper and whose ambitions more sportive than the ordinary purchaser. Cecil Kimber ran Morris Garages, the organization from which the Morris empire developed, and he modified a Morris 11.9-hp Cowley unit to push-rod ohv, put it in a light chassis frame, used Morris parts exclusively—and called it an M.G. This is the first, the 1923 experimental car, with Kimber at the wheel. Production began in 1925. (GB)

The 10-cv Type 177B *Conduite Intérieure* Peugeot. This 1.4-liter sedan with the sharp-edged body typical of the mid-twenties was a popular family car of medium price. Made at Peugeot's Beaulieu factory, some 15,000 were made between 1923 and 1926. (F)

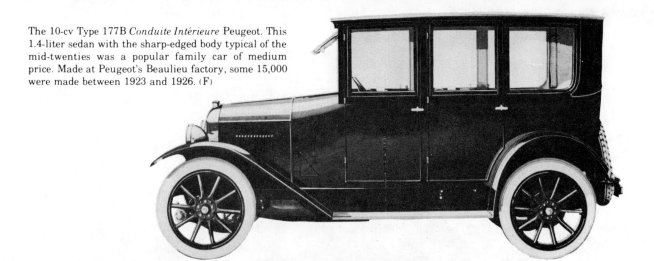

The previous year, which had seen a radical change in the outward appearance of Renault products, also saw four-wheel brakes on the larger cars from Billancourt, and in 1923 they were standard on all but one of the smaller range. This 14-hp *Coupé de Maitre* sported the new line but had a positively Edwardian attitude toward the chauffeur, whose weather protection was still minimal. (F)

Classed up in the rarified Rolls-Royce and Napier regions, the Lanchester 40, a precisely made 6-cylinder car built to the Edwardian standards and tastes, would travel, so they said, at a steady 90 mph and could use top gear from 3 to 90 mph. As more than one writer put it, "The Lanchester was designed and built to give its owner unfailing service for ever." Engine: 6,175 cc, 89-bhp at 2,000 rpm. (GB)

Economic factors and supply difficulties tended to suppress any too-ambitious venture in manufacture during the early years after the war, when wider demand for personal transport brought in a new section of buying public—the man whose purse was considerably shorter than that of the class who had bought automobiles in halcyon Edwardian days. Thus, this modest Wolsely 1.3-liter 10-hp and its like, although the company offered versions bodied in light alloy for the more *sportif*. (GB)

First seen in 1920, this was Rover's entry into the postwar small-car stakes — an 8-hp with an air-cooled flat-twin, originally of 998 cc (later enlarged to 1,130 cc), developing 14 hp. Through the years 1920-1925 17,000 of these simple little cars were sold to owners who rarely failed to sing their praises. (GB)

Just over a year after its introduction to the British public, the Austin Seven, now with a 747-cc engine, a reduced price (cheaper than many motorcycle-and-side-car combinations), and the affectionate name of "Chummy," was the increasingly popular transport for the small family who had previously imagined motoring to be well beyond their means. (GB)

Somewhere between a cycle car and light car, the A.B.C. used an air-cooled, flat-twin engine of just over a liter. The noisy and somewhat fragile unit took the car up to some creditable speeds, however, and the extremely light weight of the car helped in this performance. This is the A.B.C. "Super Sports" with a Compton body. (GB)

The Case Threshing Machine Co. of Racine, Wisconsin, had come into the automotive business in 1910, using its good name as an introduction. By 1924 this Model Y Case was available—a five-seater sedan (still with wooden wheels and rear brakes only) with a 4-liter, 6-cylinder, 4-bearing engine rated at 25 hp. Three years later the company ceased car production, although it is still alive and well and making farm machinery again. (USA)

The toy-like 5CV Citroën was first seen on the streets of Paris in 1922 and immediately proved successful. By 1924 several body styles were available: a "doctor" coupe, a three-seater tourer, and this two-seater "duck-back" tourer. Its 856-cc engine produced 11 bhp—enough to trundle it along at 39 mph, and enough to attract no less than 80,000 buyers. It was copied by several manufacturers in Europe, of which Opel's Laubfrosch was the most faithful. (F)

Balloon tires, and in some cases air suspension, were the platforms on which the Cole based its somewhat dubious claim to safety and comfort. The company offered no less than sixteen models in 1924—all of 39.2 hp—with fancy names like Aero Volante, Brouette, and Royal Limousine. (USA)

James Cunningham's company based at Rochester had produced carriages since the nineteenth century and cars from 1907. By 1915 the company made only cars, on a one-model policy. The Cunningham V-8 of 6 liters and 100 bhp was a handsome and advanced vehicle at that time and was offered for nearly eighteen years. Owned by some of the famous in entertainment and commerce, the brand was in the "prices on application" bracket. This model was first seen in 1922. (USA)

From 1914 to 1925 Ford cars could be bought in black only; the brass radiator had long since given way to a paint-job—all in the (highly successful) cause of keeping down the price. This is the 1924 Fordor Sedan (with four doors, naturally) which followed the earlier Tudor. Ford produced its 1-millionth car in 1924; now every seventh American owned an automobile. (USA)

During 1924 six models of the Dorris were still available to the public, although the company had ceased production the previous year. This 6-cylinder, overhead-valve Dorris is the four-seater Pasadena. (USA)

The Model 55 Kissel was built in eight versions, from speedster to this luxurious Berline, a seven-passenger vehicle very similar to the company's Brougham except for the dimensions of the rear compartment. Later in the 1924 model year Kissel offered 4-wheel Lockheed external contracting hydraulic brakes as optional equipment, and an alternative 8-cylinder engine. (USA)

A Gray taxi/tourer; the company (1922–1926) was formed by former Ford employees who had ideas of their own about how a car should be made—but it seemed as though many of them had previously been used by Ford. Although the engine specifications and chassis design were akin to the Model T, the company foundered after failing to fulfill ambitious plans for flooding the market with Gray products. (USA)

Sitting with the grass apparently growing up through its spokes is a 1924 McFarlan Town Car (2½ tons of it) that first suffered under the name of a Kickerbocker Cabriolet. This one housed the large TV (Twin-Valve), 6-cylinder engine with triple ignition, and a total of 18 spark plugs. (USA)

The Viennese operatic tenor and favorite of music-lovers of the Twenties, Richard Tauber steps into his supercharged Mercedes, a 24/100/140 6-cylinder tourer with an impressive 6.25 liters and 142 bhp under the hood. (D)

From 1920 the Morris Cowley price was dropped year by year, until in 1924 it could be bought quite inexpensively and, as the advertisement says — there were no extras. (GB)

This period of motoring history cannot be passed without reference to the sporting Mercedes. Superchargers had been used since 1922 and, although German racing activities were curtailed for some years after the war, 1924 proved an outstanding season, with wins at Solitude, Klausen, and Semmering—and in Sicily, where this 2-liter, 120-hp, 4-cylinder, supercharged car won the Targa and Coppa Florio. Of the 269 racing successes credited to Mercedes in 1924, 93 were scored by 1.5- and 2-liter supercharged cars. (D)

Looking very like a 5CV Citroën, the 951-cc, 4/12-PS Opel two-seater was soon called the "Laubfrosch" (treetoad) for its green color. It was immensely popular in a country that could not afford luxury models at this time, and it could travel at up to 45 mph. By 1926 Opel was able to cut the price considerably—and had sold nearly 40,000 by 1927. (D)

205

After the long success of the Silver Ghost, Rolls-Royce abandoned its one-model policy in 1922, because of economic pressures. The chassis price of the new car—the 6-cylinder, 3.1-liter Twenty—was comparatively modest, and about 3,000 were made by 1929, when it was increased in size and became the 20/25 hp. It grew even larger, into the 25/30 hp, by 1936. This landaulet may look a little old-fashioned, but Rolls-Royce never lagged behind in engineering improvements, most of which they incorporated into the cars without comment. (GB)

The Rhode was made for just fourteen years—between 1921 and 1935—and is noteworthy for its overhead-camshaft power unit, designed to attract the young sports-driver. Unusual for a small concern, all the component parts were made by the company, with the exception of the transmission. The 1¼-liter car had appeal, but as in so many cases during this period, the main bulk of the buying public ignored its undoubted qualities. (GB)

Looking as though somebody had sneaked a front-end design from Rolls-Royce, this Roamer, circa 1924, has the appearance of a solid and well-finished model — and was sold by the Barley Motor Car Company of Kalamazoo as a less-costly American-type R-R. Its 6-cylinder, 3¼ × 5¼ cu. in. engine was N.A.C.C.-rated at 25 hp. (USA)

Produced from 1920 to 1924, the 12/40-PS, 3.2-liter Type II Steyr "Waffenauto" from the Oesterreichische Waffenfabriks-Gesellschaft at Steyr (Austria) was the first motor vehicle from this former arms company which, like others in central and eastern Europe, had been forced to look around for something other than guns to make. Designed by the ubiquitous Hans Ledwinka, the Waffenauto was the first of a sound line of cars from Steyr. (A)

The 10-hp, four-seater Singer was introduced in 1923. A letter from an owner in Volo, Greece, forty years later, illustrates its character. "Dear Sirs, I have purchase directly from you in 1924 a motor car, fours seaters, four cylinder Engine S 621. It is in perfect working condition and actually in use by me since I purchase it. I am informed by many motor car industries accept to give new car in exchange of the old one which is an evidence and proof and a sample of good workmanship. If you accept my proposition please let me know your conditions: Yrs faithfully, G. A. Vafiades." Nice try, anyway. (GB)

The period of transition from two- to four-wheel brakes and larger (balloon) tires caught this rear-brakes-only, wooden-wheeled, 3.3-liter Light-Six Studebaker sedan just behind the times in 1924. However, the all-metal-bodied car caught up in 1925 (brakes all around) and in 1926 (balloon tires as standard). Choice of body colors was restricted to "Studebaker blue or maroon" with wheels and running gear in black. (USA)

Not to be confused with the French company, which had connections with Darracq and Gladiator and even Léon Bollée, the British Talbot (the last "t" is sounded to distinguish it) company had been associated with the French Clement company and later with the Rootes Group, becoming Sunbeam-Talbot, with cars based on Hillmans and Humbers. This is the 1924 12/30-hp Talbot, a 6-cylinder, 1,609-cc, ohv Coupé Cabriolet. (GB)

The 350-hp, V-12, 18.322-liter, aero-engined Sunbeam established another new world-land-speed record at 146.16 mph at Pendine Sands in Wales, with Britain's Malcolm Campbell at the wheel, in September 1924— and pushed it up to 150.87 mph a few months later in the same hands. Campbell, later knighted, created nine World Land Speed records and four World Water Speed records during his lifetime. (GB)

Almost the first true vintage Alfa-Romeo, the RL (Romeo Series L; 3-liter, 6-cylinder) was announced in 1921 and continued, in part, until 1927. This is the 22/90-hp RL SS (Super Sport) introduced in 1925, with an engine developing 83 bhp at 3,600 and a top speed of 135 km/h (84 mph). It is seen here in spider "Gran Premio" form. (I)

It may be an illustration of its versatility, but down on the farm is not exactly the place one would normally find the two-seater A.C., the car from Surrey, England, that had by this time gained a reputation for sportive performance powered by the 1½-liter British Anzani engine that had been fitted after the war. From 1925 on the power unit was A.C.'s own product. (GB)

The 3-liter Red Label (short-chassis) Bentley, considered by many to be the archetypal vintage car, made its name in sporting events. A 3-liter won both the 1924 and the 1927 Le Mans 24 Hours race, although by 1927 it was somewhat dated. A large 6½-liter model was brought out in 1925, but the 3-liter cars remained in production with detail modifications until 1929. Rolls-Royce took over in 1931. Engine: 4-cylinder, 2,996 cc, overhead valves by single overhead camshaft. (GB)

A Duesenberg had won the Indianapolis 500 Race the previous year and in 1925 Pete de Paolo broke through the "ton" with a winning race average of 101.13 mph in the event, run under the 122-cu in (c.i.) formula. (USA)

This Type 30 Bugatti, the first straight-8 to be made at the Molsheim works of Ettore Bugatti, was designed as a tourer. Bugatti, who made less than 10,000 cars during his years of production, impressed the automotive world more than almost any other single manufacturer, except Henry Royce, by his mechanical perfection in design and execution and by the performance of his racing cars, the most consistently successful ever seen on the grid. The Type 30 engine was just under 2 liters and rated at 17.8 hp by the makers and the R.A.C. (F)

Abner Doble built his first steam car in 1906 while he was still a student. A production car was first put on the market in 1917; from the start it was recognized as an excellent product, and much of its fame came from its Hollywood and European-nobility clientele. This is one of the E-series (re-bodied in 1932) which could get up steam in 80 seconds from switch-on and travel 1,500 miles on one tank of water. The car could accelerate silently (and gearlessly) to 85 mph, or slip smoothly through crowded traffic. A 4-cylinder engine, located at the rear and connected to a flash boiler, produced around 75 bhp. Luxury coupled with speed and efficiency was not, unhappily, sufficient to persuade the American public to buy in numbers large enough to keep the company alive. (USA)

Climbing up the steep villa drive is a 509 SM (Spinto Monza) Fiat, one of the many versions of this car, the company's first mass-produced model, aimed at the cheaper market. Its 990-cc engine had an overhead camshaft and produced 22 bhp at 3,400 rpm. More importantly, it could be purchased on the installment plan—and a year after its introduction it was, predictably, the most popular car in Italy. It was made in sedan, sports, taxi, and commercial variants. (I)

The seven-passenger phaeton by Hudson (the only apparent difference between this and the tourer is the way the doors open) helped the company to phenomenally high sales in 1925. Total shipments of 269,474 cars were more than double the number shipped the previous year. Hudson also announced the price of its Coach, a "high-grade commodious closed car of the best quality" at only a few dollars more than its open car. (USA)

Made by the Locomobile Company of America, the Flint was one of W. C. Durant's bargain cars. Sporting disk wheels and front bumpers, in 1925 the 6-cylinder car was equipped with four-wheel brakes for the first time. In the United States the main mechanical trend was now toward straight-8 power units, and for the first year in automotive history more closed than open cars were bought in America—and the 25-millionth U.S. car was sold. (USA)

A Peerless, one of the "three P's" of the American motoring world (the other two were Pierce-Arrow and Packard). The Peerless Motor Car Company of Cleveland, Ohio, had been in the business for a quarter of a century; this tourer housed a large V-8 unit of 3¼ × 5 in bore and stroke. (USA)

Four-wheel brakes can clearly be seen on this two-seater Oakland, introduced in 1924 as a cheaper line than earlier cars from the company. It was painted in Du Pont Duco cellulose, a significant advance, as this was a preparation that drastically cut the time needed to dry the paint, eliminating a delaying factor that had plagued many manufacturers in the past. (USA)

For the elegant and rich of France, this wooden-wheeled, long-bodied Renault 45, known as the *Queen of the Road*, must have been something of a handful in Paris traffic. Although its 6-cylinder, 9-liter engine did not even boast overhead valves (and lacked several other post-Edwardian advances), the car was an essay in the enormous in the days of small, penny-pinching products from most other European motor manufacturers. Presidents of the Republic of France hired this car for official receptions and journeys. (F)

A pit stop for a twin-camshaft, 3-liter Sunbeam at the Le Mans 24-Hour race of 1925. Filling her up is S. C. H. Davis, who won the event in a 3-liter Bentley in 1927 after surviving a multiple crash—thus creating one of the legends of Le Mans. The 6-cylinder British car produced 90 bhp and was a refreshingly mobile vehicle for its day. It took second place at Le Mans in 1925— runner up to a 3.5-liter Lorraine Dietrich. (GB)

A selection of mail-order cars for the kids. This page from a catalog of Gamages, the long-established London store, shows the type of car we could expect in our Christmas stocking in 1925.

Winston Churchill looks frustrated as he tries to start this Wolseley tourer of 1925, while a carload of politicians watch his efforts. Wolseley's wartime experience making large, V-8, overhead-valve, Hispano Suiza engines naturally influenced postwar production, and the single overhead camshafts of the 10-, 12-, and 15-hp cars were partly the result of lessons learned from the aero-engine experience. In 1925 the 15 was succeeded by a side-valve-engined car—the Wolseley 16/35. (GB)

The years 1919 – 1922 had been spent by Lionel Bamford and Robert Martin in experiment and racing, and only then did they offer a production Aston Martin (named after Aston Clinton, the British hill-climb location, and Lionel Martin). The first engines used were 1½-liter, side-valve units, intended for production cars, and several overhead-camshaft engines were made for racing. The original company lasted only until 1925, when money ran out. It was resuscitated the following year by Renwick and Bertelli, who produced a new design. This is a 1.5-liter, twin-overhead-camshaft machine, first seen in 1924. (GB)

A.C. cars had by this year been collecting world records by the fistful as part of a promotion program instigated by S. F. Edge, who had earlier joined the Thames Ditton, Surrey, Company. The bigger 6-cylinder A.C. had put up a World 24-Hours speed record in 1925 at Montlhéry with an average of 82.58 mph, and the Hon. Victor Bruce had established a new 15,000-mile figure at just over 68 mph. In 1926 the company highlighted its program with first place in the Monte Carlo Rally, the first British car to win this event. (GB)

This was an era of promotional stunts performed to obtain copy and pictures in the press. Seen here is a Chevrolet—the company's 2-millionth—taking full advantage of the 45-degree steps in front of the State Capitol Building at Jackson, Mississippi. By 1926 the deluxe models had disk wheels and nickel-plated fenders. (USA)

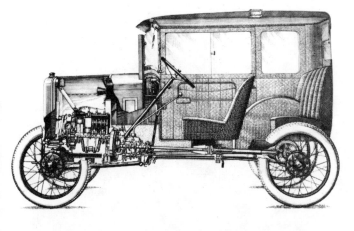

The first Austin Seven sedan had a stretched cellulosed fabric over the wood framework. This cutaway drawing shows the works and seating layout. (GB)

Two years after introducing the car bearing his name, Walter Chrysler moved into the luxury-car market with the Imperial 80, guaranteed to do 80 mph. January 1926 saw the first model, and the car soon became known for its low-gear "pull" and hill-climbing ability. The potent 92-bhp, 6-cylinder engine was the first Chrysler product to have light alloy pistons. (USA)

The driving seat and dashboard of one of America's most powerful production cars, the Chrysler Imperial 80. Among the sophistications was a small Chrysler emblem that would light up when the battery needed water. (USA)

Andre Citroën's B14 appeared in 1926, a development of the early "B" Types, now with an engine of 1,539 cc and an effective output of 22 bhp, plus an all-steel (*tout acier*) body and four-wheel servo-vacuum brakes on some versions. This is the famous wickerwork-sided landaulet taxi seen in every Paris street during this period and built just before the 1926 vehicles adopted the flat radiator. (F)

The 509 again, this time being employed as a milking machine. This, the smallest car (990 cc) Fiat had produced to date, was, by 1926, immensely popular throughout Italy and the continent. Another version, a "commercial tourer," had a detachable backseat that, when removed through an opening tailgate, converted the vehicle into a light truck. (I)

A Model T coupe, with radiator in burnished metal plate, for the first time since 1917. The lack of four-wheel brakes is noticeable—they were never offered with the American-made Model T Ford throughout its long production. In Britain in 1926 the Manchester-made, four-seater version cost less than the Austin Seven Chummy, that country's own contribution to cheaper motoring. (USA)

A right-hand-drive Marmon Big Six sedan, seen in an antique part of England. With four-wheel brakes and balloon tires, the Big Six was a luxury carriage in the best American tradition. This model's wire wheels were not standard. (USA)

Better known as "Babs," this Higham Special was bought and modified by Welshman Parry Thomas, who raced at Brooklands track in England during the twenties. He had built several "Thomas Specials," both large and small, had broken world records, and had won uncountable races with them. This, his last car, was a 27-liter Liberty V-12 aero-engined, chain-driven monster, and Thomas had set up a World Land Speed record in it before he made the attempt, on Pendine Sands in Wales, which ended in his death. (GB)

The Lanchester 40, a big 6-cylinder vehicle designed with almost Edwardian disregard for expense, remained in production through the difficult years of the mid-twenties, although the company offered a smaller 3.1-liter car for the less-opulent client. (GB)

This early M.G. was produced some three years after the first prototype was made by Cecil Kimber, and there can be no doubt of its connection with Morris Motors Limited of Cowley, near Oxford, as the next picture shows. The M.G. of 1926 was just a somewhat more elegant Morris Oxford with alloy bodywork and smarter line, and this two-seater, 14/28-hp "sports" model had its 4-cylinder, side-valve, 1,802-cc unit tuned to give it a slight edge over the Morris Oxford. (GB)

The front end is difficult to distinguish from the contemporary M.G., but the side elevation shows a more upright build. This Morris Cowley is shown here at a Shell Station in Britain in an era when the attendant pumped the fuel in by hand—and also checked tires and engine gratis. The "Bull-nosed" Morris (with a round radiator shaped something like a bullet) gave way to the flat-fronted radiator at the end of 1926. The Cowley was a cheaper, slightly smaller edition of the Morris Oxford. (GB)

A single basic model on which to hang various body styles was the production plan of most American manufacturers after World War I, and Oldsmobile pursued the policy for a time with the Model 30. This Landau Coupe was one of no less than ten bodies offered on the same chassis, using the 2.8-liter, 6-cylinder engine that was sold between 1924 and 1929. (USA)

One of the slimmest cars ever made, this Panhard "Lame de rasoir" (Razor-blade) car was built for the company's record-breaking program between the wars. The 4,800-cc, 4-cylinder single-seater was very fast and set up two records at Montlhéry near Paris, but was jetisoned after a crash. (F)

The first Pontiac made its debut at The National Automobile Show in 1926. Produced by Oakland (General Motors), it was a cheaper car, intended to fill the market gap in Oakland production. The 3-liter, 6-cylinder Pontiac was so popular that it soon consumed its parent, cutting the sales of Oakland by half in one year until, completely overshadowed by the younger make, Oakland ceased production in 1931, after which only Pontiac cars were built, and the company became the Pontiac Motor Company. This is a 1926 shot of a specially rigged Pontiac made, it seems, to give the boys a ride around the factory. (USA)

It had been a logical move for war-hero and racing-driver Eddie Rickenbacker to move into the automotive industry, and by 1926 his company was making this smooth-running brougham, a 58-hp six with two flywheels. The following year, the company's final offering was to be a straight-8 4.4-liter, giving 107 bhp in sports tune. (USA)

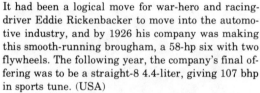

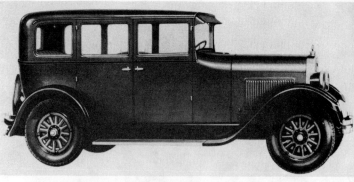

The big styling changes made by the Dodge Brothers in 1927 show in this Fast Four. Fenders, roofline, and window shapes are now much more rounded, heralding the early streamline period, and the integral sun visor is typically 1927 U.S. The Fast Four, with a 108-in wheelbase, made its debut in June 1927; its light weight and 40-hp engine gave it a top speed of over 60 mph—comfortably rapid for the type of vehicle. Four-wheel brakes appeared in November. Dodge also brought out its first 6-cylinder car this year. (USA)

The rather dilapidated car seen here in need of some front wheel alignment is a Flint, circa 1926, produced by the Locomobile Company of America, with a 6-cylinder Continental engine beefed up by a seven-bearing crankshaft. This year the company buoyantly offered a coupe-roadster, a Junior Coach, a sedan, and a Sports Touring, using three different 6-cylinder engines—2.8 liters (in the coach), 3.8 (sedan and roadster), and 4.5 liters (tourer). However, the following year was the Flint's last. (USA)

The 14-hp, 4-cylinder, side-valve Hillman was the only car on the Coventry company's production line during the years 1926–1928, when William and Reginald Rootes, controllers of Humber and Commer, took over the firm. (GB)

Aster Engineering of Wembley produced comparatively large and well-made vehicles between 1922 and 1930, the first series being 18 hp and 2.6 liters. By the time the 21-hp model seen here was produced, the power unit had been enlarged to 3 liters. The company, like many makers of quality machines during this period of rigid economy in Europe, was forced to amalgamate with another company, and joined Arrol-Johnson in 1927. The merger saved both companies for just three years. (GB)

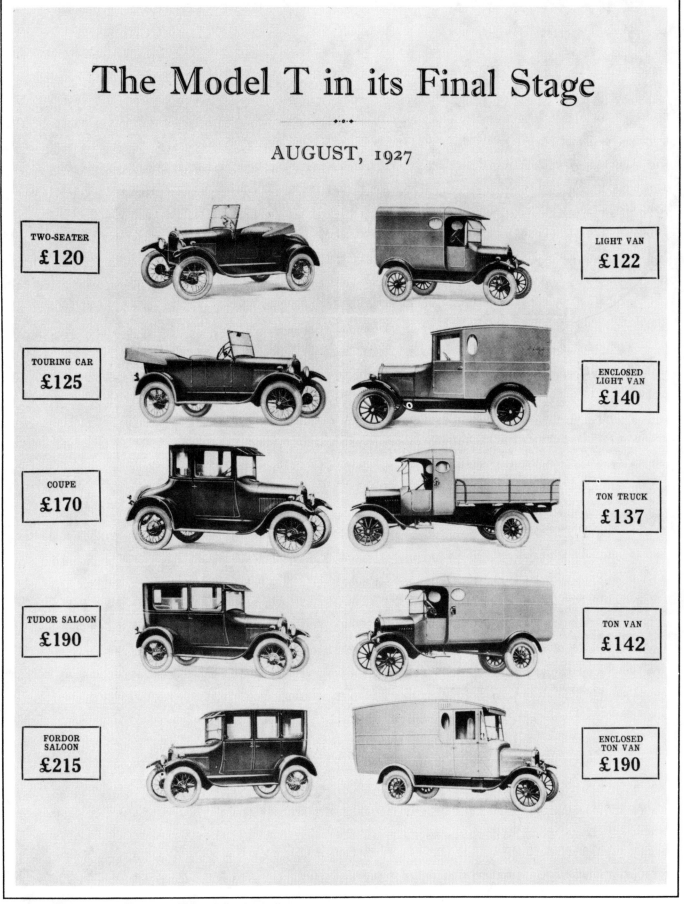

The Model T in its Final Stage

AUGUST, 1927

TWO-SEATER
£120

LIGHT VAN
£122

TOURING CAR
£125

ENCLOSED
LIGHT VAN
£140

COUPE
£170

TON TRUCK
£137

TUDOR SALOON
£190

TON VAN
£142

FORDOR
SALOON
£215

ENCLOSED
TON VAN
£190

This multiple picture shows the Model T Ford in
various forms during its final year of production. (GB)

Introduced in 1927, the La Salle was an instant success and sold some 60,000 units during the next three years. The engine was a V-8, and styles ranged from a roadster to a seven passenger Imperial Sedan. Although the car was designed as Cadillac's representative in the medium-price field, it resembled the parent car in every way, including manufacturing standards, except that some dimensions were smaller, and the La Salle weighed less. (USA)

A middle-priced American car of conventional construction, this Hupmobile seven-passenger sedan, Model E2, had a straight-8, 4-liter, side-valve engine (3 × 4¾ in), N.A.C.C.-rated at 28.8 hp. Wooden wheels and balloon tires on a long (125-in) chassis gave it a solid look and a comfortable ride. The brochure lists a very full kit, including ignition theft lock, stoplight, clock, dome light, sun visor, and VV windshield with "automatic cleaner." (USA)

Jowett had flirted with water-cooled V-twin and 3-cylinder engines since 1901, and eventually settled for an 826-cc, flat-twin, water-cooled unit which was used in very much the same form for about forty years. The car was strictly a utility job, with somewhat rough finish, but was totally reliable and enduring. In fact, in 1926–1927 the company claimed that all Jowetts ever made were still on the road—although such a statement had to be taken on faith. (GB)

Daimler and Benz, the two founding companies of the world's automotive industry, had finally amalgamated in 1926, and from that date all their cars were called Mercedes-Benz. This picture, taken in June 1927, shows a lineup on the grid at the just-completed Nürburgring in the Eiffel Mountains of Germany—17½ miles (at this date) of undulating circuit through the pine woods that form part of the Black Forest. Here, on the front line, are three Mercedes-Benz sports models; two 6.8-liter, supercharged "S" models; and an earlier "K," which used a blown 6.25-liter unit of a shattering 160 bhp. The winner, German race-driver Rudolf Caracciola, is at the wheel of No. 1. (D)

Oakland was slipping downhill by 1927—and it did not worry the company one jot. The tremendous success of its own Pontiac, introduced the previous year, was the main cause of Oakland's sales slide. However, the 6-cylinder Oakland was still offered in seven different styles, including sedans, sports roadsters, phaetons—and out-dated landaus. It seems that Miss America 1927 liked an Oakland, though. (USA)

One of the handsomest cars of its day, this Lincoln D.C. Phaeton body-builder Locke had the European touch with its dual cowl and rear-passenger windshield. Henry Leland, of Cadillac fame, had started the company but had sold out to Henry Ford in 1922, and since then all Lincolns were built by Ford. The 95-bhp, 357.8-cu in engine was a smooth V-8 designed by Leland and used until 1928, when the only modification was a ⅛-in increase in the bore. (USA)

Now with a flat front end, the Cowley, the smaller of the Morris products, still had the divided windshield and pressed-steel artillery wheels, but was fitted with front brakes. In 1927 there was still some controversy about the value of front brakes: some thought that they could constitute a danger by inspiring the driver with too much confidence! (GB)

The 1,000-hp Sunbeam, the first car to exceed 200 mph, was driven by Sir Henry Segrave at Daytona Beach, Florida, on Tuesday, March 29, 1927, when the British record car reached a two-way run of 203.79 mph. (GB)

Specification list for the 1,000-hp Sunbeam. Note that the hand brake "operates separate shoes in the rear wheel drums only." Wonder if they ever used them?

The 1000 hp. Sunbeam Car

SPECIFICATION AND DIMENSIONS.

Engines
Two 12 cylinder Sunbeam-Coatalen engines of 500 h.p. each. Bore and stroke 122 x 160 m/m respectively, giving a cubic capacity of 22,444 c.c. for each engine. Four valves to each cylinder, operated by overhead camshafts.

Lubrication
Lubrication is on the dry sump principle, two pumps, one suction and one delivery pump being fitted to each engine.

Cooling
A single radiator is fitted to the front engine and two are fitted to the rear engine. Water circulated by a centrifugal type pump fitted to each engine.

Fuel Feed and Carburation
The fuel tank has a capacity of 28 gallons and fuel is fed to the Claudel Hobson carburetters (two fitted to each engine) by air pressure supplied from the pump mounted on the rear engine.

Ignition
Four B.T.H. magnetos on each engine. Two K.L.G. sparking plugs to each cylinder.

Clutch and Gear Box
Two clutches are fitted, one being a starting clutch only. The other transmits the drive to the three speed gear box.

Gear:	3rd.	2nd.	1st.	Reverse.
Ratios :	1.017 to 1	1.56 to 1	2.968 to 1	2.6125 to 1

Brakes
Four-wheel brakes operated by Dewandre Vacuum Servo motor. Hand-brake operates separate shoes in the rear wheel drums only.

Springs
Woodhead springs, semi-elliptical front and rear, fitted with Hartford double type shock absorbers.

Wheels and Tyres
Dunlop special wire wheels fitted with thin tread type tyres, specially designed and manufactured by The Dunlop Rubber Co., Ltd.

Instruments
Among the various instruments fitted to the car are :—1 revolution counter, 3 radiator thermometers, 1 8-way magneto switch, 1 air pressure gauge, and 4 oil pressure gauges.

Chassis Frame
Specially strong channel section side members, braced by similarly sectioned cross members. The underpart of the chassis is fully protected by a steel plate attached to the bottom flange of the side members.

Body
Special streamlined body, with panels of 18 gauge aluminium sheet, built up in sections so that any part of the chassis is readily accessible by removing the section covering that particular part. Two strong steel hoops are fitted in front and behind the cockpit. Wheelbase 11' 9", track 5' 2", overall length 23' 6", overall width 6', approximate gross weight 3 tons.

Opel Laubfrosch (Tree-toad), 1924. (D)

A Hooper-bodied Rolls-Royce '20' landaulette, 1926. (GB)

Fiat Mephistopheles, 1924. Born in 1908 as the SB4
the car was extensively modified in 1923-4. It broke
the world record in 1924. (I)

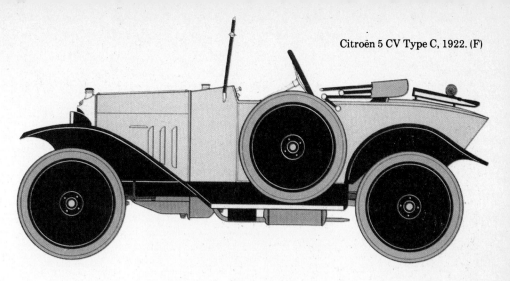

Citroën 5 CV Type C, 1922. (F)

1919 Standard 9.5 hp (GB)

1920 Aston Martin 2-4 seater with supercharged
Anzani engine. (GB)

Peugeot 5 CV, 1924. (F)

Produced both at Springfield, Massachusetts, and Derby, England, the overhead-valve, 7.6-liter Rolls-Royce Phantom I was one of the finest cars from the company and a worthy successor to the Ghost, whose run of nineteen years had seen the company become a revered name. The "New Phantom" was made until 1929 in Britain (1931 in the U.S.A.) and was followed by the Phantom II, with an entirely new chassis. This was one of the last styles in which the chauffeur got wet—and one of the first European cars to use white-wall tires. (GB)

Over a restaurant meal, Assar Gabrielsson and Gustaf Larson decided to start a Swedish car industry and by 1927 had made the first Volvo (Latin for *I roll*, but not, of course, in the way that immediately comes to mind). Nicknamed Jacob, the car had a sheet-metal body on a wood frame of ash and beech, and a 4-cylinder, 1,940-cc engine, developing around 28 bhp, with an all-out speed of 60 mph. Strong even then (Volvos have been noted for their robust build ever since), it caught the imagination of the Scandinavians and sold well. (S)

The London company producing the Windsor lasted for just three years (1927 was the last one), even though the car was well-engineered and above-standard finish. It had four-wheel brakes throughout its brief life, and its 1,353-cc power unit was highly efficient. Parts were made in the works, the transmission was well-designed, and the whole car was well-proportioned. It just cost too much. (GB)

Driven from his Molsheim factory by war, Ettore Bugatti was back again by 1920 and beginning to win sporting events with his "Brescia" Bugatti. By 1922 the 2-liter, 8-cylinder Type 30 had appeared, and 1924 saw the classic racing car, the 8-cylinder Type 35, which in modified forms was made until 1930 and subdivided into the Types 35, 35B, 35C, and 35T, of which the last two were 2,262 cc and the 35B and 35C had 3-lobed Roots superchargers. This is the 35B. (F)

During the middle twenties the most popular of all America's prestige cars in overseas countries was probably the Buick, smaller and more maneuverable than the giants from Detroit. With a 274-cu in displacement, overhead-valve engine putting out some 77 bhp, the Models 47 to 58 — all with the same general specifications — proved top sellers in the United States, too, and in terms of financial turnover were among the highest earners. This is the Model 54 2-passenger Sports Roadster. (USA)

The 4½-liter Bentley began to succeed the highly successful 3-liter model in 1927, when the latter began to be out-classed by more advanced multi-cylindered cars, both continental and British. With an output of 110 bhp, this was the "Big Six" minus 2 cylinders, and it was capable of around 93 mph. One of the first models competed in Le Mans in 1927 but was involved in the notorious White House pile-up out of which Sammy Davis and Dudley Benjafield extricated their 3-liter Bentley, limping on to win the race. (GB)

This well-engineered car of the late twenties is a Chandler, produced in Cleveland, Ohio. Noted for pioneering and technical advances, in 1928 Chandler was one of the first to offer Westinghouse vacuum brakes designed to reduce pedal pressure by two-thirds. The company was bought by Hupmobile in 1929. (USA)

"You can't go to heaven in a 507," the song should go. In fact, some could, in 1928, in this Fiat 507FA sweet chariot. Not everyone, though, for this was a funeral car, first class. Fiat produced less ornate types for second- and third-class funerals. (I)

In 1928 Cadillac offered two important advances. The company was the first to install what was then called "security-glass" windshields and windows as standard and, more significantly, the first to offer a synchro-mesh transmission. There was also a new engine this year, a 341-cu in (5.6-liter) V-8 of 90 bhp, which was used for both Cadillac and, in 5-liter form, in La Salle models. (USA)

For the living, only the best, at least for Italy's King Umberto (the one with the feather) as he smilingly prepares to descend from his flower-decked Fiat 525. The company had launched this 3.8-liter 6-cylinder earlier in 1928 in advance of the luxury 8-cylinder 530 — which was killed by the looming economic crisis of the thirties before it even reached the marketplace. (I)

Gottlieb Daimler's son Paul had worked as chief designer for Horch at Zwickau since 1923 and had produced several 8-cylinder models of which this, the 375, was the 1928 offering. Larger than it looks here, this Horch roadster had a twin-overhead camshaft, straight-8, 3,924-cc unit, developing 80 bhp at 3,200 rpm. (D)

A shorter version of the 24/100/140-PS Mercedes-Benz was built in 1926 and called the "K." With its 6.25-liter engine, it was one of the fastest tourers then in existence. The new Mercedes-Benz company decided to develop it further and brought out the "S," with 6.8 liters, a lower profile, and a larger supercharger. In 1928 the "SS" appeared with an increased capacity of 7.1 liters, followed by the SSK (Super Sports Kurz) and the SSKL (Kurz, Leicht—short, light). All had great success in sporting events. This is the 6-cylinder, 7.1-liter SS tourer. (D)

Here the Mercedes SSK takes a bend at the Semmering hill-climb during a 1928 run that culminated in a new record for its German driver, Rudolf Caracciola. The Mercedes-Benz K, S, SS, SSK, and SSKL were not built specifically as racing cars, but were in fact road sports cars, with comparatively slow-running, flexible engines, more suited to the long, fast roads of their own country than to much of the rest of Europe's twisting highways. (D)

Seen in one of the garden villages of the English Cotswold country is another British venture into the small-car world, the Morris Minor, here in family sedan version (small families preferred). Cheap motoring this, on 874 cc with a radiator thermometer thrown in. (GB)

Poised at the summit of this urban rise is a 1928 Moon from St. Louis, Missouri. In the business since 1905, the company first made high-wheel buggies and plodded on with conventional vehicles until after World War I, when they emerged as handsome, solidly constructed machines housing a Continental unit of 3.6 liters. This is the 5-seater Diana, with an sv, straight-8, 4-liter engine—and wooden wheels. (USA)

Leading the parade is an Opel tourer—a 4-cylinder, 1,100-cc car called the 4/14, and one of the last independent Opels before General Motors took over the German company. Although in 1928 Opel was Germany's largest producer, strong financial backing was needed in the face of increasing international economic difficulties, and GM's money and worldwide sales organization were saving factors. (D)

The first Plymouth by Chrysler appeared in 1928, at just about the worst time it could have chosen—a year before the U.S. stock market dropped to its lowest level in 1929. Designed to replace 4-cylinder Chryslers and to challenge the cheaper ranges of Chevrolets and Fords, some 101,000 motorists thought it a good buy. (USA)

In 1927 and 1928 Opel made a series of experiments using a rocket car of their own design and manufacture. The second, RAK II, was demonstrated at the Avus circuit on May 23, 1928, when the single-seater car—it looks modern even today, right down to the "wing" stabilizers—ran at speeds of over 125 mph. Twenty-four gunpowder rockets at the rear end of the car were fired in stages by a foot pedal operated by the driver. Here Fritz von Opel is in the hot seat; the following summer his first rocket-propelled aircraft took to the sky. (D)

The regal Reinastella, built—and really built—by Renault from 1928 to 1934 was another example of the curious compulsion by European bread-and-butter manufacturers to build castles-in-Spain luxury cars. Taking over from the "45," this was a front-radiator, 8-cylinder land-ship of just over 7 liters which in standard tune would clock 100 mph. Other models of the time by this company were less exotic: the 12.5 Monasix, the Vivasix, Monastella, and Vivastella. (F)

A Springfield Rolls-Royce Phantom, made in the Massachusetts town by skilled American mechanics under the presidency of Canadian E. J. Belnap. Although every bit as good as those made in Derby, England, a number of misguided American and Canadian buyers insisted on purchasing a "Derby Rolls," having made up their minds to buy the best that *Europe* could offer. (USA)

Riley had entered the sporting twenties with the 1½-liter, side-valve Redwing which had made its name in trials. In the same tradition — although not specifically designed for sporting work — the Riley Monaco, a version of the very advanced 9-hp, twin-cam 1,100 cc, had been brought out some two years earlier and had put a number of contemporaries in the shade. It offered an efficient and exciting car. (GB)

Living cheek-by-jowl with the giant of Billancourt, Renault, the Société des Moteurs Salmson of Paris had made aircraft engines during the war and, like so many others, had moved over to a car of their own, originally a G.N. under license. Later, using an unconventional push-and-pull rod, 4-cylinder engine, they produced home-bred vehicles. Concurrently, the company produced an overhead-camshaft engine of 1,100 cc which began to take sporting honors as early as 1922—the little car even scored an overall second place in the 1927 Le Mans event. By 1923 non-sporting Salmsons had also installed the ohc engine and had taken on a new character. Renault bought the company in 1956. (F)

Powered by a new 848-cc, chain-drive, overhead-camshaft engine, the little Singer Junior of 1928 fathered a line of highly successful small sports models of the thirties and later. Here, Junior seems to be lost in a snowdrift on its way to the south of France during the Monte Carlo Rally. (GB)

German emigrant Fred Duesenberg arrived in the United States in the 1880s and made his first competition vehicle in 1903. By 1929 his products had achieved the highest reputation for both quality and performance, culminating in the SJ (introduced in 1932), the greatest of the makes. This is the Model J; its 8-cylinder, twin-overhead-camshaft power unit of nearly 7 liters had a claimed output of 265 bhp and could travel at 90 mph—in second gear! In high it topped 110 mph, which made it the fastest production car in America—and several other superlatives as well. (USA)

The first Auburn (from Auburn, Indiana) was built in 1900, but since 1924 the company had been part of the Cord Corporation, embracing Duesenberg and Lycoming Motors in addition to Auburn. This is the boat-tailed, bucket-seat Model 120 Speedster (an almost-immoral appellation in today's safety-conscious motoring world). The straight-8, side-valve unit ($3^{1/4} \times 4^{1/2}$ cu in) from Lycoming could propel the car at 100 mph, and the low-profile design, coupled with rigid frame and good suspension, gave better road adhesion than most large sports cars of the day. (USA)

On May 6, 1928, the Detroit Free Press reported: "Probably no development of the past five years has created so profound a stir in the automobile industry as the current announcement that the new De Soto Six, which will be presented to the public in the next three months, is to be built by Chrysler." It slotted into the market gap so neatly (aimed at stealing sales from Pontiac, Nash, and other medium-priced cars) that 34,000 cars had been shipped to dealers by the end of 1928—a month before its debut at the New York Automobile Show. This is one of the first off the line— the Model K; engine displacement 174.9 cu in, rated at 55 hp. (USA)

The dignified Englishman in the so-correct bowler hat standing by his brand-new Weymann-bodied, 2.1-liter, 6-cylinder Humber 16/50, latest offering from the Coventry company, was more often seen in leather cap and goggles on a circuit, or attempting to break a world record or two. Henry O'Neal de Hans Segrave established three World Land Speed records and was at one time the only British driver to win a Grand Prix race in a British car for thirty-two years. Driving a Sunbeam, he won the 1923 French G.P. (GB)

The year of the "New Ford" was 1928, when the Model A made its appearance. Now it was in full production and geared to the thirties. Americans had made full use of the Model T, but, as standards of production and engineering increased, the Model A filled the more sophisticated bill. It still had only 4 cylinders (this time of 400 cu in), but drive control was now through conventional clutch and three-speed transmission. Orders for 400,000 had been taken before the car was seen by the public. (USA)

With a typical Italian gesture, this leather-helmeted driver shows the new Fiat 514 Coppa delle Alpi spyder to a (hopefully) admiring audience. The 514 succeeded the 509, the first of Fiat's mass-produced cars, introduced in 1925. The 1½-liter 514 car had three good years of production, selling 36,970 in various forms from a small sedan to this elegant short-wheelbase, 37-hp sports two-seater, the final development of the model. (I)

Walter Chrysler devised the Imperial range (guaranteed to reach 80 mph) in 1926 to break into the luxury-car market. By 1929 the Imperial enjoyed a high reputation. It had a 5-liter, 6-cylinder engine, developing 100 bhp, and a 136-in wheelbase. A new, slimmer-profile radiator grille fronted a hood that retained the flutes of previous Imperials. Jack Dempsey, former heavyweight boxing champion of the world, seems to be stealing most of the thunder in this picture. (USA)

Buick's smaller side-valve, 212-cu in, 6-cylinder product came out in 1929 under the name Marquette — another attempt to interest a market that was just starting to suffer before a slowly collapsing economic boom — one which saw its demise in October of that year. (USA)

The year 1929 saw the first small M.G.—the M-type Midget, based on the new overhead-camshaft engine used in the Morris Minor range. This is an 847-cc M-type, one of the first, made between 1928 and 1932, and is not much more than a warmed-up Minor with a fabric sports body. However, this modest model led to greater things: the D-type gave 7 bhp more than the M-type; the racing C-type gave 44 bhp and over 62 when fitted with a supercharger—and on through J's, PA, PB, TA, and TB. M.G. racing policy gave much information that was passed on to the Morris range from which it sprang. (GB)

Two sizes of Reo Flying Cloud were on sale in 1929, offering 3.5- or 4.4-liter engines. Here an F.C. Sedan is parked on a very fast piece of ground—Daytona Beach, Florida—next to the British-made Golden Arrow, a machine built to the design of Capt. J. S. Irving and housing a Schneider Trophy-type Napier "Lion" engine of 12 cylinders and a colossal 930 bhp. In the hands of Sir Henry Segrave the Arrow created a new World Land Speed record of 231.44 mph in 1929. (USA & GB)

Skoda, formerly Laurin & Klement, put out a new range in 1929, of which the smallest car was the 4-cylinder, 5-main bearing, 1,165-cc, 22-hp Type 422 — a very solid if uninspired piece of engineering, many of which still grace the rural highways of their country of origin. This coupe is more stylish than most of its day. (CS)

The Italian O.M. (Officine Meccaniche) Company had opened for business in 1899, making locomotives, ships, and trucks, and was doing well when it bought Zust, a smaller automotive company which had been established since the beginning of the century. By 1925 the O.M. was a highly respected vehicle; the 6-cylinder, 2-liter Tipo 665 first made in 1925 was a healthy sporting car in spite of its somewhat ordinary specifications. During the twenties it took part in numerous competitions and gained creditable places in Le Mans and the Mille Miglia. This one, an ESS 15/60 was imported into Britain in chassis-form only. (I)

Airplane pioneer Gabriel Voisin's company made cars of high finish and excellent performance—small cars (an 8CV), big cars (his first was a 12-cylinder model), Grand Prix cars (1923), record-breaking cars (1927 24-hour record)—and was a master-designer of the then new aerodynamic shape, although some of his efforts were unbelievably ugly. This is a 27/120-hp Voisin, with the wood-and-fabric body that was just beginning to lose favor in the automotive world. (F)

The Standard Motor Company brought out this little four-seater tourer with the high sides in 1929—a long wheelbase with the 9.9-hp engine that had first appeared the previous year in the Standard "Tiegnmouth" model. (GB)

Another British pioneer, the Star Motor Company (beginning date 1898) that graduated from cycles, now introduced the Luna and Nestor fabric sedans late in 1928 as successors to their earlier Diana, Athena, Cygnus, Flora, Cetus, and Eclipse (someone in the company had a classical education). This is the 6-cylinder, ohv, 69 × 110 mm, Weymann-bodied Star 18/50 Luna of 1929. (GB)

For those who may recognize the girl, the original caption reads: "Marian Marsh and her new Willys-Knight Great Six '66' coupe." Willys-Knight was one of a complex tangle of companies that included the Standard Wheel Company, Overland, Willys, Kaiser-Jeep, Crossley, and half a dozen others. Engine: 3.9-liter, 60-bhp. (USA)

WORLD ON WHEELS,
1930~1949

By 1930 the young, brave-new-world generation of men of the twenties, long returned from an almost forgotten war, were now settled family men with some ten years of work and domestic life behind them. By the mid-thirties they had weathered the depressions in both Europe and America and had come out on the (comparatively) sunny side. The long vista of genuine mobility beckoned strongly, as a little leisure time entered the lives of the peoples of the Western world.

The period also heralded a new type of motoring—not just for the enthusiasts, the skilled car-mechanics, or the traveling rich. For the middle classes keeping up with the Joneses was becoming a social game, and a family car for the front drive was essential.

This was a mass market in every respect. The cars of the thirties were not merely playthings for weekend spins, as in the previous decade, but had developed, due to the swelling of city populations and industrial regions, into serious commuting vehicles. In this, America was far ahead of Europe, and the automobile had been a workhorse there almost since its inception.

The vast potential market was answered readily by motor manufacturers, who stamped out simple mass-produced vehicles by the millions. Competition was at its most fierce, and getting the edge on a competitor was, as often as not, to dream up another bolt-on goody that would look just that much more expensive. So the gimmicks proliferated—trafficators, steering-column shifts, automatics, radios, chromium plating, free-wheeling, wrap-around this-and-that, air-flow conditioning—and hundreds of pointless sales promoters that were oriented more to the thickness of the carpet than to that of the brake shoes.

However, in their way they proved highly successful, and increased sales lifted the automotive trade out of the doldrums, substantially helping the national economy of the manufacturing nations. And if the cars' performances would make the afficionado wince, their somewhat torpid qualities passed uncriticized by the overwhelming majority of motorists and their families—and they were undoubtedly easier to drive than those of the previous decade. In Britain a middle-class dad had a Hillman Minx, a small Ford product, or a Standard Nine, while the wealthier used a Rover or Lanchester and gave MG Midgets to their sons for twenty-first birthday presents. In Germany GM turned out stolid Opels by the million, and Daimler-Benz produced (in addition to their more costly range) the economy 130H, a small, rear-engined car. There were, of course, examples of forward-thinking in most manufacturing countries. France, for instance, came up with, if not the first, the most successful front-wheel drive in 1934 "Traction Avant" Citroën. With a different basic philosophy, Germany produced the KdF, the first of the eternal Volkswagens, and Alfa Romeo and Lancia in Italy were hitting the market regularly with fine designs.

The 1930s saw the world truly on wheels. Even in the first year of the decade over 22 million cars were registered in America alone, and the year's sales of American cars totaled 2,787,465. This figure, however, was barely over half of that of the previous year and was to get worse before it recovered in 1935. Nevertheless, in 1930 no less than one in ten Americans worked for the automobile business in one way or another.

In Europe the vintage motor-car period had ended, although the actual date of December 31, 1930, after which all cars are supposed to have taken a quality nose dive, is limited to a category of vehicle qualifying for entry to the Vintage Sports Car Club, formed in 1934, the founding members of which were appalled at the trends of the current automobile design.

This all-purpose Alfa-Romeo 6C, 1,750, two-seat sports car was one of the great creations of designer Vittorio Jano and the ultimate development of a line that had begun in 1926 with a 1½-liter engine. The 1,750-cc model was offered in three forms: single-ohc, twin-ohc, and twin-ohc supercharged. The first gave 46 bhp and the last 84 bhp. The car won many races, including the Mille Miglia in the hands of Scuderia Ferrari, who ran the Alfa works team. It was withdrawn in 1934 after nearly 2,600 had been made. (I)

Refueling at a pump in Aberdeen, Scotland, the car is immediately identifiable as an Armstrong Siddeley by its V-shaped radiator, studded disk wheels, and the Sphinx mascot on the hood. The Coventry firm built solid, distinguished vehicles known for comfort and craftsmanship. The "Twenty" had a 2.8-liter engine. (GB)

The picture shows the start of the 1930 Monaco Grand Prix and a rash of cars with the horseshoe radiator that denoted a Bugatti. At the end of the day Bugatti finished first, second, and third, with winner Réné Dreyfus averaging 53.5 mph. His Type 35B had an unsupercharged, 8-cylinder engine and a two-seater body (as was still required by racing regulations) that ended in a pointed tail. It was one of a range of Type 35 derivatives that stemmed from the Grand Prix of 1924. (F)

Three-wheelers were popular in Britain in the early thirties because they offered more comfort than a motorcycle combination at a lower rate of tax than a car. The "Breeza," as this B.S.A. model was affectionately known, began when the motorcycle division of the Birmingham Small Arms Company acquired from Hotchkiss of Coventry the manufacturing rights of a 1-liter, V-twin, air-cooled engine. It was given the job of driving the front wheels. The Beeza had car-type controls, an electric starter, a detachable hood, and could reach 60 mph. The buyer could choose between a light-blue and black body. (GB)

The main claim to remembrance of this Chrysler Model 77 with a 4.3-liter, 93-bhp, 6-cylinder engine was that it was wired for an exciting new option—radio. However, factory-styled sets were still several years in the future. The car was one of the first from a major manufacturer to adopt down-draft carburetion for better fuel distribution, and the gravity-flow vacuum tank was replaced by a cam-driven fuel pump. (USA)

Two tons of motor and a real style-setter was the fabulous Cord, with its long, low look and its transmission out front to save space. The Cord was the first American front-wheel-drive car to win acclaim. It had a 4.9-liter, straight-8, Lycoming engine, developing 125 bhp. There were open and closed models and special 17-foot-long bodies, but the car was not a big seller: some 4,400 were delivered between 1929 and 1932, when production ended. (USA)

During the vintage period, the name of Delage could be seen in the lists of sporting successes all over Europe; with 5- and 10-liter cars (the latter were 12-cylinder), the Delage took many racing and hill-climb laurels. Although manufacturers rarely match the success of one field in another, Delage touring cars were of the highest quality and reputation. This is the 1930 4-liter straight-8. (F)

The Type 525 was a big, inexpensive car with a 6-cylinder, 3.7-liter, side-valve engine from Fiat. In sedan form it could seat seven and was much used at the Vatican. However, the SS version pictured here was not designed with papal dignitaries in mind; it was a tuned model with an open, two-seat sports body; wire wheels; twin-choke carb; and an 85-mph capability. It was also the first Fiat with hydraulic rather than mechanical brakes. (I)

Going down, up, and around the steps of the Duomo di Urbino, this Fiat Type 514 had a hand brake on all four wheels instead of the transmission. A 1,438-cc, 4-cylinder, side-valve engine gave 30 bhp, but the car was on the heavy side at 19 cwt and had a 26-mpg thirst. However, this picture helped sell 37,000 such cars. (I)

Drivers of Frazer Nash cars were nicknamed "the chain gang" because of the car's primitive chain drive. Virtually every car built was used in competitions, racing on sand and on roads, hill-climbing, and sprinting. The Frazer Nash was Britain's reply to continental sports cars like Bugatti. It changed little over fifteen years apart from the replacement of a 4-cylinder, 1½-liter Anzani engine by one made by Meadows. (GB)

From the Mercedes-Benz S (for sport) model of 1927 developed the SSKL pictured here. The K stood for *kurz*, or short, because of its abbreviated chassis, and the L for *leicht*, or light, because the chassis was ostentatiously perforated to save weight. It was a fierce, brutish car with a 6-cylinder, 7.1-liter engine turning out 300 bhp in supercharged form, to propel it at 140 mph. Only a few were built, and they were raced mainly by works drivers, notably Caracciola, who drove one to a number of victories, including the Irish and German Grand Prix. It raced until 1934. (D)

The 18/100 MG Tigress was developed from the MG 18/80 and intended mainly for long-distance road races. It had a close-ratio transmission, cockpit-adjusted brakes, and a four-passenger layout as required by sports-car racing regulations, but it could not equal faster machinery like the Alfa Romeo 6C 1,750. Only five were built, owing to the successful introduction of the MG Midget Brooklands. (GB)

The 6-cylinder Marquette was still Buick's cheapest range. Six models, each on a 114-inch wheelbase, included a business coupe and a four-door sedan; pictured here is the four-passenger sports roadster. The name Marquette died in the Depression later in the year. (USA)

A sporty Oldsmobile featuring a folding windshield, side-mounted spare tires, and a rumble seat. Oldsmobile made nearly 50,000 6-cylinder models in 1930, but the classic styling was to make this roadster a collector's item in later years. (USA)

One of the thoroughbred Stutz Black Hawk speedsters from Indianapolis, this model M had a 5.3-liter, straight-8 engine, giving the car a top speed of nearly 100 mph. Like all the Stutz cars, it combined comfort and beauty of line with its high performance. (USA)

The Wanderer WII had a 6-cylinder, 2.5-liter engine, giving 50 bhp; a seven-bearing crankshaft; and a low-geared, three-speed transmission. A sports version in 1931 had an extra half-liter. The car was also built under license by Martini in Switzerland, but the Swiss were not enthusiastic. In 1932 Wanderer joined the Auto Union combine, but its production ended in 1939. (D)

Half-track vehicles of the French Citroën company opened up new areas of the world to the motor vehicle in the late twenties and early thirties. Fourteen of these *Kegresse* half-tracks carried forty men 7,500 miles across Asia, from Beirut on the Mediterranean to Peking in China in 1931–1932, crossing the Himalayas (where the photograph was taken) and the Gobi Desert. The trek was known as the Croisière Jaune, or Yellow Crossing, and the name passed to the vehicles, which were also used in agriculture and the armed services. (F)

A new kind of Chrysler Imperial was introduced in 1931. A long hood with broad, sweeping fenders housed a new 6.3-liter, straight-8 engine which delivered 125 bhp. Various coach-work specialists also made bodies to order for the 154-inch wheelbase. This distinguished sedan offered good acceleration to nearly 100 mph and, as a gallon of fuel carried it only about eight miles, the Imperial was not intended for the impecunious. (USA)

Rumor had it that Britain's Austin Twelve-Six was so hard to sell that the company gave away large stocks for use as prizes in competitions. Rumor lied, but it was undeniable that this pint-sized "six," which had a 1½-liter, 31-bhp engine on an 8-foot, 10-inch chassis, lacked excitement. Yet it stayed in the catalog until 1937. By then, however, a fourth gear and a more reliable engine had been introduced. It provided 55 mph, 27 mpg, and safety glass all around. (GB)

As soon as the prototype of Hillman's Minx left the factory in 1931 it was taken on the roughest roads of Europe by the maker, William (later, Lord) Rootes, who made a practice of trying out each new model personally. Escorted by a chauffeur and a tester, he drove it through Belgium, France, Switzerland, Italy, and North Africa. (The picture was taken in the South of France.) A modest family car, the Minx was typically middle-class English, a compromise between the 8-hp "babies" and more-luxurious models. It had an 1,185-cc, 4-cylinder, side-valve engine, and a speed of 56 mph. It was highly popular. (GB)

A major motorcycle company, DKW began making cars in their Berlin works in 1928. The F1 pictured, a two-seater convertible with a 490-cc, two-stroke engine, was the first of their front-wheel-drive cars. Its companion, the F2, had a bigger engine—all of 584 cc! In 1932 the firm became part of Auto Union. (D)

The station wagon was becoming popular at this time for its load-carrying capabilities. The popular nickname was a "woody," and the solid-looking timbering on this modestly priced Dodge shows why. It had a 6-cylinder, 3.5-liter engine giving 74 bhp. The Rocky Mountain ram used as a hood ornament was introduced by Dodge in 1931 and was to remain a trademark for a quarter of a century. (USA)

The standard Invicta built by Noel Macklin delivered around 100 bhp from its 4½-liter Meadows engine (similar to one used in light tanks), but the S-type pictured here at Brooklands was "worked on" by Raymond Mays, Peter Berthon, and Murray Jamieson and gave more than half again as many horses. About fifty of these thoroughbreds were made between 1930 and 1935, and Donald Healey won the 1930 Alpine trial and the 1931 Monte Carlo rally in one. (GB)

August Horch, who began his career as a Benz engineer, started making his own cars in Cologne in 1899 and won a name for big, prestige motors. This Model 600 limousine was certainly big and also heavy and low-geared, but it had a 6-liter, V-12 engine up front. About 100 were sold. In 1932 Horch also became part of Auto Union and built its racers. (D)

Although it had been a division of Ford for nine years, the Lincoln name still represented opulence. The wheelbase of this sport phaeton was more than 12 feet long and a 6.3-liter, V-8 engine delivered 120 bhp and a comfortable 85 mph. Push-button freewheeling was incorporated. (USA)

A British "baby," the Morris Minor was Nuffield's reply to Austin's Seven. It had an 847-cc, 4-cylinder engine giving 20 bhp; a three-speed transmission; and could make 60 mph. The car was just 10 feet, 1 inch long by 4 feet, 2 inches wide and could carry five gallons of fuel. (GB)

The ultimate for pot-hunters—for this car had 16 "pots"! The V-16 was Colonel Howard Marmon's masterpiece and also his swan song, for the Indianapolis firm was wound up in 1933. The 9.1-liter, 200-bhp engine made much use of aluminum alloy, and the dashboard was genuine timber. The convertible coupe illustrated was capable of 105 mph. (USA)

Captain (later, Sir) Malcolm Campbell called this record-breaker car "Bluebird." At Daytona in 1931 he raised the World Land Speed record to 246.09 with it, and a year later he improved on that figure with 253.90 mph. Designed by Reid Railton, the Bluebird used a Napier engine built for a Schneider Trophy seaplane. It had three banks of 4 cylinders with a total capacity of 24 liters and poured out more than 1,300 bhp. (GB)

Germany's Opel had become a division of America's General Motors, and the cars had begun to acquire Chevrolet styling and specifications. Introduced in 1931 was this disk-wheeled mini-limousine with a 1.8 liter, 6-cylinder, side-valve engine giving 32 bhp and a speed in the low fifties. (D)

The makers of this Oakland claimed that the austere-looking vehicle with its 4-liter, V-8 engine offered the latest in styling and performance; the public was not convinced. Oakland sold 12,417 cars in 1931, while Pontiac moved six times as many, and the Oakland name was discontinued at the end of the year. (USA)

The Peugeot Berline was a workhorse, a simple family car with a 1.1-liter, 4-cylinder, side-valve engine that sold at a moderate price. Its production continued until 1937, incorporating independent front suspension in 1932 and synchromesh in 1934. (F)

Pierce-Arrow was still a great prestige name, although under the control of Studebaker, but demand and production were falling in 1931. This 8-cylinder model had a 6.3-liter engine producing 132 bhp, servo-assisted brakes, and synchromesh on the four-speed transmission. The notable styling feature—the way the headlights were streamlined into the wings—was still in evidence. (USA)

The Alfa-Romeo P3 was also known as the Type B and, more often, simply as "the Monoposto," because it was the first successful single-seat racing car. Designed by Vittorio Jano, it used an 8-cylinder engine from the 1931 8C2300 racing two-seater bored out to 2.65 liters and double supercharged to give 190 bhp at 5,400 rpm. It won its first grande épreuve, the Italian Grand Prix of 1932 and was beaten only twice in its first season. In succeeding years the engine was progressively increased in capacity, to 2.9, then 3.2, and finally 3.8 liters. (I)

One of a large range of Austin cars, this modest four-door Ten with a 1.1-liter, 4-cylinder, side-valve engine was made at Longbridge, Birmingham, England, from 1932 until 1947. One of its chief merits was that it gave 34 miles to the gallon. (GB)

"And first prize for elegance goes to the BMW AM4." The announcement had just been made at a motor show in Baden Baden when the picture was taken. The car, made by Munich's BMW (Bavarian Motor Works) company, which originally made engines for boats, trucks, motorcycles, and aircraft, was a baby sedan based on Britain's Austin Seven. It had a 790-cc, ohv, 4-cylinder engine, delivering just 20 bhp. (D)

The picture of two De Soto SC6s and giant seaplane suggests it was designed to appeal to the "prop set" of the day. In fact, the Depression had reached a new low, and in February 1932 De Soto production was curtailed to 6-cylinder models only. The SC6, seen in convertible and closed forms, had a 6-cylinder, 3.5-liter engine; the V grille was new in 1932, and the trumpet horns identified deluxe models. A new feature shared by other Chrysler-combine cars was "Floating Power" rubber engine mountings, and options included freewheeling and a vacuum-operated automatic clutch controlled by the accelerator pedal. (USA)

Dodge held seventh place in American sales as the auto market reached the lowest ebb of the Depression, with the whole industry barely registering one million units in sales. The 4.6-liter, 8-cylinder, 90-bhp car of that year had "Floating Power" engine mountings and freewheeling as standard equipment and the new automatic clutch as an option. (USA)

The Duesenberg was still the biggest, fastest, most sophisticated and most expensive car in America, with the comfort and prestige of a Rolls and the power and speed of a Bugatti. The car was custom built. Duesenberg made only the chassis, and bodies were made by a variety of coachbuilders—this one by Derham. Some 470 were made, but the era ended with the collapse of Errett Lobban Cord's empire in 1937. (USA)

The name given to this little Fiat sedan braving the snow was Balilla, which was apt, for it means "Plucky little one." The Balilla, with a 4-cylinder, 995-cc unit, giving 22 bhp, was plucky, and, with a wheelbase of 7 feet 4½ inches, it was certainly little. Yet it was tough and handled well and could reach 60 mph. Some 113,000 were sold between 1932 and 1937. (I)

Competition forced Henry Ford to bigger engines, and he succeeded in marketing the first mass-produced V-8 years ahead of rivals. This coupe started life with a 50-bhp, 4-cylinder engine, but from 1932 it was also available with the low-cost 70-bhp V-8 of 3.6 liters which gave it an exciting performance. A rumble seat was another option. (USA)

The 345C La Salle sedan had the same 5.8-liter, V-8 engine as a Cadillac, but it was lighter, faster, and cheaper. The wheelbase was 136 inches. Note the skirted front wings and Mercedes-Benz–style grille. (USA)

The Peugeot 301C was a 4-cylinder, 1,467-cc sports car that broke the Class F 24-hour record at Miramas, near Marseilles, between 7:00 PM on June 1 and 7:00 PM on June 2, 1932. The average speed was more than 68 mph. The driver was Andre Boillot, younger brother of Georges, the French Grand Prix winner of 1913. Andre died shortly afterward while testing another car. (F)

At this time there was a battle for supremacy in France between the conservative Renault Company and the more adventurous Citroën, a battle which was eventually won by Citroën. Renault had hitherto been known mainly for big cars and sports cars, but, to compete with Citroën, they stepped up production of small, 4-cylinder cars like the 1.3-liter Monaquatre seen here. The car was underpowered and its top speed was about 60 mph, but Renault could justifiably advertise, "There's more room in a Renault." It had three forward speeds, mechanical brakes, and disk wheels. (F)

The Rockne Motor Corporation was formed in 1931 to market cheaper cars for Studebaker, and the cars were in fact smaller models of that make. The 6-cylinder, 3-liter cars sold well—better than any other product built by Studebaker—but history was against commercial success in most fields at this date, and the Rockne disappeared after just two years. The company was named after the Notre Dame football coach, Knute Rockne. This is the 1932 sedan. (USA)

The 20/25-hp Rolls-Royce was a scaled-down version of the Phantom. It had a 3.7-liter, 6-cylinder engine, was heavy, and only reached 74 mph, yet 4,000 were made between 1929 and 1936, when it became the 25/30, with a 4.3-liter engine. Synchromesh became standard in 1932. (GB)

Swallow Sidecars (SS) moved from the manufacture of motorcycle sidecars to motor bodies and eventually grew into Britain's Jaguar firm of today. The SS1 pictured here was their version of a 16-hp Standard car. It used the Standard 6-cylinder, 2-liter engine untuned, and other Standard mechanical components, but it was given a long hood, a small coupe body, and helmet-style front wings. Engine and chassis were lowered and this "promenade sports car" looked worth double its cost, a comment which was made frequently about the firm's subsequent offerings. (GB)

Bugatti 1927; 1496 cc supercharged. (F)

Mercedes-Benz promote the Nurburg, 1928. (D)

A 4½-liter Bentley won the 1928 Le Mans race.
This is a 1929 4½-liter (4398 cc) with blower. (GB)

A 1930 3.3-liter Talbot. (GB)

Alfa Romeo P3, also known as the Type B or Monoposto. The first successful racing single-seater. (I)

Packard 1929; at a recent meeting in Britain. (USA)

Aston Martin long-chassis tourer, 1933. (GB)

ERA, 1936; 2-liter supercharged. (GB)

1927 Renault Conduite Intérieure; 951 cc, 4-cylinder. (F)

Direct descendent of the Prince Henry, the 30/98 was Vauxhall's great sports car of the Twenties. This is a 1927 car. (GB)

Mercedes-Benz, SSK 1927; 170 hp without supercharger, 225 with. (D)

The Triumph Super Seven had a miniscule 832-cc engine, but it was designed to be a cut above the mass-produced Morris and Austin "babies." It had a unit transmission and hydraulic brakes, and two-tone paint finishes were available. The car sold well in England and abroad until, in 1934, it was superseded by the Super Eight. (GB)

A Zundapp, one of the predecessors of the Volkswagen "Beetle." Designed by Ferdinand Porsche, the car had a genuine fastback and rear-wheel spats. Zundapp, who were German motorcycle manufacturers, intended to move into cars with this model, which had an air-cooled, 5-cylinder engine, but only a few prototypes were made. In fact, Zundapp did not begin to produce cars until 1956, a venture that lasted only two years. (D)

Vittorio Jano's Alfa-Romeo 8 C 2,300 was a sports tourer with a 2.3-liter, straight-8 engine giving 130 bhp and a top speed of 115 mph. From its competitive debut in the 1931 Mille Miglia, which was won in the wet by Tazio Nuvolari, it dominated long-distance sports-car races and won Le Mans every year from 1931 to 1934. It was also developed for Grand Prix events such as the Monza. (I)

The BMW Type 303 was the motorcycle company's first 6-cylinder model, a pint-sized "six" by Fritz Fielder. The wheelbase was only 8 feet and the engine only 1.1 liters giving 30 bhp, but within a year it had evolved into the Type 315 which was a more distinguished car. (D)

This 355C seven-passenger Cadillac sedan had a Y-shaped radiator which had become virtually standard in 1933. It also had a V-8 engine, swiveling ventilator windows at the rear, stylish horns, and the whitewall tires that were fashionable at the time. (USA)

The 15CV Citroën of 1933 was the company's first 6-cylinder car. Its 15CV was, of course, a purely nominal rating, and the 2,650-cc engine developed 49 bhp, to give effortless, restful long-distance motoring. (F)

A very different kind of Citroën, "Petite Rosalie" was a special, based on an 8CV sedan with a 4-cylinder, 1,452-cc, side-valve engine, one of a series of Rosalies which began in 1931. The Petite weighed more than a ton and had a top speed of 70 mph, but at Montlhéry a team of drivers ran it day and night for 133 days, covering 300,000 km (around 187,500 miles) at an average speed of 58 mph and establishing some 300 new and assorted records. (F)

The plucky little Balilla with its 995-cc engine developed into the 508S sports car. The body was still only 7 feet, 6½ inches long, but the tuned engine gave 48 bhp and 75 mph. It was an advanced small car, and it dominated 1,100-cc sports-car racing. About 1,000 Fiat 508S's were built. (I)

The Ford Company had been building cars in Britain since the Model T in 1911, but this was the first Ford designed in Britain and aimed specifically at the British market. Instead of a big, thirsty, American power plant it had an economical 4-cylinder, 993-cc engine which gave it 58-mph performance. A two-door four-seater just under 12 feet long, it offered more space than established British small cars. It was christened the Popular, and popular it was. (GB)

The Framo Stromer was a three-wheeler, with its two front wheels driven by water-cooled DKW engines of 200, 400, or 600 cc. It weighed only 6¾ cwt and so could manage 50 mph, yet it was a real car, like a scaled-down Meisterklasse, which was not surprising, since Framo was controlled by DKW, but outside the Auto Union combine. Remarkable features were its rubber cord suspension and a tubular backbone frame which also served as an exhaust pipe. (D)

Made in Milan, this Isotta-Fraschini was a luxury model aimed mainly at the American market. It had a straight-8 engine of 7.4 liters which made use of light alloys. Lightly tuned, it gave up to 150 bhp and could reach 100 mph. But the Depression crippled American sales. Only thirty of the Type 8B were made, and the firm shifted its efforts to aircraft and marine engines and commercial vehicles. (I)

Like many popular British cars the 1,185-cc Hillman Minx spawned a number of derivatives. The most striking was the Aero Minx, so-called because of its advanced, low-slung aerodynamic lines. It was not popular, but it formed the basis for Talbot and Sunbeam Talbot Tens when Rootes acquired that firm. (GB)

The Lancia Augusta was a rather ordinary-looking model with a 1.2-liter engine giving a stolid 35 bhp and 30 mpg. Its top speed was around 65 mph, but it was lightweight at 16½ cwt; it had good road-holding and hydraulic brakes and could drive quite briskly. Racing driver Tazio Nuvolari used one when he was not scorching around the race circuits. (I)

The KB seven-passenger car was the last great Lincoln produced in the lifetime of Henry Leland; the grand old man of the American car industry died soon after its announcement in 1932. The tourer pictured here was a lot of car. Its V-12, side-valve engine of 7.2 liters gave it an 80-mph cruising speed and 100-mph top speed. A V-grille replaced the traditional Lincoln front end, and there were servo-assisted brakes and freewheeling controlled by a dashboard lever. (USA)

Wilhelm Maybach was a close associate of Gottlieb Daimler, but he left Daimler in 1907 to join Count Zeppelin in establishing a factory to make airship engines. The factory later began to make cars that were acclaimed as the Rolls-Royces of Germany. The name Zeppelin was a natural choice for a range of giant Maybach limousines in which the shortest wheelbase was 12 feet. The hood was seven feet long, the radiator three feet wide, the car's weight was over 3 tons, and there were eight forward speeds. The Zeppelin's power plant was an 8-liter V-12 giving 200 bhp. (D)

Cheapest of the 6-cylinder Morris range was the Ten-Six which had a 1,378-cc engine. Object of the picture showing it fording a stream with its sunshine roof open was to demonstrate its rugged dependability and no doubt to draw attention to the sliding roof, which had been introduced in 1932. (GB)

Under General Motors, Germany's Opel company ranked first in European production in the thirties. This attractive two-seater sports car had a 1,790-cc, 6-cylinder, in-line engine. (D)

261

The French firm of Panhard & Levassor was one of motoring's oldest and most respected, and the 6CS2 2.3-liter model was appropriately dignified and conservative. Yet it had at least two unusual features. Instead of an oil-pressure warning light, it had a device that cut the ignition if the oil pump failed. More obviously, it had a so-called "Panoramique" windshield, an early version of the wrap-around windshield to improve vision. (F)

Few cars in the medium-powered class were as esteemed in Britain as the Riley, and few were to be mourned more when it lost its individual identity in the giant Morris group in 1938. It was an enthusiast's car, with a name for quality and performance, ride, and road-holding. More than 20,000 Riley Nines had been made by 1934. The car had a 1,087-cc engine and a speed of just over 60 mph. (GB)

Beside the Singer 9-hp sports coupe stands the late Stanley Fruin of Cheltenham, England—one of the most successful Singer drivers of the mid-thirties. The Nine Sports had a 972-cc engine giving 33 bhp and ran in many reliability trials over such courses as London to Lands End and Edinburgh. Among them 578 cars collected 495 awards in trials in 1933–1934. (GB)

It was not very rewarding to be a motoring enthusiast in Japan in the thirties. It has been estimated that there were only about 40,000 private cars, most of them of American origin, when the decade began, and the poor-quality roads were far from crowded with cars in 1933. Motoring was just not available to the general public. This H-type Sumida was a four-door sedan similar to the American La Salle. (J)

The name Terraplane had replaced that of Essex on inexpensive Hudsons. The car was virtually the same as a Hudson in styling, with a 6-cylinder, 3.2-liter engine and three-speed transmission. However, despite the use of woman aviator Amelia Earhart in pictures publicizing this compact convertible, the Terraplane name failed to excite customers, and it was dropped in 1937. (USA)

Rally driver Donald Healey worked for a time for Triumph, and the association resulted in the Gloria range introduced in 1933. Keenest to his heart must have been the Triumph Gloria Southern Cross, pictured, which was a sporting two-seater fitted with a Coventry-Climax engine of either 4 cylinders, 1,087 cc and 40 bhp or 6 cylinders, 1.8 liters and 70 bhp. It was a good all-around competition car, much used in trialing. (GB)

The terrain might have been impracticable, as the notice board said, but not impossible, as the Vauxhall Light Six A-type proved. Based in Luton, England, Vauxhall had been a division of General Motors since 1925, and the car looked something like a German Opel, although the hood's fluting was a distinctive Vauxhall trademark. The car was offered with a 1.5-liter engine or an optional 1.8-liter engine. Brakes were cable-operated, but by 1935 the car incorporated the General Motors "knee action" independent front suspension. (GB)

The Swallow was another car tailored by William Lyons' Swallow Coachbuilding company from a popular existing model, a two-seat runabout body on the chassis and using the mechanical components of a Wolseley Hornet. (GB)

The 4-cylinder, 1.4-liter Walter Bijou was the product of J. Walter of Jinonice, a town once in Austria, then, after national boundary moves following the first world war, in Czechoslovakia. In 1933 the company, established since 1908, offered the Bijou, the Junior (980 cc), and a 3-liter, 6-cylinder car. (CS)

The Wolseley Hornet was an inexpensive, sportingly inclined, 75-mph English car that was produced for five years in a variety of body styles—from open two-seater to four-seater sedan—in lengths from 10 feet, 6 inches to 11 feet. It had a 6-cylinder, 1.3-liter engine. Sliding windows were an unusual feature. (GB)

The Hurlock brothers, who ran A.C. Cars Limited, made custom-made cars. All the cars used a 6-cylinder, 2-liter engine that was introduced in 1919 and continued in production for half a century. The cars were thoroughbreds and the engines spent 12 hours on a bench test before they turned wheels on a road. Any combination of body, color, and engine tune could be selected if you were prepared to wait a month for delivery. This was a touring model. (GB)

Designer Jano's 6C 2,300 Alfa Romeo had a 2,309-cc engine of 6 cylinders, which replaced the 1,750-cc engine and gave 68 bhp. The Gran Turismo car shown here was a long-distance traveler and an expensive, semi-custom-made machine. (I)

Another picture to underline the importance of a designer and coachbuilder. This is the 6-cylinder, 2300B Alfa Romeo chassis with a Pinin Farina cabriolet mounted on it. Farina's influence on automobile design was to be large. (I)

The Austin Seven, with its 747-cc engine, was to continue until World War II. Among the many variants was this four-seater body, built by Swallow Sidecars, which was 9 feet, 10 inches long and 4 feet, 1 inch wide. The car had a speed of 55 mph. (GB)

Encouraged by Hitler, the Horch, Audi, DKW, and Wanderer companies combined to form Auto Union to seek prestige for Germany through motor racing. The first Auto Union, designed by Ferdinand Porsche, was revolutionary in that the engine was behind the driver, for it was to take a quarter of a century for this position to become standard. The 4.3-liter, super-charged, V-16 engine gave 295 bhp at 4,500 rpm. Hans Stuck broke several records with it on the Avus track, averaging more than 134 mph, and then won the German, Swiss, and Czech Grand Prix. (D)

The Type 315 BMW, which followed the 303 in 1934, was a two-seat touring version with the 6-cylinder engine increased to 1½ liters. The 315/1, as shown, had three carburetors, as compared with the standard two, and gave 40 bhp, as compared with the 34 of the standard model. It had a top speed of 125 mph and was the first BMW to succeed in competitions. After its auspicious debut in the 1934 Alpine Trial, Frazer Nash took over the concession for the car in Britain. (D)

The picture shows a big day for Buick, the occasion when the first Buick Special left the assembly line. A keen eye will note that it was still without front fenders, but it did have "knee action" Dubonnet-type independent front suspension and synchromesh as standard. (USA)

Haute couture comes to the auto industry. The Coventry-based Humber firm called in Captain Molyneux, the couturier, to advise on design and as a result was able to advertise, with an eye on the women's market: "There was a rumour that all new body styles came from across the Atlantic — until Molyneux of Paris and London collaborated with Humber. Molyneux' flair for line and color and Humber's 35 years experience of chassis and body building have now produced the ideal sports car for those who want something out of the ordinary — a model of intriguing performance and unusual beauty of outline." It was called the Vogue sedan. Mechanically it was a scaled-down (13 feet, 4 inches long) Snipe with a 4-cylinder, 1,669-cc engine. (GB)

The last long-stroke 6-cylinder-engined model from Fiat was the Type 527. It had a 2½-liter unit, synchromesh, and freewheeling. The picture shows the Ardita S (for sports) version, a grand touring car with extra power and luggage space, not to mention two spare wheels. (I)

Carl Borgward controlled the small-car firm of Hansa which built in Bremen. The coupe pictured here had a 2-cylinder, two-stroke, rear-mounted engine of 400 cc. The car was later made available with 500 cc, but the firm died in 1939. (D)

The 7CV was the first of Citroën's "traction avant" (front-wheel-drive) cars and the first mass-produced fwd model. Other innovations were unit construction, torsion-bar suspension, independent front suspension, and removable cylinder liners. The car had a flat welded floor which gave good accommodation; it was strong, had 68-mph performance, and handled well. Originally it had a 4-cylinder, 1.3-liter engine, but in 1935 it became 1.6 liters. Apart from this, the car continued virtually unchanged until 1956, and 700,000 were made. (F)

Humber also produced more-rugged, open-air publicity material. This picture was taken in the Sahara Desert to promote the de Normanville safety gear, an epicyclic type of easy-change gear system named after the inventor and developed by Humber, who called it "Motoring's sixth sense." A 3½-liter Snipe to which it was fitted towed a heavy caravan and transported six passengers—a gross weight of more than 3 tons—across North Africa and the Sahara to prove it. But the de Normanville transmission disappeared from Humber cars in 1937, and the company reverted to synchromesh. (GB)

The Mercedes-Benx 500K was a supercharged roadster. (In this case the "K" stood for Kompressor, or supercharger.) It was a high-speed touring machine with sporting lines and an 8-cylinder, 5-liter engine which gave 160 bhp and 100 mph when blown. It also drank fuel at the rate of a gallon every 11 miles. (D)

A small but expensive semi-sporting car, the Lagonda Rapier had a 1,104-cc, twin-ohc engine giving 46 bhp. It also had a rather heavy body which came in convertible or closed form, two-passenger sports models, and four-passenger tourers. This is an Abbott-bodied, four-seat tourer capable of 80 mph. In 1936 rights were passed to a small company set up for the purpose and called Rapier, and the car was additionally offered in supercharged form, but it was never competitive, and only about 300 of all types were made. (GB)

Supercharging was virtually obligatory for racing cars at this time, and this picture shows a racing Mercedes, with front-mounted supercharger, in action at the twisty Nurburgring. Racing was under the 750-kg formula at this time, and in 1934 the car had an 8-cylinder engine of 3.36 liters, giving 354 bhp. By 1937 it had been increased to 5.66 liters and a howling 646 bhp. (D)

Captain George Eyston drove this car; it was known as EX135 and was an M.G. K3 model Magic Magnette, a supercharged, 1,100-cc, 6-cylinder racer, with special offset transmission. It had two bodies: one for racing and one for record-breaking. The picture shows the record shell that Eyston used when he put the Class G flying-start record to 128.7 mph in 1934. (GB)

M.G. two-seat sports cars were deservedly popular with less-wealthy young men who wanted the thrill of sports-cars performance on a small budget. This Magnette N-type aimed to make this kind of experience possible for the young family man. It had room (just about) for the children, but it lacked the appeal of the bachelor car. (GB)

"Wild Bill" Cummings, age twenty, won the Indianapolis 500 at a record-breaking 104.8 mph in this Miller, the first winner there to be powered by a 4-cylinder engine since 1920. It was, in fact, a 3.6-liter Miller which was the ancestor of the Offenhauser units that were later so successful at Indianapolis. Miller-engined cars won every Indy from 1930 to 1938. (USA)

There was still an embarrassingly large range of Morris models at this time. The Family Minor was a quality family sedan on a lengthened Minor chassis which was built in order to utilize stocks of 847-cc, ohc engines. (GB)

Another Panhard record-breaker used by George Eyston. The narrow, knife-like car began life with a 6.4-liter, straight-8 engine and traveled at 120.24 mph, but in 1932 it was bored out to 8 liters and Eyston set a new hour record at 130.73 mph. In 1934 it reached 133.01 mph and then went into honorable retirement. (F)

The one-millionth Plymouth rolled off the assembly lines in August 1934, and this was it. When Walter Chrysler produced the first one in 1928, he said the name Plymouth had been chosen "to symbolize the endurance and strength, rugged honesty, enterprise and determination . . . of the Pilgrim band who were the first American colonialists." Plymouth represented the low-priced end of the Chrysler family, and only 4-cylinder units were used in them until 1933. However, the model shown was a 6-cylinder of 3.3 liters and 77 bhp. There were 258 combinations of bodywork and color that could be specified on the 107¾-inch wheelbase of the Six. (USA)

The 4.8-liter Nervasport was a French record-breaker built by Renault in 1932. In 1934 it was fitted with a streamlined body, and at Montlhéry it traveled 5,000 miles at an average speed of 101.979 mph to create a world 48-hour record—breaking nine other records in the process. (F)

Racing driver Freddie Dixon is seen during a 500-mile race at Brooklands in 1934; he won at a speed of 104.8 mph. The car was one of his "aluminium Rileys," so-called because of their light, polished finish. It had a 2-liter, 6-cylinder engine in an offset single-seater with a long tail. Dixon won the Brooklands 500 again in 1936, just before the ERA successes ended the Riley reign. (GB)

The Singer Airstream was an imitative tribute to Chrysler's Airflow models; like them it had a full-width aerodynamic body. Mechanically the car was a 1½-liter, ohc Eleven with independent front suspension, fluid-drive transmission, and perm-mesh clutchless gear change. It weighed nearly a ton. Some 750 were built, but the British public was as wary of the Airstream as the American public was of the Airflow. (GB)

The SS II was built on a modified Standard Little Nine chassis and used a 4-cylinder, 1-liter, Little Nine engine. It never sold as well as the 6-cylinder SS I. (GB)

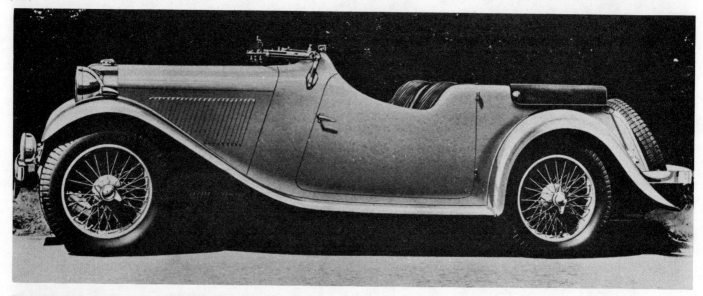

Ranking slightly higher in the social scale than Austin or Morris, Standard was a growing concern in the Thirties. The deluxe model, with chromium-plated lights and leather-upholstery "extras" held a curious snob appeal for the British until the Fifties. (GB)

The Austin Ruby was a comparatively stylish derivative of the original baby Austin Seven. The four-seat sedan was more refined than the original, but without any fundamental change in engine or chassis. (GB)

The Brewster coachbuilding company of Springfield, Massachusetts, built town cars under its own name, as well as limousines and convertibles on chassis made by Ford, Buick, and other manufacturers. This car used a Ford chassis, with its wheelbase extended to 10 feet, 7 inches. It conveyed tycoons to boardrooms and, as a hearse, carried deceased of all classes to cemeteries. It had a cow-catcher type of grille, flared wings, and a V-8 engine behind the heart-shaped grille. Approximately 300 Brewsters were built. (USA)

273

Among the most popular cars in Germany in 1935 were those of the DKW Schwebeklasse range of 1,054-cc, V-4 engined, rear-driven vehicles. The car was the first DKW with synchromesh and hydraulic brakes. DKW had become part of Auto Union in 1932. (D)

Heralding the shape of things to come was the Fiat 1500 with a 44-bhp, 6-cylinder, short-stroke engine. The one-ton aerodynamically styled car had a downward curving hood to give good forward vision. Headlights and door handles were recessed. Synchromesh, hydraulic brakes, and a headlight flasher were standard, and the speed was 70 mph. Nearly 24,000 were made in three seasons, but the 1500 was most important because the famous 500-cc Topolino was to be based on it. (I)

Ford produced its millionth V-8 in 1935; this was one of them—a Model 48 with a 3.6-liter engine giving 65 bhp. Britain's Model 60 looked identical, but had a more economical 2.2-liter unit. The engine had been moved forward to contain all the seating within the 112-inch wheelbase. Two Rumanians won the Monte Carlo rally of 1936 in a modified version. (USA)

The Frazer Nash Shelsley model was named after Shelsley Walsh, the most famous British hill-climb course, at which Frazer Nash cars scored many victories. The Shelsley was the ultimate in the FN range, a two-seater with a twin, supercharged, 1½-liter, Gough engine, designed by one of the company engineers. The name actually applied to the chassis rather than to the car, and some models utilized a more flexible 1.6-liter, Blackburne power unit. However, by the time the Shelsley began winning, Frazer Nash had decided to concentrate on the importation of BMWs from Germany. (GB)

The state-subsidized Mercedes-Benz W25 Grand Prix car of 1935 was built without regard to expense. Germany was determined to be supreme in motor racing. Its debut as a team car was at Monaco (illustrated), where Luigi Fagioli won at 58.2 mph from Italy's Alfa Romeos. The W25 went on to win nine out of the ten races for which it was entered, proving, if proof were needed, the importance of money in motor racing. (The tenth race was, ironically, the German GP, in which the Merc came in only third!) The car had a 4-liter unit delivering 430 bhp and was capable of nearly 200 mph. (D)

An economy-class Mercedes which was to set a style in years to come was the 68-mph Model 170 with a rear-mounted, 6-cylinder, 1.7-liter engine. The first Mercedes with independent wheel suspension, it was highly successful on its home market. It was a mass seller until production ended in 1938. (D)

Less successful was another rear-engined car by Mercedes-Benz—the oddly shaped Type 150S which had a 4-cylinder, 1.5-liter engine developing 55 bhp. However, Mercedes could claim that it was basically an experimental car, since only a handful were built. (D)

The best-seller in the Morris range was the Eight, an inexpensive family car that helped the firm to high success. It had a 4-cylinder, 918-cc, side-valve engine, and was 12 feet long. Many were made with left-hand drive for export; others appeared in the guise of vans to be used by post office engineers. (GB)

A much-publicized feature of the other current Morris fast-selling sedan, the Ten-Four, was a built-in-jacking system. It was a considerably bigger car than the Eight, weighing 21 cwt, with 4-cylinder, 1,292-cc, side-valve engine, a three-speed transmission, and a maximum velocity of between 60 and 65 mph. Sedan and special coupe bodies were available with two-tone-paint finishes. (GB)

The La Fayette name was revived by Nash in 1934 for use on their cheapest models, a decade after the original Milwaukee company ceased production. By 1935 there were eight body styles, among them this sleek coupe built around a 6-cylinder, 3½-liter engine. (USA)

In their bid for the low-price market, Packard introduced the clean-lined 120 touring sedan. It had a straight-8, 3.7-liter engine, hydraulic brakes, and independent front suspension. (USA)

The Prague company that produced this Praga Picollo had been in the business for thirty-one years by 1935 and had made light cars based on Renault principles, with behind-the-engine radiators. This smart convertible coupe had a 4-cylinder, 1,670-cc, 35-hp power pack and a top speed of 110 km/h (68 mph). (CS)

THE RAILTON

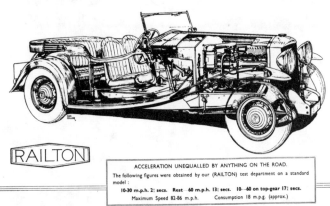

RAILTON

ACCELERATION UNEQUALLED BY ANYTHING ON THE ROAD.
The following figures were obtained by our (RAILTON) test department on a standard model :
10-30 m.p.h. 2½ secs.   Rest   60 m.p.h. 13½ secs.   10—60 on top-gear 17½ secs.
Maximum Speed 82-86 m.p.h.   Consumption 18 m.p.g. (approx.)

"Acceleration unequalled by anything on the road," claimed the advertising for this Railton, made in England by Noel Macklin around a Hudson 8-cylinder, 4.1-liter engine giving 124 bhp. The standard model took just over 13 seconds to reach 60 mph and was flat out in the eighties, but, modified by Reid Railton, who designed the Brooklands Riley, it got to 60 mph in less than 9 seconds and could reach 107 mph. This Anglo-American hybrid was a stark four-seater. (GB)

The SS90 was a sporting, slab-tank two-seater with a
2,664-cc, Standard engine in an 8-foot, 8-inch wheelbase. Only a few were made, and its main importance
was that it prepared the way for the more significant
100 model. (GB)

Another German motor manufacturer that started in
the nineteenth century, Stoewer of Stettin made its
first car in 1899, after producing lighter mechanical
transport. This 1935 Stoewer Greif is a 2½-liter, V-8,
front-wheel-drive model with a nice turn to the wings
in a clean attempt at aerodynamics. The company
stopped making private cars in 1939, and the plant was
destroyed during the war. (D)

Made in Czechoslovakia, the big, smooth, 90-mph Tatra 77 was designed by Hans Ledwinka. It had an air-cooled, V-8 unit of 2,970 cc over the back axle, giving 60 bhp, and the aerodynamic bodywork concealed two spare wheels under the front hood. The first cars produced had a central driving position, but later models had conventional front seating. (CS)

Volvo, the Gothenburg-based Swedish company, had already acquired a reputation for building solid sedans, but it was not yet a major exporter. The PV36 Carioca was a trendy fastback with recessed headlights and rear-wheel spats. It also had an all-steel body (new to Volvo) and independent front suspension. (S)

An illuminated radiator badge was a trademark of Britain's Wolseley Company; the power came from two batteries under the front seats. The Wolseley Ten had a 4-cylinder, 1,292-cc engine of 41 bhp in an 8-foot, 4-inch wheelbase; it represented respectable conservatism. It does not take an expert to notice its similarity to the 1935 Morris Ten. The company had been bought by William Morris in 1927. (GB)

This was the final year of the Alvis Silver Eagle range, first introduced in 1929. It was most often seen as a very British touring limousine as pictured, although there was also a tuned sports version. The engine was a 6-cylinder of 2,148 cc, although from 1932 a 2½-liter engine was available as an option. (GB)

A guarantee that accompanied the Auburn 852 Speedster attested that the boat-tailed, 150-bhp car had been test-driven at more than 100 mph. However, its life was short. A year after the Indiana company introduced the car in 1935 the firm ceased production when the Cord-Duesenberg-Auburn empire disbanded. (USA)

One of the last of the genuine Berliet models made in Lyons, France, this was the 2-liter Dauphine with independent front suspension and rack-and-pinion steering. Although the firm did not shut down until 1939, the final cars were equipped with the same body as the Peugeot 402. (F)

The BMW 328 was one of the most successful sports cars ever built, with good performance, road-holding, and power-to-weight ratio. A 6-cylinder, 2-liter engine gave 80 bhp and 95 mph—or as much as 120 mph when modified. The brakes were hydraulic. It yielded so much performance that it could often beat true racing cars. Factory teams had class wins in the 1936 and 1937 TT races and won the 1940 Mille Miglia. In 1937, running on pump gasoline, a BMW covered 102 miles in an hour at Brooklands. The car went on winning until after World War II. (D)

A car for the Cognocenti was the Type 57 Bugatti—touring equivalent of the Type 59 racer. It was the last Molsheim model produced, and 800 were made between 1934 and the outbreak of war in 1939. A twin-ohc, 3.3-liter, 8-cylinder engine yielded a devastating 135 bhp, yet it was a quiet and refined carriage—built with traditional Bugatti excellence, to travel the roads at speed. (F)

The De Soto was the only Chrysler make devoted entirely to Airflows. This was a 6-cylinder version with a 4-liter, 100-bhp engine, and it was just as unsuccessful as the Chrysler-labeled cars. Five thousand De Soto Airflows were produced in 1936, but it was their last year. An interesting feature was a steel roof panel insert that was acoustically treated and electrically insulated to serve as a radio antenna. (USA)

"Detroit's most Successful failure" was the tag applied to the Chrysler Airflow. Six years of study and wind-tunnel tests preceded the introduction of the Airflow range in 1934. The cars featured aerodynamically smooth, sweeping contours, a lower silhouette, improved weight distribution, and an integral body and chassis. This C9 sedan of 1936, with an 8-cylinder, 5.3-liter, 115-bhp engine, added a built-in luggage compartment, a front seat that adjusted up and down as well as back and forth, and Life Guard tires (a heavy-duty tube containing a second tube floating inside) as standard. The Airflow was successful in that all its features were accepted in time; it was a failure in that a more gradual evolution was required. The public was not ready for the Airflow, declined to buy, and the range ended in 1937. (USA)

ERA—the initials stood for English Racing Automobile, and the cars were built by Raymond Mays, Peter Berthon, and Reid Railton to win prestige for Britain in motor racing. Grand Prix events were dominated by continentals; the ERA was designed to run in voiturette or light-car classes, and it was highly successful. Most famous of the nineteen cars of various types built were Romulus and Remus, driven by "B. Bira" (Prince Birabongse of Siam), and the picture shows Remus, a B-type with a 6-cylinder, 1,488-cc, supercharged engine offering between 130 and 150 bhp. The ERA was a highly reliable car, and several still race at vintage club meetings. (GB)

Nicknamed Topolino (little Mouse), this Italian baby from Fiat caused a sensation and was hailed as the greatest development in tiny cars since the Austin Seven. The two-seater was ideal for shopping and parking, being only 10 feet, 8½ inches long and 4 feet, 3 inches wide and able to turn in 28 feet. It had a canvas roll-top roof, yet it was a real car in miniature, with a 4-cylinder, 569-cc engine giving 55 mph and the same number of miles per gallon. The picture shows it being acclaimed in Hungary. (I)

The cutaway picture of the Topolino shows the compact layout and, in particular, how the engine was positioned in front of the radiator. (I)

The name of Lincoln still stood for luxury travel; this model had a 6.9-liter, V-12 engine giving 150 bhp and 95 mph. The tank held 23 gallons of fuel. A new feature was the under-dash hand brake, and there were new-pattern disk wheels, but streamlining was still to come to the headlights. It arrived at a time when the luxury-car market was still dwindling, and later in the year Lincoln introduced the more modest Zephyr range with a 4.4-liter engine. (USA)

The 540K model Mercedes succeeded the 500K; its engine had been increased in size to 5.4 liters giving 180 bhp with the supercharger in use. Weight had also gone up, and the top gear ratio had gone down, so it was little faster (though it could reach 106 mph), but it was quieter and more comfortable. Some 700 were built in limousine, sedan, and convertible form (as illustrated) by 1939, when the 5.8-liter, 140-mph 580K model was unwrapped. Because of the war, however, it was never put into production. (D)

The Railton light sports tourer of 1936 could reach 80 in second gear and 107 mph in top gear. It was still an Anglo-American hybrid, with an 8-cylinder, 4.2-liter Hudson engine, but 1936 brought hydraulic brakes, a longer (10-foot) wheelbase, a remote-control floor change, more weight, and a higher price tag. (GB)

The Rolls-Royce Phantom III was the last prewar Rolls and, by general agreement, a vintage one. Several coachbuilders made bodies, and the picture shows a seven-seat touring limousine by Park Ward. The engine was a V-12 of 7.3 liters, giving 165 bhp and 100 mph, although Rolls-Royce dignity did not permit the company to shout about performance. It was nearly 16 feet long and 6½ feet wide, and weighed 51 cwt; the fuel tank held 33 gallons. One was driven across the Sahara from London to Kano and back without using any water. (GB)

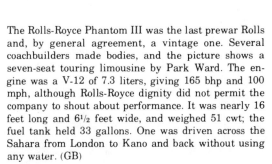

The name Jaguar was used for the first time in 1936, although it was 1945 before the prefix SS was dropped. The SS Jaguar 100 was a shortened version of the standard 2,663-cc car joined in 1938 by a 3,485-cc model. The two-seaters performed well in sprints and rallies, although only about 300 had been made when production ceased because of the war; later they were much sought after by enthusiasts, particularly in the United States. (GB)

The Flying Twenty, one of the "Flying Standard" range launched in 1936, had a 6-cylinder, 2,664-cc engine of 64 bhp. The picture shows a variant that resulted from the chassis being made available to the Avon coach-building company. (GB)

Produced between 1936 and 1939, this supercharged, 2-liter, 6-cylinder two-seater with the advanced line was the W 25 K Wanderer from Auto Union. Top speed was well over 90 mph from its 83-bhp unit. (D)

The Aero from Prague was derived from a series of small, two-stroke vehicles with origins in the 1920s. By 1937 they had grown somewhat, yet they still retained their two-stroke units (this Aero A30 model had a 1-liter, twin-cylinder engine with 30 bhp) coupled with front-wheel drive. Smart in appearance, they had something of an English air about them. (CS)

George Brough of Nottingham, England, is best remembered as the maker of what was known as "the Rolls-Royce of motorcycles," but from 1933 to 1939 he also built cars, using American Hudson engines. This was the 8-cylinder, 4.1-liter Brough Superior convertible coupe, capable of 90 mph; there was also a 6-cylinder, 3½-liter model. (GB)

The Buick Roadmaster Model 81 was a big (10-foot, 11-inch wheelbase) 6-passenger, four-door touring sedan. It had a 5.2-liter engine. (USA)

The 812 marked the end of the Cord range. It had a Lycoming V-8 engine giving nearly 200 bhp, with the optional supercharger, and over 100 mph. It retained the Cord front-wheel drive, but had a new, eye-catching feature—retractable headlights. Sales were small. (USA)

Another midget from Berlin—a DKW convertible coupe with a 2-cylinder, 684-cc engine giving 20 bhp. It was part of the front-wheel-drive Meisterklasse range. The radiator was similar to that of the big Horch. (D)

During 1936 the 6-cylinder Type 135 Delahaye won just about every sports-car race in sight and took second and third places in the 1937 Le Mans, as well as winning a highly-publicized international sports-car race in England. One of the options on the 135 was the fingertip, clutchless, Cotal electric gear-change system which offered a selection of three or four gears—in either direction. History does not record the opinion of drivers who may have chosen the 100-mph top gear in reverse. (F)

A French 3½-liter car, the Hotchkiss 686GS was based on the Hotchkiss that won the Monte Carlo rally in 1933 and 1934. It was austerely simple, but the Gran Sport pictured, the most powerful model in the range, could accelerate from 0 to 50 in just over 11 seconds and go on to 93 mph. Later in 1937 the Hotchkiss firm, based at St. Denis near Paris, merged with Amilcar. The 686 range was re-introduced and developed further after the war, but Hotchkiss ended in 1955 after a merger with Delahaye. (F)

HRG—first of a range of competition cars from this firm, whose initials stood for Halford, Robins, and Godfrey, this two-seater had a 1,496-cc Meadows engine. It could hit 92 mph in road trim or 100 mph when stripped for action, and it ran in a variety of events, achieving second place in the 1½-liter class at Le Mans in 1937, 1938, and 1939. The car was still competing in a hill-climb in 1971 when the picture was shot. (GB)

The Jensen brothers, Richard and Allan, were clever body stylists. In 1937 they began a new line in Anglo-American hybrids, using a 3.6-liter Ford V-8 engine and a Columbia two-speed rear axle giving effectively six forward speeds. The 31-cwt Jensen had twin carburetors and overdrive and produced 120 bhp and 85 mph on the road. (CB)

The Mercedes-Benz W125 was the most powerful Grand Prix car to have been built. The 8-cylinder, supercharged engine of 1936 was enlarged in 1937 to 5.7 liters to give 640 bhp at 5,800 rpm and a speed of nearly 200 mph. The chassis of the car was lengthened to give better road-holding, and independent rear suspension was abandoned in favor of a return to the de Dion axle of the turn of the century. This consisted of jointed half-shafts to each wheel, with the wheels linked by a floating tube. (D)

The 2½-liter Panhard & Levassor "Dynamic" coupe was an extraordinary example of the stylist's art, with its curvaceous body, flared headlights, and spatted wheels. The driver was required to occupy a central driving position, which necessitated the provision of three wipers to sweep the panoramic windshield. A year later, however, the car was produced with a choice of left-hand or right-hand driving positions. Engines of 2.7 or 3.8 liters were available as options. (F)

From Kenosha, Wisconsin, came the Nash Ambassador 8, a high-speed cruiser that was the biggest in the Nash range. The 8-cylinder, 4,270-cc engine developed 105 bhp. Its sales feature in 1936 was its "weather eye" air conditioning, with heated air ducted to the windshield or the feet. (USA)

After the Sunbeam-Talbot-Darracq group disbanded in 1935, Major Anthony Lago took over the French factory and continued to race cars under the Talbot name. Lago Talbots dominated the French Grand Prix for sports cars at Montlhéry in 1937, finishing first, second, and third. The car had a 4-liter engine developing 165 bhp, and Louis Chiron, who won the race, averaged 82.5 mph. (F)

Early post-war single-seater racer, a 2-liter Connaught, 1952. (GB)

Allard 30 hp, 1948. (GB)

Reliant Sabre 6 cresting a hill during the 1963 RAC Rally. (GB)

Plymouth Fury, 1961, and 1928 Plymouth. (USA)

Two Renaults of the emergent post war period. A 5 CV Dauphine of 1956, and Renault's attempt at a record-breaking turbine, the 270 CV *Etoile Filant* of the same date. (F)

Maserati 250F, 1955. Often called the most handsome racing car of all. (I)

Ford Anglia, 1953. (GB)

BMW 507 Touring Sport (3.2-liter V8), produced
1955-59. (D)

Volkswagen prototypes take to the road. Ferdinand Porsche had been working for years on the design of a small, economical "people's car." Then, in 1934, the German government gave him the backing to make it a reality. Thirty prototypes were built in 1937 by Daimler-Benz and in Porsche workshops at Zuffenhausen. The model shown—one in which the driver had to look through the engine louvers to see traffic approaching from the rear—was designated the VW 30, but it was not, needless to say, the final version. (D)

Low and elegant, the Triumph Gloria Continental was a 2-liter sedan with handsome coach work inspired by the SS Jaguar. Otherwise it was a Dolomite model with the radiator of a Vitesse. (GB)

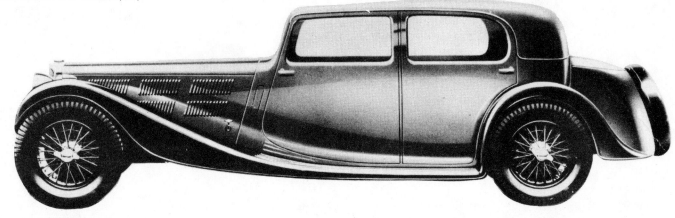

The Allard stemmed from a trials special evolved by England's Sydney Allard from a 1934 Ford V-8 engine and a Bugatti body. A dozen were built using a Ford V-8 of 3.6 liters or a Lincoln Zephyr V-12 of 4.3 liters. The car had a two-seat body with flared wings, a large slab gasoline tank, and twin spare wheels at the rear. It was capable of speeds in the nineties and was used for trials and sprints. (GB)

The single-seat racing car shown here was the last of the Austin Seven racers designed by Murray Jamieson. It was like a miniature Grand Prix car on 16-inch-diameter wheels. The 4-cylinder, 750-cc engine, which appeared in both unsupercharged and in blown forms, could rev up to 9,000 rpm and was capable of 125 mph. The little cars raced with considerable success until the outbreak of the war and continued after the war in hill-climbs and club races. (GB)

Auto Union—at the wheel sits Bernd Rosemeyer, twenty-eight years old and the fastest racing driver of the day. Talking to him is Ferdinand Porsche, designer of the streamlined car in which Rosemeyer attacked two class B records on the Frankfurt autobahn. Tragedy followed. A gust of wind caught the car when it was traveling at 260 mph; it crashed, and Rosemeyer was killed. Auto Union made no more record bids. (D)

In addition to the Auto Union racing cars made at the Horch plant in Zwickau, the company produced a line of distinguished cars, numbers of which had been designed by Gottlieb Daimler's son Paul. This is a large, solidly built, V-8, 4,911-cc Type 853A Horch, giving 120 bhp at 3,400 rpm. (D)

W. O. Bentley himself designed the 4½-liter V-12 for this Lagonda (he had been chief designer of Lagondas since 1935), a unit that was reputed to be one of his best. It developed 180 bhp and was smooth enough to take the car from a walking pace to 103 mph in top gear without discomfort. This 1938 car belonged to race- and record-driver Goldie Gardner. (GB)

The Lincoln Zephyr model had aerodynamic lines and a V-12 engine of 4.3 liters and 110 bhp for prestige. It had a 90-mph performance and was comparatively light and economical compared with other Lincolns, but it was never a best-seller. (USA)

The 1938 Grand Prix formula restricted supercharged engines to 3 liters. The Mercedes-Benz W154 produced for this formula had a V-12 engine giving 483 bhp at 7,800 rpm, which was a sizable increase in revs over previous models. There were two superchargers, and the bodies were lower, wider, and more streamlined. Among them, Lang, Caracciola, and Brauchitsch won the Tripoli, German, and Swiss Grand Prix. The W163 model of 1939 was similar. (D)

The aerodynamic body of the 402B limousine was a new style for Peugeot. The headlights were located with the battery between the front grille and the radiator. The engine was a 4-cylinder of 2,142 cc, giving 55 bhp. A dashboard gearshift operated the three-speed transmission, although a four-speed transmission was available as an option. (F)

Reid Railton designed this 3-ton, streamlined, Railton-Mobil special for John Cobb to use in World Land Speed record attempts. Cobb was housed in the nose of the car which had a body that lifted off in one piece to give access to the engine room. That was occupied by two 24-liter, 12-cylinder, supercharged, Napier Lion engines, each of which developed 1,250 bhp and drove a pair of wheels—a drive system used to give maximum acceleration. At Bonneville in 1938 Cobb raised the record to 350.2 mph. On the eve of World War II he advanced it to 369.7 mph, and in 1947 he made it 394.2. (GB)

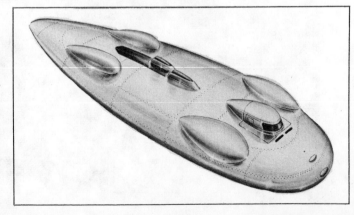

From 1935 Simca (Société Industrielle de Mécanique et Carrosserie Automobile) made Fiat cars at Nanterre in France under license from the Italian company. The Simca shown here was essentially a Fiat 508C, a four-door sedan equipped with a 1,089-cc engine that gave it a top speed of 70 mph. (F)

The 1½-liter SS Jaguar was one of the best-looking cars on the roads of England in the prewar period. The lines were modern and stylish, yet dignified. This model was the smallest in the range. (GB)

The 3½-liter SS Jaguar—largest of the range. The engine gave 125 bhp and 100 mph. Over 5,000 were sold. (GB)

Looking little like the aerodynamic Tatra 77 of four years earlier, this model 57A had something of the Citroën "Traction Avant" shape, although it was powered by an air-cooled, 1,256-cc engine of 4 cylinders. This car was a direct development of the Type 57 first seen in 1932 and now producing 25 bhp. (CS)

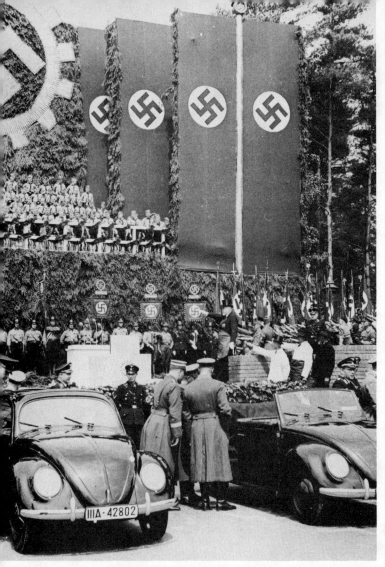

Swastikas dominate the scene; Nazi dignitaries heil Hitler, and troops salute. But the heroes of the occasion were Porsche's Volkswagens, in the foreground; the parade was to mark the opening of a factory to put the people's car into mass production. (D)

From 1937 on all Standard cars were designated Flying Standards; they carried a small Union Jack emblem on the hood. The "fencer's mask" grille was an additional Flying Standard motif. This Flying Twelve convertible coupe was an attractive five-seater with a 4-cylinder, side-valve engine of 1,343 cc in an 8-foot, 4-inch wheelbase. (GB)

This was the final realization of Dr. Porsche's dream, the Volkswagen 38 with a 704- or 984-cc, air-cooled engine and (unlike the prototypes) a rear window. Officially, the car was known as a KdF *wagen,* KdF standing for *"Kraft durch Freude"* or "Strength through Joy," which was the name of the Nazi organization that sponsored the car. (D)

The Volvo P53/56, first seen in 1938, continued in production during the war. It was the Swedes' version of a medium-sized American automobile, and the American influence was so strong that the car might have been thought to be American. It could run on domestic gas—hence the towed container. (S)

Baroque setting for a 1938 Wanderer, the W23, a 6-cylinder, side-valve, 2,632-cc convertible coupe with engineering inherited from the W25K. With a claimed 62 bhp and a *höchstgeschwindigkeit* (top speed) of 118 km/h (73 mph), this was a breezy car for a long-distance trip on the autobahn, but without much else to commend it. (D)

Developing 82 bhp from its 1,650-cc, 4-cylinder unit, this British Atalanta was an exclusive sports car with a number of options. A Gough engine of 1½ or 2 liters was offered at first (later the smaller was upgraded to the 1,650-cc unit). A Supercharger and later a 4.3 Lincoln Zephyr engine were also offered. The make lasted for only two years because of its high cost. (GB)

The last prewar Audi, the 920, had a rear-driven, 6-cylinder, 3,281-cc engine and was made under the same roof as Horch in the Auto Union organization. It was large and roomy, on the Wanderer pattern, and capable of 85 mph, but production lasted only six months. (D)

The last of the great Auto Union racers was this 12-cylinder, 2,990-cc model with Roots superchargers—capable of 185 mph. It was longer in the nose and the driver sat farther back than in previous models. Nuvolari won the last prewar Grand Prix in this car in Belgrade on the day war was declared, and, as the Auto Union racing department was in East Germany, racing was never resumed. (D)

The Chrysler New Yorker was an aggressively styled Imperial model with a straight-8, 5.3-liter engine developing 130 bhp and giving a speed of 90 mph. Dual overdrive was standard, and there was a column gearshift. The wheelbase was 125 inches. The car also had "Superfinish," a process in which all major chassis components subject to wear were finished to a mirror-like surface. Other features new to Chrysler were push-button inside door locks and rotary-type door latches. (USA)

Wilbur Shaw poses in the Maserati in which he won the Indianapolis 500 in 1939 and 1940 at 115 and 114 mph, respectively. The 8-cylinder, 3-liter, double-super-charged car was the last prewar Maserati Grand Prix model. It was fast but unreliable in Europe, although it triumphed at Indy. (USA)

A new product of Ford's Lincoln division, introduced in 1938, the Mercury was aimed at the medium-price field to compete with the Oldsmobile and Buick of General Motors. A 3,917-cc version of the Ford V-8 engine gave 95 bhp and 90 mph, and 90,000 cars a year were being made by 1941. (USA)

The range of Skoda models in 1939 included the small Popular—a novelty for this year. Its 995-cc engine put out 22 hp and was basically identical with side-valve units of previous Popular models, but was now mounted ahead of the front axle, with the radiator behind the engine. The larger Type 1100 Popular, shown here, featured the ohv unit of 1,088 cc, developing 32 bhp. (CS)

Amédée Gordini, an Italian living in France, raced Fiat cars, but achieved more fame as a preparer of sports racing cars. He was nicknamed "le sorcier" (the wizard) because of his work on Simca cars, which were really Fiats made in France under license. His 1939 Simca-Gordini extracted 65 bhp from a 1,100-cc engine, had a speed of 110 mph, and was a class winner at Le Mans. (F)

The Cadillac 60 Special which had been introduced in 1938 was a trend-setter. It had a V-8 engine, four-seat bodywork, chrome grilles, and column gearshift on a 10-foot, 7-inch wheelbase. Running boards had van-ished. "Trouble is," said a writer of the time, "that every car now looks like a teardrop on a movie queen's face." (USA)

The 122.5-inch wheelbase of the Custom 57 was De Soto's longest up to this time. The car had a 6-cylinder, 3.7-liter, 100-bhp engine. Sealed-beam headlights became standard equipment on all Chrysler-combine cars at this time, while also new to De Soto was the optional all-weather air-control system with dual blower and heater units. (USA)

It was farewell to La Salle in 1940. The Model 52 sedan with its 5.3-liter, V-8 engine cost nearly as much as the parent Cadillac which outsold it, and the name ended that year. (USA)

The Oldsmobile "Woody" station wagon sported a 6-cylinder engine and was available with two-pedal Hydra-Matic transmission, the first efficient automatic system. This was advertised as "the most important engineering advancement since the self-starter ... no gears to shift; no clutch to press." (USA)

Buick's cheapest car, the fastbacked 48 special sports coupe had built-in headlights, and it housed an 8-cylinder engine in a 120-inch wheelbase. (USA)

The last Chevrolet to be produced at the company's Buffalo plant, this special deluxe town sedan was powered by a 6-cylinder, valve-in-head engine. There was a full-width front bench seat with a divided back, and running boards had shrunk almost to the disappearing point. (USA)

The Chrysler Newport was what the makers termed an "idea car." Only six were built—for exhibition and display purposes. They were put on view at trade fairs and in dealers' showrooms, and one served as pace car at the start of the 1941 Indianapolis 500-mile race. The most striking features of the Newport were the dual cockpits with separate folding windshields. The "idea car" also had a hydraulically controlled disappearing top and push-button door handles. The chassis was that of the current Imperial. (USA)

Interchangeable engines and extras were features of the Oldsmobile Dynamic Cruiser 76 sedan. The customary engine was a 6-cylinder, but an 8-cylinder could be supplied for little extra cost. The wheelbase was 125 inches, and 89,000 were built. (USA)

By 1942 America's automobile factories were following the example of Europe's and were changing over to war production. This picture shows the last Nash car coming off the production line on February 4. It did not appear again until 1945. A unit-construction model with a 6-cylinder, 2.8-liter engine, it was an ancestor of the Rambler series. (USA)

A major production item for the war years was the Willys-Overland quarter-ton 4 x 4 truck that became known as the Jeep (from the initials GP, for General Purpose). The first production vehicles left the Toledo, Ohio, factory in December 1941; then Ford began building Jeeps to the Willys pattern. Altogether 639,245 were made during the war. The Jeeps used a 4-cylinder engine with six forward and two reverse gears. With alternative units of two, three, and four liters, Jeeps served in every theater of war in every kind of role. Some were front-line ambulances, some were gun-carriers, some were amphibians, and some were equipped with flanged wheels to tow trucks on railway lines. (USA)

Available with the option of Hydramatic transmission, the 3,903-cc, 6-cylinder Oldsmobile Special shown in 1946 was basically the 1941 "Dynamic" and continued in production through the 1947 model year. For 1948 it received the "Futuramic" styling treatment, and by 1949, when the 4.9-liter "Rocket" was introduced, the old six had only two more years to run. (USA)

The old Triumph Company went into receivership in 1939 and was taken over by Standard in 1945, which at that time was still making the 1.8-liter, 4-cylinder engine for Jaguar. This unit was used to power the classic 1800 Triumph Roadster illustrated, but by 1949 it had been replaced by the 2.1-liter Standard Vanguard Four. Despite a peculiar right-hand gearshift, the aluminum content in the bodywork and its classic lines ensured an enthusiastic following, and, although ousted by the TR series, a good many have survived on both sides of the Atlantic. (GB)

Winner of the last Indianapolis Classic before Pearl Harbor, Mauri Rose had returned in 1946, with the Offenhauser-engined Blue Crown Special, to try a repeat performance. Unfortunately, his postwar debut was not auspicious, and he had to withdraw from the race after colliding with a wall. He was not badly hurt, however, and returned in 1947 to pilot the 4 1/2-liter car to victory with an average speed of 116.34 mph. (USA)

A few "independents" managed to stagger through the Depression in America only to expire, like Cord and Pierce-Arrow, in the late thirties. Those that managed to hang on until the outbreak of war included Graham-Paige, and, although their last offering—the Hollywood—would undoubtedly have bankrupted the company eventually, war contracts ensured the survival of Joseph Frazer's empire. Joining forces with Liberty-ship builder Henry J. Kaiser in 1946, he produced the Frazer, an attractive car that became something of a style-setter, powered by the Graham-Paige version of the old prewar Continental Red Seal 3.7 sv six. (USA)

The prestige car of the Ford stable, the Lincoln Continental, emerged in 1945 little changed from the 1941 models. Apart from a revamped frontal treatment, the car shown—the last of Edsel Ford's Continentals—was a '41 in all other respects. By 1949, with the introduc- tion of the Cosmopolitan, Lincoln followed the common Ford engineering theme of "L"-head, V-8 engines, ladder frame with coil and wishbone ifs, and entirely new bodywork. (USA)

The Standard company's first new postwar design, the rugged "humpty back" Vanguard, was first introduced in 1947 and spearheaded a "one model" policy that lasted until the introduction of the "eight" in 1953. Its 4-cylinder, ohv, 2,088-cc engine was virtually indestructible, but the six-seater, unitary-construction body was prone to rust. (GB)

Developed secretly during World War II, the 760-cc, rear-engined 4 CV was the main postwar offering from the now government-controlled Renault concern. Its ohv engine produced 19 bhp and a top speed of 60 mph, and, with all-around independent suspension and hydraulic brakes, it was an instant success. (F)

Introduced during 1939, the Colombo-designed Alfa-Romeo Type 158 was a 1½-liter scaled-down version of the company's earlier and unsuccessful 16-cylinder Grand Prix car. Its 8-cylinder unit with identical bore and stroke was virtually half of the larger car's engine and was successful in competition in 1939 and 1940. It was still unbeatable in 1946, 1947, and 1948, and the team was withdrawn in 1949 because there was no worthwhile competition from rival stables. Slightly modified, the car was re-introduced as the Type 159 in 1950, eventually being beaten in 1951, by which time the engine was producing over 380 bhp. Here Count Trossi and Jean Pierre Wimille are shown at the 1948 Grand Prix d'Europa in which they finished first and second, respectively. (I)

Like most of its competitors, the postwar Chevrolet was basically the 1942 offering, and the Stylemaster shown here did not receive a face-lift until 1949, when it was extensively re-styled, lowered, and re-named the Style-line. The old 3,548-cc six, however, continued in use; the fiberglass Corvette, introduced in 1953, employed a 160-bhp version of this unit. (USA)

Bodybuilders even in the 1920s, Holden was taken over by General Motors before the war and, under their aegis, assembled both American and British GM vehicles for the home market. Basically a Buick, the "FX," introduced in 1948 as the first fully Australian Holden (it wasn't—there was a Holden built there in 1911) was a conventional GM offering, with unitary-construction body and a 6-cylinder, ohv, 2.2-liter engine. Unlike the previous "assembly" jobs, it was truly 92% Australian, and over 7,000 cars were sold in 1949. Firmly established, Holden is now Australia's most popular car-maker. (AUS)

Introduced at the 1948 Motor Show, production of the Jaguar XK 120 began in 1949, although few Britons saw any, since the majority were exported. The aerodynamic sports two-seater created a sensation and, with a 6-cylinder, 3.4-liter, twin-ohc engine, represented a remarkable value for its price. Capable of 120 mph in production form, the cars were successful in almost every sphere of motor sport, and Jaguar's showings at Le Mans in 1951, 1953, 1955, 1956, and 1957 are now legendary. (GB)

By the time this rather ugly Lagonda coupe appeared, the company had been taken over by the David Brown organization. It did, however, clothe the last of W. O. Bentley's designs—a beautifully engineered 2.6-liter, 6-cylinder, twin-cam engine in an unconventional cruciform chassis with irs by torsion bar, in addition to coil and wishbone ifs. With column gearshift, it still attracted few buyers, but some months later the same engine, plus the Aston-Martin chassis, spelled DB 2 . . . a different story. (GB)

First introduced in 1938 during one of the Lea-Francis company's numerous reorganizations, the Hugh Rose–designed, 14-hp, 4-cylinder engine continued in production after the war both in sedan versions and as a "station wagon," in addition to the sports model shown here, which appeared in 1948.

The push-rod-operated ohv arrangement with two high camshafts was similar to the smaller prewar Riley Nine unit, which Rose had also designed. The company had financial troubles like other specialist independents in austere Britain, and by 1952 production had fallen to six cars a week; the company ceased operations shortly afterward. (GB)

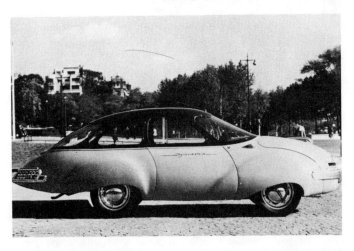

Introduced in 1946, the Panhard "Dyna" range represented not only a complete change of direction for Panhard & Levassor, but also illustrated that it was still possible to introduce a radical design and make a success of it. The special streamlined sedan seen here was not generally available, the standard offering being a small four-door sedan with light alloy bodywork by Facel-Metallon. A Gregoire design, the car originally used an air-cooled, fwd, flat-twin engine of only 610 cc, four-speed transmission with dashboard change, and ifs. (F)

Introduced in 1947 as a successor to the prewar 1,100-cc 202 model, the Peugeot 203 proved to be a best-seller. Powered by a 1.3-liter engine with hemispherical head and wet liners driving through a four-speed transmission to a somewhat dated worm-drive back axle, the car featured unitary construction and all-around coil suspension with ifs. (F)

First shown in 1948 as a replacement for the Hillman 14-engined, 2-liter car that first appeared in 1940, the Sunbeam Talbot "80" and "90" (of 1,185 cc and 1,944 cc, respectively) were attractive cars housing ohv engines, wrap-around windshields, column gearshifts, and hypoid rear axles. While both cars still adhered to semi-elliptics, when the smaller "80" was dropped in 1950, the "90" was given ifs and a 70-bhp engine. Following successes in the Alpine Rally, a sports two-seater version of the "90" was introduced in 1953 as the Sunbeam Alpine, and the Talbot name was dropped. (GB)

Basically the staple Grand Prix Ferrari offering from 1948 until 1950, this Colombo-designed 1½-liter progressed from a single-ohc V-12 with single supercharger to twin ohc with two-stage supercharging. In 1950 development of an unsupercharged 4½-liter V-12 resulted in the realization of Ferrari's ambition to vanquish the Alfa Romeo team in 1951. (I)

Based on Vincenzo Lancia's last design, the 1,352-cc Aprilia, this little 903-cc Ardea 4a first appeared just before World War II. Re-introduced in 1949 with a five-speed transmission, the car boasted semi-elliptic rear suspension and produced 29 bhp. It was replaced in 1953 by the 1,100-cc Appia. (I)

With 104,593 units sold in 1949, Packard might be permitted this backward glance. The Clipper line—available with either 6- or 8-cylinder engines—still retained some of its former elegance. The chromium excesses of the late fifties were in the future, and the company could not know that in less than ten years the Packard name would no longer exist. The older car is the first Packard—the 1899 Model A. (USA)

Although "export only" in 1949 (note the left-hand drive), this Rolls-Royce Silver Dawn was significant in that it was the first "cooking" Rolls; i.e., it was supplied with a factory-built body. With a 6-cylinder engine (enlarged to 4.6 liters in 1952) and steering-column gearshift, the car was also available cheaper with a Bentley radiator. (GB)

Developed from the prewar 4-liter that had taken part in the French Grand Prix in 1939 driven by Raymond Mays, the 4.5-liter Talbot Lago G.P. was introduced by Anthony Lago in 1948 to comply with the current limits of Formula 1. With channel-section chassis frame, ifs, and one-piece rear axle mounted on semi-elliptics, this 6-cylinder car was certainly an improvement and, although not outstandingly fast (it was unblown), achieved success through sheer reliability. (F)

BRINK OF TODAY: 1950-1969

The early Fifties, in Britain at least, continued the frustrations of the past six years since the war had ended. The public still waited for the motor industry to produce the goods, and waited...and waited. Exports had taken priority, and the automobile industry had established itself as the country's number one exporter (albeit of cars of mainly prewar design). At home, shortages of steel and an overabundance of government control kept supplies at a trickle.

However, by 1951 manufacturers were throwing away their fifteen-year-old blueprints, and the Motor Show saw no less than thirty-two British models on the market, compared with Italy's four, France's ten, and Germany's lone Porsche. American vehicles, however, included the Dodge, De Soto, Buick, Cadillac, Chevrolet, Chrysler, Plymouth, Hudson, Kaiser, Lincoln, Ford of Canada, Mercury, Nash, Pontiac, Packard, Oldsmobile, and Studebaker—most of them showing more than one model and illustrating to the rest of the world that USA production, at least, was in full force once more.

The Fifties were years of looking forward to better things—and of eventually getting them, although with several large mergers in several countries, the choice of models was somewhat reduced. In the USA similar circumstances prevailed, with the loss of some smaller independents such as Kaiser (1955), Hudson and Nash (1957), Packard (1958), and others. Technical changes were made rapidly—some not always for the better—and automatics became universal in America, weights increased to a soft-riding 4,500 lbs. with as much roadholding on a corner as a feather on a skating rink,

and brake efficiency degenerated badly. Bodies grew a permanent "Japanese grin." The Americans were not alone; in the first part of the decade most run-of-the-mill British cars were heading the same way.

However, the early Fifties heralded a new crop of designs, probably the most significant of which in Britain was the Jaguar XK 120. In America a genuine attempt at a "sports" car (with the engineering that the word conveys) was Chevrolet's Corvette. Born as the Motorama dream car in 1952, it rapidly evolved into the 160-bhp Corvette and was bought by a quarter of a million Americans in 1953. In Germany Daimler-Benz produced the Mercedes 300 SL, a car that was to prove, with only the minimum of changes, a racing world-beater. France developed the traction avant into the DS, which in 1955 looked as though it belonged to the Sixties or later.

The period also saw the mass introduction of unit construction in place of the conventional chassis frame, and later, suspensions for smaller cars became more sophisticated. Michelin brought a complete new concept to tires with a steel-braced radial-ply.

Disc brakes, introduced by Dunlop in the Fifties, tested in use by the BRM and Jaguar, became the norm on high-performance cars and began to filter slowly through to the family product. Almost the last model to be introduced in the Fifties was the Mini (1960 model), then called either an Austin Seven or a Morris Mini Minor, and now known throughout the world simply as the Mini, a small jewel familiar to every country and used by every class of motorist.

Jano's 1934 unsupercharged, 6-cylinder, twin-ohc, 2.3-liter car remained Alfa Romeo's staple offering until 1939 when, developed by Treviso, it became the 2500 and remained in custom-made production until 1950.

As a result of Alfa Romeo's "volte-face" in that year, the 1900 shown was introduced—a unitary-construction sedan produced on mass-production lines—and since 1950 over 30,000 have been sold. (I)

Aston Martin DB2. Originally designed for the Lagonda branch of David Brown's empire in 1948 by W. O. Bentley, the 2.6-liter, twin-ohc "six" finally achieved production installed in a chassis originally designed by Claud Hill for Gordon Sutherland's experimental post-war Atom. Sutherland sold out to David Brown in 1947, and by 1950 the cars had shown they could perform well at Le Mans, repeating the performance in 1951. (GB)

Never a big seller, the Austin A40 Sports was introduced in 1950; more expensive than the Saloon Devon with which it shared a common basic specification, it could not be called a real sports car. Fitted with the 1,200-cc, ohv engine and with ifs, the Sports was somewhat longer than the Devon. It lived in the shadow of the A90 sports models and was withdrawn in 1953. (GB)

Although the prestige car of the Chrysler range, this 1950 Imperial is typical of the malaise which affected postwar Chrysler styling. Not only does the conservative "high-hipped" line date the car—the mechanics were also due for a face-lift. This came a year later when the old 5.3-liter "eight" was replaced by a 5,426-cc, ohv V-8, and not too soon, for the "eight" was basically a 1937 design. (USA)

Members of the Chrysler Corporation empire from 1928, Dodge became rather submerged during the Forties and differed little from De Sotos and deluxe Plymouths from the same stable. This 1950 version of the Dodge Coronet was still using the 3,769-cc "six" introduced in the early forties on the D22 De Luxe and Custom models. President Tex Colbert had spent about 90,000,000 dollars on retooling and styling in 1949, and the introduction of the "Red Ram" ohv, V-8 unit helped Dodge sales in 1952. (USA)

After a war in which it built armored and scout cars, Daimler never quite recovered its prewar position in the motor industry. Two limousine models were offered, a 4-liter six and a 5½-liter eight, the latter finding some favor with undertakers for hearse and funeral-car duties. This was perhaps a portent for the future, but in the immediate postwar period a number of the old carriage firms were still building custom-made bodies for those who could afford them, and this Daimler Sedanca by Hooper is typical of the period. (GB)

No matter how chic the models may have looked, it was the car that brought the customers—a lesson which Hudson was to learn the hard way. From a postwar high in 1950, Hudson production dwindled to 32,000 in 1954. Nevertheless, this Pacemaker—an example of the revolutionary "Step down" series, with a high-compression, sv, in-line engine—was a brave attempt to fight off the "big three." Low-built, with unitary construction, coil-spring ifs, and the rear wheels mounted *inside* the chassis frame, it deserved a better fate. (USA)

Descended from the prewar 1100S aerodynamic coupe, the Fiat 1100 ES was unveiled at the 1949 Geneva Salon and became available to the public in 1950. Capable of 150 km/h (93 mph), it was, however, never sold in large numbers, and production ceased in 1951. This is the 1100 ES with a coupe body by Pinin Farina. (I)

Clean and relatively unadorned lines characterized this 1950 Ford convertible. Automatic transmission became available during the year, and, together with the '49 line—longer and lower—and coil-spring ifs, ensured plenty of customers—well over a million in 1950. (USA)

Although an affinity with earlier Lancias can be seen from this photo of the Lancia Aurelia in the year of its introduction in 1950, overhead camshafts were "out," and push rods were "in," with an entirely new 1,754-cc, V-6 engine. The transmission—now located in the back axle—had synchromesh on the top three ratios, and in 1951 the car was available with an alternative 2-liter engine. (I)

The Moskvitch 400 "son of Moscow" was not a son of Moscow at all, but the outgrowth of the prewar German Opel "Olympic" which grew into the Kadett. Under the terms of reparation settlements after the war, the Kadett production lines were dismantled and shipped to Russia, where the car reappeared as the Moskvitch. With a 4-cylinder, 23-hp engine, the design was "dated" even in 1950, and no attempt was made to disguise the car's pedigree. (SU)

Emerging in the postwar years as the most innovative division of General Motors, Oldsmobile celebrated its half-centennial in 1948 (a little late) and introduced the "88" the following year. Its 4.9-liter, over-square, ohv, "Rocket" V-8 engine was the first of its type, and a year after the car shown was built, the old sixes had been completely phased-out. (USA)

Still using the old "L"-head "six," which was basically a prewar design, the Plymouth (Special deluxe) shown here had to wait another five years before receiving the alternative "over-square," ohv V-8 that heralded the introduction of Chrysler's "Flight sweep" lines. Thereafter, Plymouth—the rather staid and respectable family car of the Chrysler family—became the testing ground for new ideas. (USA)

The first Porsche to be built in the Stuttgart factory, the Type 356 heralded series production after 50 prototypes had been built in Austria. Based on the Volkswagen, which Porsche had also designed, the 356 was propelled by a rear-mounted, VW-based, air-cooled, 4-cylinder unit of 1,086 cc, producing 40 bhp. As in the parent VW, this proved to be a successful formula, and the basic design survived with little outward change until 1964, by which time 130 bhp was being given by an enlarged engine of 1,966 cc. (D)

The "Cyclops" Rover 75—so-called because of its central headlight in the grille—was a completely re-styled version of the ifs, 2.1-liter six first introduced in 1948 with traditional bodywork. This "P4" range—known affectionately as the "Aunty" Rover—was beloved by bank managers and other genteel folk, which probably accounts for the larger number of good specimens still on the roads. (GB)

During the war the Rover Company had worked on gas turbines, and they later drew on this experience to produce, in 1950, the world's first successful turbocar, JET 1, seen here. With a 200-bhp engine mounted in the rear of a standard "75" chassis, it recorded over 151 mph. It was followed by the T3 coupe which was exhibited at Earls Court in 1956, the T4 in 1962, and the Rover-B.R.M. which ran (unofficially) in the 1963 Le Mans 24 Hour race. (GB)

Originally based on the prewar Fiat 1100 which Simca built under license in France, the postwar Simca 8CV seen here was redesigned in 1949, the standard offering being a smart sports coupe with bodywork by Facel Metallon. By the time this convertible had been built, the 1100 had been replaced by a new 40-bhp, 1,200-cc engine, and in 1951, producing 45 bhp, the same unit was used to power an entirely new car, the Aronde. (F)

Based on the prewar 1100 ohv model, this transient postwar Skoda 1101 was extracting 45 bhp from its 1,089-cc engine, which in 1939 had been giving only 32 bhp; a sedan version was also available, and this was developed into the Octavia range which continued in production until the introduction of the 1000 MB in 1964. (CS)

Introduced in 1946, the Mk VI Bentley utilized the old 4,257-cc "six" first used for the 1937 season—an engine it shared with the postwar Rolls-Royce "Silver Wraith" until it was replaced in 1960. However, the designation Mk VI was dropped at the end of 1953, and thereafter the standard offerings were the Sports Saloon and Continental. The former was dropped in favor of the "S" series in 1957. This is an Mk V by James Young, seen here parked in a quiet French village. (GB)

Another variation of the successful prewar Fiat "Topolino" theme, the Fiat Belvedere was introduced in 1951 and used the 569-cc, ohv engine which had first appeared in 1948. Producing 16.5 bhp at 4,400 rpm, the little Belvedere boasted an all-metal station wagon-type body beloved of parish priests, and with a maximum of 90 km/h (55½ mph) available even with four up, the model was popular. (I)

Introduced in 1951 together with the larger Zephyr to replace the old V-8 Pilot, the Ford Consul followed the fashion of the period with its slab-sided styling. With a 1½-liter, ohv, 4-cylinder engine and ifs, however, it was a full five-seater and represented good value for its price. Convertible versions were later available, and the car was not replaced by the Mk 2 Consul until 1956. (GB)

Although the body lines of this Ford Custom represented a completely new style when introduced in 1949 (the old 1942 line persisted for three years after the war), the engine was still the old sv, 3.9-liter V-8. This was supplemented in 1952 by a new "square" 3½-liter, ohv six, and in 1954 the V-8 was dropped. The Custom was also available with automatic transmission. (USA)

It was still "export or die" in 1951 when Rootes chartered the 11,000-ton "Hoperidge" for this biggest shipment ever of cars and commercials to Australia. Differing little from the 1950 model apart from the chrome side flashes and spats, the Minx was the first really new postwar Hillman design, developed in 1949. Initially fitted with the prewar 1,185-cc, sv engine, the model shown here acquired a more powerful 1¼-liter engine in 1950, producing 37.5 bhp at 4,200 rpm, and had full-width 5–6 seater bodywork. (GB)

The first entirely new postwar Jaguar *saloon* to appear after the war, the Mk VII eschewed the push-rod engines of its predecessors and employed the 3.4-liter, twin-ohc unit. It was not replaced until 1957 when the Mk VIII was introduced, won the 1956 Monte Carlo Rally, and consolidated the Jaguar tradition of combining luxury and performance at a price other manufacturers could not match. (GB)

Originally appearing as the XK120C in 1951, the Jaguar "C" type evolved as a sports/racing car with an all-enveloping body and a tuned version of the famous twin-cam XK 120 engine delivering 210 bhp. The disk-braked "C" type won at Le Mans in 1953 and was replaced shortly afterward by the "D" type. The latter car produced 250 bhp, and even though road-holding was not up to some of its competitors' standards, this was enough to ensure wins at Le Mans again and again. (GB)

Toyota Corona Mkl, 1968. (J)

Ubiquitous Mini. (GB)

An Alpine A110 coupé brakes into a control in the 1970
Monte Carlo Rally. (F)

The greatest invention
since the wheel.

Ferrari Dino 246 GT, 1972. (I)

Racing in the Seventies; Jackie Stewart in a 1972
Formula 1 Tyrrell Ford. (GB)

Aggressive Peugeot 504 on the East African Safari Rally.
The marque won this event in 1966, '67 and '68. (F)

Fiat 128, 1973. (I)

Sophisticated British Ford. The 1974 Capri
3000 Ghia. (GB)

Lincoln luxury. A 1974 Continental. (USA)

Popular American: Ford Mustang, 1974. (USA)

Locating his plant in the Willow Run complex built by Ford for manufacture of the B-24 Liberator, Henry J. Kaiser joined forces with Joseph Frazer of Graham-Paige in an attempt to repeat the success he had enjoyed with his Liberty ships by launching an entirely new make of car in 1946. The K-F combine started well, and at one stage built more cars than the established "independents" (including Studebaker, Hudson, and Nash) but was never able to consolidate this lead. The Kaiser shown here used an improved side-valve, 3.7-liter straight-6 of continental design. (USA)

The first completely new Lancia to appear after the war, the Aurelia was the result of the combined design talents of Jano (previously with Alfa-Romeo) and Gianni Lancia (Vincenzo Lancia, the founder of the firm, died in 1937) and was introduced in 1950. The production cars retained the shell and suspension of earlier models, but the engine was a new 1,754-cc, push-rod V-6 producing 56 bhp. The example pictured is the 2-liter version cloaked with a special body by Pininfarina. (I)

Prewar styling heavily influenced this Mercedes-Benz 220 convertible offered by Stuttgart in 1951, and no hint was given of the exciting 300 SL sports car the company marketed the following year. With a 2,195-cc engine, the 220 was one of two sixes introduced by Mercedes in 1951, the other being the 300 of 2,996-cc capacity. (D)

Following the same successful theme introduced by Ford in 1949, there was little to distinguish '51 Mercuries from the previous year's offerings. With hypoid back axle, coil-spring ifs, and a 4,185-cc, V-8 engine, the pattern was continued until 1955, when customers had the option of two V-8 engines producing 188 and 198 bhp. (USA)

In addition to the Mini and its transverse-engined derivatives, Alec Issigonis was also responsible for the design of the ageless Morris "Moggie" Minor seen here. First conceived as the "Mosquito" in 1948, the first production models appeared in 1949 as the MM series, powered by the prewar side-valve, 918-cc engine. After the formation of the British Motor Corporation in 1952, the Austin A30 engine—an 803, ohv unit—was substituted in 1953, and by 1960 the car had grown up into the "1000," with a 1,098-cc power plant. (GB)

The last "dirt" car to win at Indianapolis, Troy Ruttman's Agajanian Special was never farther than third from the lead car in the 1952 event, and by the tenth lap was second to Vukovich. There he stayed, gradually overtaking him, until by the 200-mile mark he was leading Vukovich by some 34 seconds. A pit stop reversed the order, and by the 170th lap Ruttman was 31 seconds behind again. It looked like Vukovich's race until his steering gear collapsed and he hit the north wall. Ruttman went on to win at a new record average of 138.992 mph. (USA)

This 1952 Alfa-Romeo Disco Volante (Flying Saucer) was one of only nine built. The car employed a bored-out version of the "1900" engine originally intended as a design study for a 3-liter sedan which was eventually abandoned. Four coupes were entered for the 1953 Mille Miglia—one fitted with a 4-cylinder, 2-liter engine and the others with the 6-cylinder unit. The larger versions also raced at Le Mans, Spa, and the Nurburgring, but without success. (I)

Despite the rather bulbous "new line" that characterized Austins from 1948 onward, the large 4-cylinder A90 Atlantic power-top convertible shown here was a fast car, and, in a bid to attract transatlantic customers, a series of long-distance record bids were made at Indianapolis. Despite a good showing, sales were disappointing, although the engine—in Austin-Healey guise—gave the Triumph TR series a run for its money until 1956. (GB)

Representing one of the last individual Bentley designs at a time when Rolls-Royce and Bentley identities were being merged in a common manufacturing program, this 2-liter, 120-mph Continental by H. J. Mulliner showed that the coachbuilder's art was by no means dead. Continued until 1966, the Continental acquired a 4.9-liter engine in 1955, in which year automatic transmissions, previously optional, became standard. (GB)

Victims of the partition of Germany after the war, BMW lost the works at Eisenach that they had acquired from Dixi in 1928. Motorcycle production was taken up in 1945 in Munich, and in 1952 their first postwar car (shown here), the 501 sedan, appeared. Based on their last prewar designs, it utilized a 6-cylinder, 1,971-cc engine. (D)

One of the first successful commercially produced trials specials, the Dellow was introduced in 1949 and employed the British Ford "ten" engine in an "A" frame with a very spartan two-seater body. The Mk II shown here was followed by a four-seater (Mk III), while the Mk V boasted coil front suspension in place of the transverse semi-elliptics of the earlier models. The last Dellow was made in 1959. (GB)

1952 De Soto Firedome 8. Looking at this slab-sided monument to the mouth-organ grille with the hindsight of later years, it is surprising that De Soto managed to unload over 97,000 units in 1952. The car typified all that was wrong with Chrysler styling during this period. Although the 4½-liter, 160-bhp, over-square V-8 introduced this year boosted sales in 1953 to nearly 130,000, they never managed to repeat this, and even Chrysler's "Flight sweep" line could do little to prevent De Soto's decline throughout the Fifties. (USA)

The postwar Frazer-Nash was a far cry from the chain-driven cars descended from the GN cycle car that had established the reputation of the brand during the Twenties and Thirties. Powered by a 2-liter Bristol engine, this Le Mans version, in the hands of Ken Wharton, notched up numerous competition successes. A Frazer-Nash won the 12-hour Sebring race in 1952, and this gave rise to another model of that name. (GB)

Launched at the Geneva Salon in 1952, the Fiat 8V was totally out of line with the company's general manufacturing policy at this time and was produced in small numbers until 1954. The ohv, 110-bhp, V-8 engine of 1,996 cc was developed by Siata of Turin—well-known tuners of Fiats since before the war and builders of their own mainly Fiat-based cars—and was capable of propelling the car at 120 mph. Despite this, it was unsuccessful in competition in the hands of various private owners. (I)

Developing 82 bhp from its 1,650-cc, 4-cylinder unit, this British Atalanta was an exclusive sports car with a number of options. A Gough engine of 1½ or 2 liters was offered at first (later the smaller was upgraded to cylinder TD developed 57½ bhp and continued in production until 1953 and was the last MG model to appear with "traditional" bodywork. (GB)

The Packard Patrician 400—an example of the unfortunate postwar styling that dogged the company's products in its last years. The Patrician utilized the old straight-8 engine (eventually discontinued in 1954) and was not dissimilar in outward appearance to the later Clippers. These, however, were but a pale shadow of the handsome 1941 Clipper line, and, with the introduction of the Caribbean convertible, nemesis was virtually unavoidable. It was delayed only by a brief liaison with Studebaker. (USA)

Reflecting the complete re-styling operation in 1949, this Pontiac looks quite handsome when compared with its competitors from the Chrysler stable. It was, however, a sheep in wolf's clothing—the old 127-bhp, sv straight-8 continued to live under Pontiac hoods until 1955, when the 4.7-liter, ohv V-8 supplanted it on American-produced cars. (USA)

When the old Sunbeam-Talbot-Darracq combine finally folded in 1935, Major A. F. Lago took control of the Suresnes factory, while Rootes got the British end and combined Sunbeam and Talbot. The French factory had been known as Automobiles Talbot since 1920, however, so when Lago produced this postwar 4½-liter sedan, the French called it a Talbot (this is a Talbot Lago Record Type T26), and the English called it a Darracq—all very confusing. Despite racing successes (including the 1950 Le Mans), postwar France was no place to be producing luxury cars with large engines, no matter how economical they might be, and taxation crippled the already financially weak company. (F)

Introduced in 1948, the Vauxhall Velox shared a standardized hull with the smaller Wyvern and employed a long-stroke, 6-cylinder, 2.3-liter engine producing 54 bhp. By this time all Vauxhalls for the home market were of unitary construction, and the model shown was the first of a re-styled version introduced in 1952. (GB)

Basically the Morris Six, this, the 6/80, was the larger of two Wolseley models introduced when the works moved to Cowley in 1949. The last vestiges of Wolseley independence disappeared in 1955 with the introduction of the Austin-engined 2.6-liter 6/90. (GB)

Brink of Today: 1950-1969

The 4-cylinder "1900" Alfa Romeo was introduced in 1950 as a unitary-construction sedan and marked the turning point in the company's history. The curiously shaped Astral (illustrated), like the tubular chassis Disco Volante (Flying Saucer) cars introduced in 1953, was derived from the "1900." (I) .

Evolved from prewar Ford V-8 trials specials of Sydney Allard, the postwar Allard was the only really successful Anglo-American produced after the war. Whatever sold them, it wasn't good looks, and even if, as the poem went, they did eat Jaguars for breakfast and Bentleys for tea, it was not the big type-M convertible (shown here) that attracted 75% of Allard production to the United States, but the J2 introduced in 1950, which utilized (for export) the 5.4 Cadillac V-8 and similar units. (GB)

The ubiquitous 2 CV Citroën (affectionately known as the "deux chevaux") was designed by Pierre Boulanger, and 250 prototypes were tested during 1938 and 1939, but further development was prevented during the war. Making its debut at the Paris Salon in 1948, it quickly caught the imagination of the French despite its spartan appearance. Like the larger "traction avant" Citroëns, it had fwd and unitary construction. The 375-cc, ohv, flat-twin engine was enlarged to 425 cc in 1955. (F)

Available also with the old 3.8-liter, side-valve six, the Dodge Coronet illustrated housed the ohv, "Red Ram," 3.8-liter unit introduced a year earlier. While it is doubtful that this model Dodge would, as John Steinbeck asserted, "go to hell and back on its belly," it was a tough car with a reputation for longevity. After a period during which it was virtually indistinguishable from other lower-priced products in the Chrysler range, the Coronet once more gave Dodge an individuality of its own. (USA)

Unlike other European manufacturers, Fiat had emerged from the war years virtually unscathed, and by the time this 1100/103 was produced, postwar recovery was complete. Producing 35 bhp, the car was augmented by a 48-bhp turismo veloce (fast touring) type and continued in production until 1956. (I)

The immortal "Traction Avante" seen here in the Rallye de Sestrières had, by 1953, begun to look more than a little dated. This is scarcely surprising, since in outward appearance it differed little from the 7 CV Citroën first introduced in 1934. The latter created a sensation when introduced, but it almost bankrupted Andre Citroën, who sold out to Michelin in 1935. Finally ousted by the Citroën DS19 (introduced in 1955) in 1957, the car still has a devoted following. (F)

In 1953, the smaller cars in the UK Ford range (such as the Anglia seen here) were re-styled on lines similar to the Consul and Zephyr models, but were fitted with 1,172-cc engines. The exception was the Popular, which inherited the old prewar "sit-up-and-beg" bodywork of the Anglia married to the 1172 unit. This antique design, renowned for its uncertain directional stability, was made until 1959. (GB)

Whether or not it was a result of the British Government's exhortation to "export or die" in the immediate postwar years, a number of British manufacturers slanted their products toward the American market either in terms of styling or nomenclature. The Austin Atlantic was one that deserved a better reception than it received, but it is unlikely that the Hillman Californian seen here tempted many paying customers. Following as it did, however, the well-tried Rootes formula of cloaking conventional mechanics (in this case the enlarged 1¼-liter, Minx-based engine introduced in 1950) with attractive bodywork—a two-tone hardtop coupe—the car found favor with home buyers. (GB)

One of the best known of the American "independents," Hudson had established its reputation during the 1920s with the Super Six and Essex Coach models. Although it had managed to weather the Depression years, the 1930s were a trying time for the company. It managed a brief revival in the car-starved postwar years, and the Hornet, introduced in 1951, was the most successful of its postwar models. The car shown was one of the last Hornets produced by the company before its amalgamation with American Motors in 1954; it boasted a 5-liter, 145-bhp, 6-cylinder engine. (USA)

Although the name "Rambler" was derived from the first cars built by the old Thos. B. Jeffery Co. from 1902–1913, there was nothing old-fashioned about this "Custom" model. With its 2.8-liter, sv-six, unitary construction, short chassis, and low weight, it was the first of the postwar "compacts" and was largely responsible for the survival of Nash (now American Motors) as the lone American "independent." Parentage of the Austin-produced Metropolitan is unmistakable in this photo. (USA)

The Standard Ten first appeared in 803-cc, ohv guise late in 1953, at a time when the Standard Company was building more tractors than cars. The 948-cc Ten followed shortly afterward and could be distinguished from its smaller brother by the chrome grille and more luxurious trim. (GB)

The first Toyota cars appeared in 1937, built by an offshoot of a company making power looms and spinning machinery in Koromo. Spearheading its re-entry into the market after the war was the model SA, a two-door sedan producing 27 bhp from its 4-cylinder engine and boasting a backbone chassis and independent coil-spring suspension. It was followed in 1952 by the RHK (1953 model shown here), and by 1955 some 700 cars a month were being produced, at which time the Crown, giving 48 bhp from its 1,453-cc, push-rod, ohv engine, was introduced. (J)

Joining the sedan and convertible Sunbeam-Talbot "90" models which had distinguished themselves in the Alpine Rally, this two-seater Sunbeam Alpine was introduced in March 1953. Using a modified "90" engine of 2,267 cc, it was capable of 100 mph, and, driving a stripped version with a high axle ratio, rally driver Sheila Van Damm set up the Belgian and women's records in the 2-liter class at 120.135 mph at Jabbeke. (GB)

Utilizing the versatile Standard Vanguard engine in 1,991-cc form, the Triumph TR2 was an instant success when introduced in 1953. Like the Vanguard, the engine proved economical (even when coupled with a performance in excess of 100 mph) and was renowned for its lack of temperament. (GB)

First introduced by the Bristol Aeroplane Company as the type 400 in 1947, the Bristol was based on the prewar BMW 328. By 1953 the 403 was giving a genuine 100 mph and developed 100 bhp at 5,000 rpm. The 404 Sports coupe was available with either 105- or 125-bhp engines, the more powerful being that used in the Cooper-Bristol Formula II racing cars, and a team of experimental coupes based on the 404 won the 2-liter class and team prize at Le Mans in 1954. One of them is shown here. (GB)

The 1,300-cc Alfa Romeo Giuletta was introduced in 1954 as a companion for the 1900 from which it evolved. Despite the reduced engine capacity, the classic twin-cam head was retained, and the power unit developed 80, 90, or 100 bhp, depending on whether you opted for the Sprint (illustrated here with body by Bertone), Sprint Veloce, or Sprint Speciale. The latter was capable of speeds of 124 mph when fitted with twin Weber carburetors. (I)

Fiat hitched on to the gas-turbine bandwagon in the mid-fifties with this Fiat Turbina, although we have yet to see a production model so-powered from any company. This futuristic coupe utilized the chassis of Fiat's limited-production V-8 sports car, first introduced in 1952. (I)

Continuing the frontal styling of the sedan Holden FX model which had received a minor face-lift with the introduction of the FJ series of 1954, this "ute" was a purpose-built version of a type of vehicle that has become synonymous with the Australian way of life. The "utility" has been an essential vehicle ever since pioneer days when someone chopped the back off a Model T sedan to make a truck. (AUS)

Sometimes unkindly referred to as the "lumber" Hawk, the MK VI Humber Hawk shown here featured a new 4-cylinder, ohv engine of 2,267 cc which developed 70 bhp and was capable of speeds in excess of 80 mph. Earlier examples were, however, descended from the 1938–1940 Hillman Fourteen, powered by 1.9-liter, sv engines and endowed with heavy bodies beloved of rental-car proprietors. (GB)

Of unitary construction, the "D"-type Jaguar was a development of the successful "C"-type — itself a version of the twin-cam XK 120. Jaguar's successes at Le Mans are now legendary, but it is worth noting that, after replacing the "C"-types in the works team with "D"-types, the company fielded five cars for the 1957 event, all of which finished — in first, second, third, fourth, and sixth places! A few "C"- and "D"-types were sold to the public, but the standard offering for non-racing customers was the XK 140 (an improved 190-bhp XK 120, also available with the "C"-type engine) until the advent of the "E"-type in 1961. (GB)

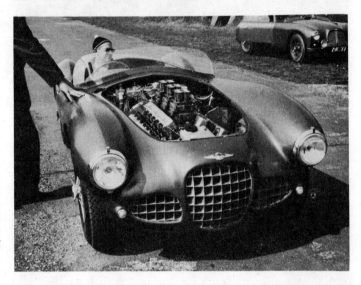

Designed by Howard A. Darrin in Los Angeles, on Henry J. Kaiser's chassis, this sliding-door Kaiser-Darrin roadster created a minor sensation when first introduced. The concave grille echoed those on the larger '54–'55 Manhattans and Specials designed by A. B. Grisinger, and the Darrin is distinguished by its lack of chrome at a time when other U.S. manufacturers were passing unhappily through their "mouth-organ" stage. (USA)

Ferraris were not the only 12-cylinder cars entered for the 1954 Le Mans event; David Brown fielded this 4½-liter Lagonda V-12 with two plugs per cylinder and triple twin-choke Webers. The body, mounted on a space frame, was similar to the Aston Martin DB3S (three of which also ran at Le Mans that year), but the car, which made its debut at Silverstone driven by Reg Parnell, did not, unfortunately, go into production. (GB)

The first Lancia Grand Prix car, designated the D 50, was designed by Jano for the 1954 season and incorporated many new features. The V-8 engine formed part of the space frame and was mounted diagonally; suspension was by wishbones at the front, employing a very thin transverse leaf spring, and de Dion at the rear, also with transverse leaf spring and a complicated system of telescopic shock absorbers. The fuel tanks were slung on outriggers between the wheels. This promising design was handed over to Ferrari when Lancia sold out to Fiat in 1955. (I)

When Maserati returned to racing in 1952, their unblown, 6-cylinder, 2-liter, Formula II cars very quickly established a challenge to Ferrari's domination. The car was developed through 1953, and, when a new Formula I car was announced for 1954—the 250 F— much of that development was incorporated in it. Four came to England (for Moss, Salvadori, Bira, and BRM), and here Moss is seen in his 250 F winning the Goodwood Trophy at the International Car Race Meeting in September 1954. (I)

Introduced for the 1952 Le Mans, the Mercedes-Benz 300 SL utilized the 300S engine tuned to give 215 bhp (increased to 240 bhp in the production cars), and production began in 1954. Fitted with fuel injection, they were the fastest road cars then available, giving 150 mph. Although the "gull wing" doors were phased out in 1956, the model remained in production until 1963. (D)

Mercedes-Benz won the Manufacturers Championship in both 1954 and 1955, in addition to providing the car for Fangio, who was World Champion in both years. For the 1954 season they built the 2½-liter, W 196, fuel-injection straight-8. The cars came first and second in their first race—the French Grand Prix. A 3-liter version of the same engine powered the 300SLR in sports-car racing during 1955. Here, Fangio is shown at the Reims circuit in 1954 in an aerodynamically bodied W196. (D)

The Series II Morris Oxford differed little in outward appearance from the MO that it succeeded and which was introduced in 1949. Following the merger with Austin in 1952 and the formation of the British Motor Corporation, the Austin A50 unit was used in place of the 1,477-cc Morris. Unitary construction was introduced in 1955, and the model remained in production until the advent of the Farina-styled 1½-liter sedans in 1959. (GB)

Harley Earl produced the first GM "dream car" in 1938 on a Buick Roadmaster chassis, and, although the public never actually had the opportunity to buy one "off the peg," subsequent Buick models incorporated more than a modicum of engineering and body design directly inherited from Earl's design exercise. Since then there have been others, including this futuristic Pontiac Firebird in 1954. (USA)

Originally a product of Ford's factory at Poissy, the Simca Vedette in original form was powered by the old 2.2-liter V-8, introduced in 1936 for the Mathis-built Matford. This engine continued in use until 1954, when a larger 3.9-liter unit was listed. However, Ford had not operated over-successfully in postwar France, largely owing to the system of taxation that heavily penalized the larger-engined cars, and later in 1954 they sold out to Simca. The Chambord version shown here was still in production under license in Brazil as late as 1967. (F)

Utilizing the same body shell as the prewar Kapitans, with revised frontal styling, the postwar model shown here was an updated version of the car that heralded Opel's re-entry into the market in 1948. Its 2,473-cc, 6-cylinder engine was also a prewar design, and, although there were changes in body styling, this unit was retained until 1959. (D)

By the time this Singer Special Saloon, a cheaper version of the Hunter, appeared, the sands were running out for the Singer company. While capable of impressive performance when tuned (as in the postwar H.R.G.), the chain-driven, overhead-cam, 1½-liter engine was basically an updated 1920s design, and Singer could not afford the retooling necessary to rid itself of the dated slab-sided sedan first introduced in 1948. Rootes took over in 1956, and the first Gazelles utilized the old 1½-liter unit. (GB)

A Volvo that never went into production was this experimental 179, with both body and 1,400-cc, 4-cylinder power unit from the rugged PV444—although the body was considerably revamped. The final design finished among the prototypes that did not come up to standard in Volvo's severe test program, and it was scrapped. It looked handsome, though. (S)

Developed by Alec Issigonis, during a brief sojourn at Alvis, from the earlier 2,993-cc, 90-bhp TA21, the Alvis TC21/100 produced 100 bhp and carried a 100-mph guarantee. When, in 1955, Graber designed new bodywork on this chassis (illustrated), the shape of all future Alvis production crystalized. Despite detail improvements, the TD and TE series followed the same handsome lines, but, after the Rover take-over in 1965, all private-car production ceased in 1967. (GB)

Sharing its 1,500-cc power unit with the Morris Oxford, the Austin A50 Cambridge shown here was also available initially with the 1,200-cc, A 40 engine. It was still recognizably Austin, became known as the A55 in 1958, and in 1959 adopted Farina styling common to Morris, M.G., Wolseley, and Riley. (GB)

This was the last year in which the Austin-Healey used the 2.7-liter, ohv, 4-cylinder Austin A90 engine. By this time, fitted with disk brakes and developing 132 bhp, the original 100 series had reached the limit of development, and in 1956 the 100-6 was introduced. Powered by Austin's 2.6-liter unit, this was in turn superseded in 1960 by the 3000 with a 2.9-liter six. Always popular with the "heavy brigade," the "big" Healeys did well in competition, but suffered from low ground clearance which hampered them in some events. Worthy competitors of Triumph's TR series, the "big" Healeys were discontinued in 1968, by which time they were being made in M.G.'s factory at Abingdon. (GB)

Introduced in coupe and convertible forms in 1955 to compete with Ford's Thunderbird, the Chrysler 300 illustrated shows graphically the result of Chrysler's "Flight sweep" lines. The 4.9-liter, 188-bhp engines had by 1957 been enlarged to 6,423 cc and developed more power than any of their competitors. (USA)

Financed by the wealthy MacAlpine building family, the racing Connaught started life as a "special" with a much-modified Lea Francis 1750 engine. By 1954 the firm was building cars for resale, and their Type B, utilizing the 2½-liter, twin-ohc Alta engine (seen here), won the Syracuse G.P. in 1955, driven by Tony Brooks. Financial difficulties forced the closing of the firm in 1957. (GB)

When Citroën at last supplemented the prewar "Traction Avante" models with a new car, it created almost as great an impact as had its predecessor in 1934. A foretaste of things to come had been the introduction of hydropneumatic suspension on the old "six" in 1954, but when the DS 19 (illustrated) was introduced, its only affinity with the old order was fwd and the old long-stroke, 4-cylinder engine, now producing 65 bhp. Lines that still look advanced today were combined with self-leveling suspension and power assistance for brakes, steering, and gearshift. (F)

Destined to become sought by collectors as a postwar "classic," the Ford Thunderbird was introduced in 1954, and at that time was a genuine attempt by the American Ford company to market a sports car. Ohv, V-8 engines of 4.8 or 5.1 liters were available, the larger of which would propel the car at 113 mph, but later T-birds lost their sports-car image and were never as popular. (USA)

Introduced in 1955 as a companion to the Minx and California hard-top coupe, the Hillman Husky short-wheelbase station wagon was an immediate success. In this year, the Californian and Minx deluxe acquired 1,395-cc, ohv engines, but the Husky shared the basic Minx 1,265-cc unit and was not to inherit the larger engine until 1959. By that time all the rest of the Hillman range were wearing 1½-liter engines, and the Husky continued to lag behind until it was discontinued in 1967. (GB)

Designed by the versatile Spaniard, Wilfredo Ricart, the Pegaso in original form was introduced in 1951 by the Spanish E.N.A.S.A. firm in Barcelona. The factory was located in part of the old Hispano-Suiza works, and, despite E.N.A.S.A.'s reputation as primarily commercial-vehicle manufacturers, this gave rise to hopes of great things to come. Only about 125 Pegasos were built, three or four of which were Z 103s (illustrated) fitted with the firm's own push-rod–operated V-8, available in 4-, 4½-, or 4.7-liter form. (E)

Introduced in 1956 as a successor to the traditional TF, the M.G.A. was the first fully streamlined production M.G. Utilizing an Austin-designed, 68-bhp, 1½-liter engine, it proved faster and more economical than its predecessor and was publicized by some very convincing record-breaking activity. A twin-cam engine briefly introduced as an option proved to be very fast indeed, at the expense of a prodigious thirst for oil and uncertain temperament, and the 1,600-cc, push-rod, ohv, 78-bhp engine that subsequently replaced it as standard proved almost as fast and totally dependable. (GB)

Developed from the W196 Formula I car, the Mercedes-Benz 300 SLR, with a straight-8, 3-liter, fuel-injection engine, was an outstandingly successful sports/racing car. Not only did it provide Fangio, in 2½-liter form, with the car in which he won the World Championship in 1954 and 1955, but also enabled Stirling Moss to win the 1955 Mille Miglia—the first time since the race began in 1927 that this had been achieved by a British driver. Here, Fangio is seen in his car at the commencement of that epic 1955 race at Brescia. (D)

Only twelve months of independence remained to the Salmson Company when this "2300" was produced in 1955, Renault taking over in 1956. Developed from the 2.2-liter Randonnée model introduced in 1951, the 2300 used a tuned version of the twin-camshaft, light-alloy engine, producing 105 bhp and speeds in excess of 100 mph. But the writing was on the wall, and, although Renault sponsored a long-wheelbase version with four-door sedan bodywork in 1957, no more Salmsons appeared thereafter. (F)

Introduced in 1955 as a companion to the popular but aging 203, the 1½-liter Peugeot 403 was another winner that quickly established a high reputation. Fitted with all-synchromesh transmission, it was available with two-pedal control in 1958, and, for those who wanted one, an Indenor diesel engine was offered in 1959. (F)

Derived from BMW's 502 and 503, themselves a continuation of the postwar prestige theme that began in 1952 with the 501, the 507 Sportwagen seen here employed a 3.2-liter version of the sedan's V-8 engine. Bearing a striking resemblance to the contemporary Mercedes, this two-seater was no mean performer, being capable of 70 mph from rest in just over 10 seconds and with a top speed of about 130 mph. (D)

A 1956 Allard Palm Beach Mk II. By the time this Jaguar "C"-engined model was produced, Sydney Allard was building cars to special order only. Boasting a tubular frame, torsion bar, wishbone ifs, and a rigid axle, the car had been available earlier with the 3.6-liter, sv, Ford V-8 unit, but the firm's heyday (they won the 1952 Monte Carlo Rally with their "P"-type sedan) was now over, and no cars were built after 1960. (GB)

Swapping its 3,858-cc, 6-cylinder engine for the 4.3-liter V-8 which the company had introduced the previous year, this Chevrolet Bel Air represented the larger group of cars in the Chevrolet range. The previous year Chevrolet production had accounted for more than half the total private cars sold in the United States. (USA)

Replacing the Lotus Mk 9 for the 1956 season, Colin Chapman's enthusiastic little company tried hard to live down the reputation for unreliability they had earned (albeit somewhat unfairly) with previous models. By now fitted with disk brakes, the cars clocked 156 wins during 1956, and Mackay Fraser took the 1,100-cc class records at Monza. Sold also in kit form, the cars (this is the Lotus MK XI) were available with Ford, M.G. Coventry-Climax, and even 2-liter Bristol engines. (GB)

Fitted with bell and central aerial as illustrated, this Wolseley Six-Ninety was the car no British motorist wanted to see in his rearview mirror, for ever since Scotland Yard adopted the 18-hp model in 1937, Wolseley sixes had been synonymous with the police force. The model shown here employed the Austin 2.6-liter engine and shared its body shell with Riley's Pathfinder. In 1956 it was available with overdrive or automatic transmission. (GB)

Possibly as a result of the work carried out by Rover on their "Jet 1," T3, and T4 models, interest in alternative methods of propulsion became widespread in the early and mid-fifties—certainly Chrysler was running a gas turbine in 1954—and among the hopefuls to appear about this time was the experimental Renault "L'Étoile Filante" which achieved some success in establishing turbine records. At one time or another, Austin, Ford, and General Motors have also concentrated research effort in this direction, and all have produced individual prototypes. (F)

When the PV 444 was finally pensioned-off in 1965, its engine had increased in size to 1.8 liters, but this limited-production, 70-bhp P1900 Volvo Sports Roadster introduced in 1956 used the original 1.4-liter engine. Coinciding with the introduction of the Model 122 with completely new four-door sedan bodywork married to the 444 engine, the Sports lasted barely two seasons, despite the novelty of a five-speed transmission. (S)

Introduced in 1956, the 845-cc Dauphine continued Renault's policy of rear-engined small cars and proved an even greater success than the 4 CV. Over 2 million were sold, and this might have been more. With a 30-bhp engine, the car was developed further during Amédée Gordini's spell with Renault, and this resulted in the 38-bhp Dauphine Gordini and, in 1959, the Floride Sports coupe. Dauphines were finally discontinued in 1968. (F)

By the time this Rambler appeared, American Motors was really beginning to "think small." Introduced in 1950 by the then Nash-Kelvinator Corporation, the Rambler—indeed the whole "compact" image—had become American Motors' biggest asset. They dropped the large Nash and Hudson lines the following year (1957) and put almost all their eggs in the compact basket. As it was, the 2.8-liter, sv "six," weighing only 2,576 lbs, saved the day, and when compact "fever" really hit the American buying public in the late fifties, the Rambler scooped the sales. Naturally, the "big guns" followed suit, but, nevertheless, 400,000 Ramblers were sold in 1959, and in 1960 Chrysler was forced down into fourth place in the production table. (USA)

An updated version of the immortal Mk 6 Lotus—the first regular production Lotus—the Mk 7 of 1957 followed the same stark functional layout of the earlier cars, but adopted the frame of the larger 1.2-liter Mk 11 sports car. Normally fitted with the Ford 100E engine, a Super Seven was also available with Coventry Climax engine and disk brakes, the Ford proving the more successful. Here designer Colin Chapman poses with an Mk 7 on its introduction in 1957. (GB)

Following the same general lines as the Buick Special of 1955, this car was typical of the period. With Buick once again in third place in the production and sales race with Chevrolet and Ford, 1955 had been a good year. Unfortunately, quality control could not keep up with the pace, and both the 1957 and 1958 Buicks developed serious weaknesses in their braking systems, which necessitated a major engineering change. (USA)

Originally introduced in 1938 to fill the gap in the Ford program, by 1957 Mercury was offering this stylish convertible with a 5.1-liter V-8. Producing 255 bhp, this was augmented by the option of a de-tuned Lincoln unit. To avoid an overlap with the unfortunate Edsel range, 1958 and 1959 Mercuries became larger and more expensive, fielding a 6.3-liter V-8 in addition to the existing engine. With the Edsel's demise, Mercury could afford to come down a peg, and 1961 saw the introduction of their 2.4-liter Comet. (USA)

Posing here with members of the East Sussex Constabulary, the 2½-liter Riley Pathfinder was a remarkable car in that its 2,443-cc engine survived not only the rationalization of the Nuffield take-over of the old Riley Company in 1939 (it had been introduced as the 85-bhp "Big Four" in 1937), but also that of the B.M.C. merger in 1952, in postwar form developing first 90 and then 100 bhp. By 1954 the handsome fabric-topped Riley bodywork had been exchanged for Wolseley's 6/90 body well; 1957 saw the last of the old Riley 2½-liter engines, and in 1958 they were replaced by Austin's 2.6-liter, ohv six. (GB)

Heralding the re-entry of the nationalized Tatra company into private-car production after the lapse of three years, the 603 appeared in 1957 and reverted to the rear-engined principle that had dominated their products during the thirties. Once again, an air-cooled V-8 was employed—this time of 2,472 cc—and this continued in production until 1972, by which time the model was designated the T3-603 and boasted the refinements of twin carburetors, servo-assisted brakes, and power steering. (CS)

Performance was the watchword at Pontiac during the late fifties, and this 5,189-cc, ohv, V-8-engined Pontiac Star Chief was a fast car when introduced in 1956. When the model shown here appeared in 1957, capacity had been increased to 5,687 cc; it went up again to 6,063 cc in 1958, and, when Pontiac introduced their wide-track chassis in 1959, a 6.4-liter unit with output ranging up to 345 bhp was available. (USA)

After winning the Manufacturers' Championship with the improved Lancia/Ferraris he had inherited from Gianni Lancia in 1956, Enzo Ferrari embarked on the development of a new G.P. car with a V-6 engine of his own design. Designated the Dino, after his son who had just died, this new 2½-liter Ferrari was outstandingly successful, giving Mike Hawthorn (seen here at Goodwood in 1958) his 1958 World Championship and coming within a whisker of once again winning the Manufacturers' Championship for Ferrari. (I)

When Air Vice-Marshall ("Pathfinder") Bennett introduced his first Fairthorpe — an unprepossessing 650-cc minicar — in 1954, its chances of survival seemed slim, and no hint was given of the exciting and successful little sports car that was to emerge (and is still emerging) from the same stable. The Fairthorpe Electron Minor seen here, with Standard 10 engine/transmission and running gear in a conventional ladder chassis, was the cheaper running mate to the 1,098-cc, Coventry-Climax-engined Electron. The EM 3, fitted with a Triumph Spitfire engine, was still selling well nine years later and in 1972 was being offered with the triumph 1300 engine. (GB)

Probably the largest and most expensive brick the Ford Motor Company has ever dropped, the Edsel was the result of extensive market research that went wrong. By the time 250 million dollars had been spent in tooling up for a full-size car to fill an assumed market gap between Ford and Mercury, public taste had swung over to compacts, and after three seasons total sales barely achieved one-third of the planned annual production of 300,000 units. With a choice of two V-8s—a 5.9-liter and a 6.7-liter—it had its virtues, and, ironically, the Edsel is now becoming a "cult" in America. The distinctive grille—sometimes likened to a horse collar by unkind critics—set the car apart but did not help sales, and production ceased in 1960. (USA)

Developed from the smaller 3.4-liter Armstrong-Siddeley Star Sapphire introduced in 1953, this was the last of the Armstrong-Siddeley models and was sold in both sedan and limousine forms with a 4-liter engine. When the parent Hawker-Siddeley aircraft firm amalgamated with the Bristol Aircraft Company, the new combine decided to concentrate on its aviation interests, and, although an independent company was formed to build and sell Bristol's cars, the Armstrong-Siddeley—an admirable car with an enthusiastic following—found no takers and by the end of 1960 had disappeared from the Buyer's Guides. (GB)

The name Auto Union was resurrected in 1958 and applied to the 981-cc "1000" D.K.W. cars which continued in production until 1962. D.K.W's in all but name, the 1000s were a development of the earlier D.K.W. Sonderklasse model which had engines of only 896 cc, but employed the same principle of a front-mounted, 3-cylinder, two-stroke engine and fwd. (D)

Taken in 1959, this picture shows Stirling Moss on a bend during the Monaco Grand Prix in one of a long line of rear-engined cars. Developed from the earlier Cooper-Bristols, the Cooper-Climax initially used the 1½-liter Coventry-Climax engine for Formula II, and a car so-equipped was ready before the 1957 season commenced. Larger engines were later used of 2-, 2.2-, and finally 2½-liter capacity—the latter the 4-cylinder Climax unit. With the advent of the larger engines, the cars became heavier and more complicated, culminating with the 1960 G.P. car. By 1962, the V-8, 1½-liter Climax unit was being employed in the same rear-engined layout. (GB)

Introduced in prototype form as the Nash NX1 by American Motors in 1950, production Austin Metropolitans first appeared in 1954 as the result of a transatlantic deal with the British Motor Corporation whereby the cars were built in Austin's plant in England. In reality Nash Airflytes in miniature, there were some who said that the transition was an unhappy one, but, nevertheless, little change was made in the styling of either the convertible or coupe models during their seven-year life span. Powered by the Austin 1,200-cc, A 40 engine, they later inherited the A50 Cambridge unit. (GB)

Normally offered as a hardtop coupe, the XK 140 version of the original Jaguar XK 120 theme was extended in 1959, and the XK 150 model shown here was available with 2.4-, 3.4-, and 3.8-liter engines (the latter producing up to 250 bhp) and disk brakes all around. (GB)

Initially establishing a reputation with trailers and commercial vehicles, D.A.F. (Van Doorne's Automobielfabrik) introduced their first private car in 1958, and production began in 1959. Despite their angular lines and eccentric specification, they rapidly gained acceptance—particularly with women drivers and those for whom conventional gear-changing held unknown terrors. Publicized as "the cheapest automatic," the D.A.F. employed a unique vee-belt drive with centrifugal clutch and limited-slip differential and was powered as fast by a 600-cc, front-mounted, ohv, air-cooled, flat-twin engine. (NL)

In 1953 the Ardea was replaced by the Appia (a scaled-down Aurelia) with a 1,100-cc, 38-bhp engine. This small unit with 9½-inch block and two-bearing crankshaft could nevertheless propel the Appia at speeds in excess of 75 mph, but the car was hopelessly uncompetitive pricewise with the products of several other manufacturers in the 1,100-cc bracket. It was replaced in 1964 by the Fulvia, based on the Fessia-designed Flavia. (I)

Introduced in 1959, the Triumph Herald reverted to a separate chassis and was the first British small sedan to be equipped with all-around independent suspension. Initially powered by the old 948-cc Standard "ten" unit, it was fitted with a larger 1,147-cc engine after the Leyland take-over in 1961, at which time optional front disk brakes were also offered, while in 1962 a 1.6-liter, 6-cylinder "Vitesse" model was available. The Herald range was eventually replaced in 1971 by the Toledo two-door sedan. (GB)

Re-styled for the last time in 1959, the Standard Vanguard model shown here represented the final development of the old 2,088-cc "four" Vanguard unit. By the time this model appeared, wearing Triumph's "world" badge, the basic formula was somewhat out of date, although still popular in Australia, where the name survived a little longer than in England. The company joined the ranks of "lost causes" in 1963, partly because by that time the word "standard" had come to mean something less than best quality in our debased advertising language. (GB)

Entering Formula II racing in 1957 with this very light, single-seat, Climax-powered Lotus, Colin Chapman concentrated initially on weight reduction. Although relatively successful, his cars never quite equaled the performance of their greatest rivals, the rear-engined Cooper-Climaxes. Throughout 1957, 1958, and 1959 he persisted with a front-engined layout, but, although this facilitated better road-holding, the cars suffered from poor reliability. For the 1960 season, Chapman—probably on the principle that if you can't beat 'em, join 'em—introduced the obviously Cooper-inspired rear-engined layout which resulted in a highly effective car, almost unbeatable in its class. (GB)

After leaving the B.R.M. project in 1947, G. A. (Tony) Vandervell, the wealthy owner of the VP Bearing factory, formed his own racing team, fielding various Ferraris. Deriving its name from a combination of his own name and his "Thinwall" bearings, the first Vanwall appeared in 2-liter, 4-cylinder form and was built in the racing department of Norton motorcycles. Enlarged to 2½ liters to conform with the Formula I rules, the cars were eventually completely redesigned and, with new chassis suspension and bodywork, embarked on a successful 1957 season which was to culminate in 1958 with the realization of Vandervell's ambition—winning the coveted Manufacturer's Championship. The pictures show Tony Brooks in a 1958 car. (GB)

After the Volkswagen works were returned to German administration in 1949, only the sedan version of the Beetle was made by the company, but alternative bodywork was offered by a variety of coachbuilders. Karmann, an old-established German company, offered a four-seater convertible, and eventually the Karmann-Ghia coupe (seen here) and convertible two-seat versions that evolved became generally available and adopted as factory alternatives. Employing the well-known and tried VW formula of rear-mounted, air-cooled, 1,131-cc (1,192 cc from 1954), horizontally opposed engines, the Karmann-Ghia proved popular, and updated versions were still being offered in 1973. (D)

Designed by the Italian Piaggio aircraft company, and bearing the same name as their successful scooter, the Vespa was built in France by A.C.M.A. Enjoying some currency in the economy-conscious days following the Suez crisis, it boasted unitary construction and a rear-mounted, air-cooled, vertical-twin two-stroke. It was ousted by the BMC Mini which made its appearance in 1960, and the last Vespas were made in 1961. (F)

Derived from the Aurelia-based Florida exhibited by Pininfarina at Turin in 1955, the standard six light sedan Lancia Flaminia was introduced in 1956 and represented a complete reconsideration at Lancia following the loss of control by the Lancia family. Still a V-6 of 2½ liters with transmission housed in the hypoid rear axle, the car employed not only unitary construction but also coil and wishbone ifs. Output was raised from 98 bhp to 126 bhp with the introduction of the short chassis G.T. in 1958, which year also heralded disk brakes on all Flaminias. Shown is the Flaminia sports coupe. (I)

Equally at home outside the front door of a Chelsea flat or at London's Buckingham Palace for a Garden Party, the ubiquitous Mini, designed by Alec Issigonis and introduced in 1960, revolutionized small-car motoring for millions. Ousting the many nasty "bubble" and post-Suez economy cars that abounded in the late fifties in much the same way as its illustrious namesake the Austin Seven (also shown here) had killed the cycle car, the car bristled with innovation. Its 848-cc, ohv, 4-cylinder engine was mounted transversely and drove the front wheels. The sump contained not only the oil, but the four-speed transmission, and all four wheels had independent suspension by rubber in torsion. Not only did it pave the way for the larger 1100, 1300, and 1800 models with similar layout, but distinguished itself in numerous competitions, frequently beating the "heavy brigade." The Morris and Austin versions, differing in detail only, lost their separate identity, and the car survives as a "make" in its own right as the "Mini." (GB)

Coinciding with the introduction of the V-8, 623-cc, ohv engine in 1960 and the discontinuation of the old "six," this attractive Park Ward convertible coupe on the Bentley S 2 Continental chassis graced the Bentley stand at the 1960 Motor Show. Despite its bulk, the use of lightweight steel and alloy in the body construction ensured brisk and comfortable performance when allied to the new V-8, the output of which was stated by the makers to be "adequate." (GB)

Moving to a new factory in 1959, Colin Chapman formed Lotus Cars Limited, and one of the first fruits of the upheaval was the Lotus Elite. A coupe built almost entirely of plastic materials, with a 1,216-cc Coventry-Climax engine, the car employed coil and wishbone ifs, suspension at the rear being taken care of by a unique system whereby the coil-spring struts protruded into the passenger compartment. This latter innovation caused some headaches (literally) through the hammering of the struts on their stops. Despite an early reputation for unreliability, almost a thousand were built before production ceased in 1963. The Elite is seen here being challenged by an M.G.A. (GB)

Looking for all the world like the purposeful cockpit of its World War II namesake—the ME 109 fighter—the Messerschmidt Tiger, produced between 1958 and 1960, was one of the better minicars. A four-wheeler, it was powered by a 500-cc Sachs engine and was developed from the earlier three-wheelers built to Fend design from 1953. The three-wheelers, using 175-cc and 200-cc engines (the latter introduced in 1955), continued to be made in one of the aircraft company's works until 1962. (D)

A Park Ward limousine on the Rolls-Royce Phantom V chassis. With a wheelbase of 12 feet, passengers had plenty of leg room even when the two forward-facing occasional seats were unfolded behind the front seat. It shared its newly introduced 6¼-liter, V-8 engine with the Silver Cloud sedan and remained in production until it was replaced in 1970 by the Phantom VI after a ten-year production run. (GB)

Following the mechanical design as the model F9 previously built at the old Audi works at Zwickau and later at Eisenach, the Wartburg (reviving a name last-used in 1904 for the products of Fahrzeugfabrik Eisenach) was basically a prewar D.K.W. of a type that never went into production. After the partition of Germany in 1945, East Germany nationalized its motor industry and revived the design. With front-mounted, 889-cc (later 991-cc), 3-cylinder, two-stroke engine and front wheel drive, the format was familiar, albeit cloaked in the not-unattractive Wartburg bodywork. The Wartburg Sport model illustrated here used the same engine with the standard bhp increased from 40 to 50. (D)

Retaining the Bentley-designed, twin-cam engine (by now with alloy head), the 3.7-liter Aston Martin DB4 was probably one of the fastest sports cars of its day. The G.T. version developed 302 bhp, and in coupe form 240 bhp was sufficient to propel it from 0–100 mph in 26 seconds. Here, British driver Innes Ireland conducts the car through Goodwood's chicane in 1961. (GB)

Carl Borgward was perhaps the last of the original breed of car manufacturers, and he clung tenaciously to absolute ownership and control of his company until the end in 1961, at which time this 2.3-liter Grosse limousine had been in production for only a few months. It housed a 6-cylinder engine with an output of 100 bhp, and customers had the option of air suspension; like the earlier Borgward Isabella model, it was a good, stable car. By 1961, Borgward's company—always short of capital—was, however, unable to survive in the highly competitive passenger-car market. (D)

The Monte Carlo Rally has attracted some unusual entries in the years since it was first held by the Sporting Club of Monaco in 1911, but probably none so bizarre as this Austin taxi entered for the 1961 event. An almost standard FX3 model, differing little outwardly from the first models introduced in 1948, it had already been superseded by the FX4 at the time of the Rally, in which it was entered by the British Broadcasting Corporation and driven by Peter Dimmock and Tony Brooks. Predictably, its performance was no match for the prevailing conditions. (GB)

Although Buicks of the late **Fifties** made their mark with flamboyant delta tails and extravagant fins, this 1961 Invicta displays quite restrained clean lines, although the distinctive Buick "portholes" are retained. Despite the swing away from larger cars to compacts (catered to by Buick's "Special"), the Invicta sported a 6,570-cc, V-8 engine which it shared with the Electra 225 series. (USA)

The end of the road came for De Soto with this 1961 model, introduced late in 1960. The Chrysler Corporation had managed to unload only about 19,000 in the latter year, which was well below the break-even point, and the Buick-inspired fins did nothing to bolster sagging sales. Available with 5,907-cc V-8 or 3,686-cc, "Slant Six" engines, very few '61 models reached the public before production ceased. (USA)

By 1961, when this trio of Formula 1 Coopers (driven by Brabham, McLaren, and Surtees) were built, the company's highly successful era in the late Fifties—culminating in the World Championship in 1959— was past its peak, and a period of slow decline was setting in. Having set the pattern with their rear-engined designs, Coopers were placed in the invidious position of watching their competitors adopt their principles, catch up, and eventually overtake them. With the introduction of a new 1½-liter formula in 1961 which precluded the continued use of the 2,462-cc, Coventry-Climax engine, Coopers found themselves without a suitable engine with which to compete with Ferrari, and the V-8 1½-liter introduced in 1962 for Formula 1 came too late for them. (GB)

It might be thought that the diminutive 105E Anglia introduced by Ford of Dagenham in 1960 was an unlikely contender for laurels in the grueling conditions of winter rallies. However, Lloyd Howell and Bill Silvera brought their Anglia home first-equal in the 1961 Canadian Winter Rally, out of 190 starters, and in the '61 Monte Carlo Sutcliffe and Crabtree they put up a creditable performance. Despite its unconventional rear sloping window, the 997-cc sedan—the first Anglia to sport a four-speed transmission—proved to be a best seller. (GB)

Not the best-looking Renault to come from Billancourt, the Fregate, first introduced in 1951, nevertheless enjoyed a production run of over a decade. Eschewing the more successful rear-engined layout of its smaller sister, the Dauphine, the Fregate initially appeared with a 1,996-cc engine that, by the time this 1961 example arrived, had been enlarged to 2,141 cc. It was, however, the last of the line, its shape already dated. (F)

One of the advantages of being the son of Woolworth heiress Barbara Hutton was illustrated by Lance Reventlow when he began building Scarab sports cars in 1957. A Formula 1 G.P. car, begun in 1959, failed to make its mark in the 1960 season, despite considerable development expenditure, and the 3-liter example shown, constructed for the 1961 Inter-Continental formula, was another expensive mistake. No more success attended a Buick-engined, rear-engined car, built in 1962, and thereafter Reventlow closed his factory, and no more Scarabs were made. (USA)

The F85 Cutlass sports coupe illustrated here represented a complete breakaway from the traditional Oldsmobile image. Featuring an aluminum V-8 Rockette engine of only 3,525 cc, it could, nevertheless, push out 185 bhp and represented Oldsmobile's entry into the low-price field in 1961, at a time when the "compact" fever was at its height. The standard F85 compact used the same engine, but with a lower output of 155 bhp, and the V-8 unit was replaced by GM's V-6 unit (as shared by Buick) in 1964. (USA)

Derived from the 1,300-cc Giuletta, the Alfa Romeo Sprint first appeared in 2600 form in 1962. With a 6-cylinder, twin-camshaft, aluminum engine of 2,584 cc, it was also available as the Berlina and Spider. With this model Alfa introduced disk brakes as standard, and, with a five-speed transmission, the car offered luxury coupled with superlative performance. (I)

Introduced in 1962, the B.M.W. 3200 CS represented the final development of the Munich-built range of prestige cars which commenced with the 501 in 1952. Its V-8 engine of 3,168 cc produced 160 bhp; the car was available only in two-door coupe form, but by 1962 B.M.W. had decided to re-enter the medium-price market and for some years concentrated mainly on their 4-cylinder 1500. (D)

By 1962 the successful rear-engined formula pioneered by Cooper had been almost universally accepted for G.P. cars, and this is graphically illustrated by the similarity of the cars shown on the grid of the French Grand Prix in July 1962. Left to right, they are: Jim Clark in a Lotus, Graham Hill in a B.R.M., and Bruce McLaren in a Cooper. The race was won by Dan Gurney driving a Porsche (No. 30 in the third row).

Making its first appearance at Zandvoort in May 1962, the Lotus Mk25 followed the introduction of the Mk24 very rapidly and created a sensation. Representing Lotus' first essay in monocoque construction, the "25" featured a stressed skin and a rear-mounted, 1½-liter, Coventry-Climax, V-8 engine. If imitation is the sincerest form of flattery, then Colin Chapman must have felt flattered, because the "25" set a pattern that was copied by virtually all contenders in Formula 1 racing. Jim Clark (seen here) drove the car successfully throughout its first season—although Graham Hill in a BRM won the Dutch Grand Prix at Zandvoort—and both he and Lotus finished 1962 runners-up in their respective Championships. (GB)

Employing the successful Mundy/Ansdale–designed, twin-ohc version of the Ford Classic 116E engine first-used in the rear-engined Mark 25 racing car, the Mark 26 Lotus Elan was introduced in 1962. A front-engined car, it had a backbone chassis of box-section sheet steel, coupled with the Chapman rear-strut suspension which had been well tried on the racing models. The body-work featured vacuum-operated, retractable headlights (echoing the Buehrig-designed Cord 812), and the Elan earned itself an enviable reputation for road-holding; standard models offered a 105-bhp, 1,558-cc engine. (GB)

Basically a badge-engineered version of the Wolseley 1500, the 1962 Riley One-point-five (rear left) shown here racing with a Sunbeam Rapier and 3.8-liter Jaguar was, however, capable of considerable development. Little larger than BMC's Morris Minor, its 1,489-cc, 4-cylinder engine gave it a good power-to-weight ratio, and this, coupled with its close-ratio, four-speed transmission, prompted some owners to fit high-lift cam conversions for competition. In this form the car was able to acquit itself quite well, but even in standard trim it was a rapid compact sedan. (GB)

Introduced at the 1962 Olympia Motor Show, Reliant's Sabre represented a complete departure for the Tamworth Company, which had previously concentrated on economy three-wheelers, a field in which they still excel. Developed in conjunction with Sabra of Haifa, it was also marketed in Israel as the Sabra, shown here. Powered by a Ford Consul engine of 1,703 cc, it sported front-disk brakes and coil-spring ifs. Its somewhat unappealing fiberglass styling was later replaced by the handsome Scimitar on the British versions, and the model evolved into the Cortina-powered Sussita in Israel. (GB)

In the early Sixties it was compacts all the way, and Pontiac got in on the act with their Tempest in 1961. It sold 116,000, and the successful formula was continued for this 1962 model. Following the normal GM recipe of unitary construction, the car was unusual in having its three-speed transmission located in the back axle, power being provided by a 3.2-liter, ohv, 4-cylinder engine. With a wheelbase of 9 feet, 4 inches, its overall length was over 2 feet less than that of its larger sisters, the Bonneville and Star Chief, but this was apparently what the public wanted, and Pontiac moved into third place in the U.S. sales race. (USA)

Although it suffered from a slant-eyed squint, the Triumph Vitesse was nevertheless able to show a clean pair of heels to most other traffic when the need arose. Derived from the Alick Dick-designed Herald and introduced in 1962, it squeezed a 1,596-cc, 6-cylinder engine into the space previously occupied by the Herald's 1,147-cc unit. Later versions utilized the 2-liter engine introduced in the 1964 Triumph 2000 sedan, and in this 90-bhp form, the Vitesse found favor with those who wished to combine sporting proclivities with sedan-car comfort. (GB)

Probably no other driver did more to popularize the BMC Mini in competition than Paddy Hopkirk, seen here driving his Mini-Cooper "S" in the 1963 R.A.C. Rally. Originally introduced in 1961, the Mini-Cooper employed a standard Mini engine bored out to 997 cc and fitted with twin S.U. carburetors, but during its career this was successively enlarged to 1,293 cc in final form. In the hands of Makinen, Aaltonen, and Hopkirk, these cars notched-up numerous rally successes, culminating in the European Rally Championship. (GB)

This 1963 Ferrari 250 Pininfarina coupe was one of a line of 12-cylinder, luxury G.T. cars introduced in 1951 by the Modena-based company, which was to continue until the end of the sixties, when flat sixes and flat twelves were adopted. A relatively small engine of 2,953 cc powered the car which, with an overall length of 15 feet, 5 inches, was of reasonably modest proportions, but few could afford the price required for one in England. (I)

Repeating his success in the 1962 Spa-Sofia-Liege Rally in a Mercedes-Benz 220SE, German rally driver Eugen Bohringer is seen here with teammate Kaiser driving to victory in the 1963 event in a 230SL. First shown in England at the October 1963 Olympia Motor Show and housing a 6-cylinder engine of 2,306 cc, the 230SL won this, its first event, leading the 22 finishers from a field of 129 starters in this grueling marathon—an impressive debut. (D)

Developed from the Mercedes-Benz 220 introduced in 1951, the 220SE was becoming somewhat dated by 1963. Nevertheless, its 2,195-cc, 6-cylinder engine—basically the same unit used in the original model—was still capable of acquitting itself well in competition, although the car was primarily intended as a luxury sedan. Following Bohringer's success in the 1962 Spa-Sofia-Liege Rally, Ewy Rosqvist is seen here nearing the end of the 1963 Monte Carlo Rally in which she won the Coupe des Dames. (D)

A badge-engineered BMC "110," the 1963 M.G. shown here continued BMC's somewhat unfortunate policy of sticking the M.G. octagon on smaller sedans in the company's range. Sharing its 1,098-cc 4-cylinder with Austin and Morris, it followed the transverse engine layout and front-wheel drive pioneered in the Issigonis-designed Mini, later inheriting the 1,275-cc "1300" unit. The model was dropped after the formation of British Leyland. (GB)

Four generations of Rover turbines are shown in this unusual photograph: JET 1, the P4-based car built in 1950; the T3 exhibited at the 1956 Earl's Court Motor Show; the T4 of 1962, a 140-bhp sedan with front-wheel drive which, although it did not achieve series production, provided the prototype for the later and successful "2000" introduced in 1964, with which its shape is readily identifiable; and the Rover-B.R.M. The latter car is driven here by Graham Hill who, together with Richie Ginther, completed the 1963 Le Mans race at an average speed of 107.84 mph, winning a special award for the first gas-turbine car to complete the 24-hour event. (GB)

Illustrated here is a Type 93 Saab, being driven in characteristic fashion by champion rally driver Eric Carlsson in the 1963 Rally of the Midnight Sun, in which he came in second. Then staunch adherents of the fwd, two-stroke formula pioneered by D.K.W., Saabs of this period employed a 3-cylinder, 748-cc engine producing 38 bhp and in Carlsson's hands dominated Rally events in the early Sixties. (S)

Almost a last-ditch attempt to bolster sagging sales and cash in on the compact market, Studebaker's Lark was introduced for the 1959 season, and initially employed a 2,779-cc, side-valve, 6-cylinder unit derived from the old Champion range. It was also available with a 4,244-cc, V-8 engine as the Lark Cruiser. By the time this 1963 Lark Daytona was introduced, the "six" had acquired overhead valves, but, with only some 68,000 cars sold, even the revolutionary fiberglass Avanti could not avert the inevitable, and the last Studebaker left the (Canadian) plant some three years later. (USA)

The result of a marriage of ideas by American Carol Shelby and the old-established Thames Ditton firm of A.C., the Cobra was based on the Tojeiro-designed, tubular-framed Ace, which had already been in production nine years with a variety of engines. Shelby's suggestion that A.C. should drop a 330-bhp, 4.7-liter, Ford V-8 unit into this chassis produced a potent contender for the 1964 Le Mans, in which the Cobra finished fourth. It also paved the way for a line of Ford-engined cars, marketed by Shelby in America as Cobras until 1968, and culminating in the 7-liter A.C. 428. (GB)

An independent company set up by M. Redele in 1955, Alpine's development has always been closely allied to that of Renault, upon whose components they have been heavily dependent, and since 1969, when Renault withdrew from competition, they have become more and more the unofficial competition arm of Renault. By 1964, when this Berlinette was produced, 87 bhp was available from the 1,108-cc, 4-cylinder engine in Gordini-tuned form, and the little cars were capable of well over 100 mph, a formula which helped them to a class win in the 1964 Tour de France. (F)

Representing the final development of the "big" Austin-Healey, the 3000 Mk III shown here employed a 2,912-cc version of the Austin Westminster engine. 3,000s performed consistently well in international rallies, and, in the year this photograph was taken, won the G.T. class in the 1964 Tulip Rally, among others. The model was discontinued in 1968, and the Austin-Healey name was dropped from the British Leyland range when Donald Healey joined the Jensen organization to produce the Jensen-Healey. (GB)

Built by the Advanced Vehicle Division of the British Ford company, and partly based on Eric Broadley's Lola G.T., the Ford GT 40, put together by Roy Lunn's design team at Slough, represented the British end of a determined effort by Henry Ford II to commit his company—on both sides of the Atlantic—to a racing program. In America this took the form of assaults on the Indianapolis 500, but for Europe Ford had his eye on the Le Mans 24 Hour Race. The first prototype—a semi-monocoque construction mid-engined coupe, was completed in April 1964, and, after initial problems of rear-end instability, a single car was entered in the 1,000-km (620-mile) Race at Nurburgring, driven by Hill and McLaren. Although it retired with suspension failure, the car's potential was amply demonstrated, and a team of three cars was entered for the 1964 Le Mans. All three retired this time—two with transmission failure, and the Attwood/Schlesser car catching fire—but not before estimated speeds of almost 200 mph had been attained. (GB)

In reality a D.K.W., the 1964 Auto Union 1000 shown here was the only model in the D.K.W. range to adopt the old prewar corporate name. Despite fins and other attempts to update it, the car followed the time-honored D.K.W. formula of front-wheel drive and two-stroke engine—in this case a 3-cylinder unit of 981 cc. The model was dropped at the end of 1964, although a cross-country version with the same engine was available in 1965, and it formed the basis of the Rural 1000 built by Auto Union (Brazil) the same year. (D)

Whatever design exercise Virgil Exner undertakes, the end product is bound to be unusual, and frequently bizarre. No exception is this Mercer-Cobra exhibited at the 1964 Paris Motor Show. Bodied by Sibona-Bassano of Turin to Exner's design, the car employed a modified A.C. Cobra chassis and Ford engine and appeared on the French Ford stand. Nicknamed the "Copper Car," it was apparently designed for the express purpose of demonstrating the colorful warmth and beauty of copper and brass in car design, and it boasted a copper radiator; brass-trimmed, swiveling headlights; brass wheel embellishments; and a copper exhaust cover. (USA)

Eric Broadley's Lola Company adopted monocoque construction for its Formula 1 cars in 1965 and continued its close association with Ford (which had resulted in Broadley's work on the Ford G.T. 40 cars), employing Ford V-8 engines, mounted behind the driver. 1966 was a good year for them, Graham Hill (shown here) winning the fiftieth Indianapolis "500" race in the V-8–engined Type 90, with very little difficulty, and no real opposition from the Offenhauser-engined contingent. Stewart managed sixth place in another Lola-Ford. (GB)

Voted the "Car of the Year" when it was introduced in 1965, the Renault 16 bristled with innovations. A full four-door sedan, but with large rear-opening door on shooting brake lines, it featured front-wheel drive and a 1,470-cc, 4-cylinder engine, with removable wet liners and overhead valves. Like other Renaults, the 16 continued the practice of sealing the coolant, pioneered by the firm. Suspension was independent all around, and front disk brakes were fitted as standard. (F)

Specially designed to give the impression of more motor car for the money, this 1965 Cadillac Calais coupe employed a massive 7,030-cc, V-8 engine (later enlarged to 7,736 cc) mounted in General Motors "perimeter"-type chassis and had an overall length of almost 19 feet. For the man who had everything, this model (and the larger Fleetwood and Eldorado) was available with such refinements as air conditioning, variable power-steering, and a steering wheel with six positions. (USA)

The 1965 Amphicar shown here represented the culmination of a series of amphibious vehicle designs by Hans Trippel, whose first effort had appeared as early as 1932. Powered by the 1,147-cc, 4-cylinder, Triumph Herald engine, the car had rear-wheel drive, with a special gear driving two propellers at the rear of the vehicle when in water. The car was not fitted with a rudder as such, steering being accomplished while water-borne by normal turning of the front road-wheels. The viability of the design was amply demonstrated by a cross-channel trip in 1962. (D)

Introduced at the 1965 Motor Show, the Rolls-Royce Silver Shadow represented an entirely new concept from Crewe. Lower lines combined with the traditional "Greek temple" radiator and unitary construction to disguise the vintage of the engine (the V-8, 6,230-cc unit introduced for the 1960 season). Although the larger separate-chassis Phantoms were continued, the bulk of production activity was concentrated on the Shadow and its Bentley equivalent, and there can be no doubt that the popularity of the model was largely responsible for the survival of the motor-car division when the parent aviation company went bankrupt in 1971. (GB)

Better known for their commercial vehicles, Isuzu began postwar series production of motor cars with a license to build the Rootes Hillman Minx. In 1961 the Minx gave way to a wholly Japanese design—the 2-liter Bellel—and in 1966 this was supplemented by the Bellett 1500, powered by a 1,491-cc, 4-cylinder engine. In G.T. form, and fitted with twin carburetors, the Bellett was imported into England, primarily, so it is said, to challenge the supremacy of the Ford Lotus-Cortina in sedan-car racing. Producing 90 bhp, the car was capable of a genuine 100 mph, while the "cooking" version produced 75 bhp, but, while road-holding was enhanced by independent suspension, front and rear, general finish, and the transmission in particular, came in for criticism. (J)

The late fifties and early sixties saw the emergence of a new luxury G.T. class—the American-engined, European-produced sedans. This Iso Grifo, a two-plus-two-seater coupe version of the Rivolta sedan, was powered by a 5,359-cc, V-8, Chevrolet engine mounted in a platform-type chassis of Bizzarini design. By the time this 1966 Grifo was produced, the engine was capable of propelling the car at up to 142 mph. Iso, who began car production in the fifties with the miniature Isetta "bubble car," had come a long way. (I)

After the war, Oldsmobile tended to become the proving ground for G.M.'s technical innovations, and thus the division spawned a number of advanced features, some of which were taken up throughout the group. The front-wheel-drive Toronado introduced in 1966 caused something of a sensation. A six-passenger, hardtop coupe with fwd allowing a flat floor, it was spacious and, fitted with the 6,965-cc Toronado V-8 engine driving through Turbo Hydramatic transmission, it was fast. The model was still in production seven years later, although after a spree with 7½-liter engines producing 360 bhp plus in 1968, power plants became more modest in size, and by 1972 output was down to 265 bhp. (USA)

At first closely following the styling of the prewar and highly successful B.M.W. 328, Bristol styling went through a slab-sided period of the doldrums during the middle sixties, and this Type 408 of early 1966 was typical. Bristol had switched to American engines in 1962, and the 408 used a 5,130-cc, ohv, Chrysler V-8 (enlarged to 5,211 cc on the 409 introduced later in 1966) and adopted Torque-flight automatic transmission. (GB)

Owing little to its predecessor, the wartime "vehicle general purpose," this 1966 Kaiser Jeep Wagoneer was nevertheless a rugged multi-purpose vehicle. The station wagon shown here was powered by a 5,359-cc, V-8, Rambler engine (a case of one independent supporting another), anticipating the merger with American Motors in 1970, but was also available in two- or four-wheel drive or with 2,199-cc, 4-cylinder engines or 3,802-cc sixes. The range was further complicated by the Jeep Universal utility, for which a choice of Perkins diesel, Buick V-6, or the old 2.2-liter Jeep unit existed. (USA)

Two years after the Audi name was revived by the Auto Union combine at Ingolstadt in 1965, the original offering of a 1,696-cc, medium-sized sedan had been augmented by the "Variant" station wagon shown here. Employing the same inclined 4-cylinder engine, the car followed the front-wheel-drive formula of its predecessor, the D.K.W., but there the similarity ended. The fwd layout permitted a beam back axle, and disk brakes on the front wheels and ifs had been standardized on the first 1965 offerings. (D)

Continuing its policy of applying successful innovations to other group products, G.M. gave the 1967 Cadillac Fleetwood Eldorado front-wheel drive on the lines of that which had been so successfully developed in the Toronado in G.M.'s "guinea pig" division—Oldsmobile. The distinctive coffin nose which first appeared in the forties was retained, and the car boasted independent front suspension by torsion bar, disk-braking on the front wheels only, and self-leveling suspension. Power was supplied by a hefty 7,030-cc V-8, enlarged to 7,736 cc in 1968, and a massive 8.2 liters by 1970. (USA)

The larger of the two red Wildcats shown here was Buick's contribution to the sporting idiom for 1967. Wielding a hefty 7,048-cc, V-8 engine—the largest in the Buick range—the Wildcat followed a more dashing trend introduced the previous year but, with an overall length of 18 feet, 4 inches, was still a large car. Engine sizes were up to 7½ liters by 1970, but thereafter, as with most manufacturers, pollution and safety factors (Ralph Nader, et. al.) dictated that outputs should be reduced to more manageable proportions. (USA)

Problems of pollution and diminishing world-energy supplies which were highlighted during the Arab-Israeli war have been occupying the minds of most of the larger manufacturers for several years, and this Ford "Comuta" Electric first saw the light of day in 1967. So-called because it was intended for city use, this tiny two-seater (plus child/luggage) was just over 6 feet long and only 4 feet high, and Ford persevered with it until 1971, when the project was abandoned. (GB)

Under the enthusiastic and capable management of Kjell Qvale the Jensen concern has grown from strength to strength and the Interceptor Mk III introduced in 1967 represents the better features of Anglo-American cooperation in car construction. Returning to steel bodywork, after using fiberglass, the Mk III was designed by Vignale and used a husky 6,276-cc, Chrysler V-8 engine producing 330 bhp. Also available was the revolutionary FF (Ferguson Formula) which used the same body and engine but which also employed four-wheel drive and anti-lock braking. The FF was discontinued in 1972, but Interceptors are still selling steadily. (GB)

Introduced in 1963 as a sports derivative of the Triumph Herald, the Spitfire followed Herald practice with its forward-opening hood which encompassed the front wings, headlights, and grille, affording excellent accessibility. The Mark III shown here was fitted with an enlarged 1,296-cc version of the 4-cylinder, 1,147-cc Herald engine and appealed to younger enthusiasts who could not afford the more sophisticated 2½-liter TR5. (GB)

Following a period after the war when they built Austin A40s and A50s under license, the giant Japanese Nissan concern introduced the first Cedric model in 1960. By 1967 this had evolved into the Cedric Special Six shown here, fitted with a 1,998-cc, 6-cylinder engine, although a smaller version with a 1,982-cc, 95-bhp, 4-cylinder, ohv unit was also available. (J)

Intended primarily as a utility cross-country vehicle, this 1967 4 × 4 version of B.M.C.'s Mini, called the Moke, was a spartan development of the Issigonis theme. Its rugged simplicity and ease of maintenance quickly endeared it to a wider public, and examples could be seen competing in Autocross events, in the hands of the "dune-buggy" set, and, painted in dazzling hues, spreading the word of "flower power." (GB)

Based on the Nuova 500 introduced in 1957, the Fiat Giardiniera station wagon shown here in 1968 provided real miniature motoring, but with a surprising amount of space. Powered by an overhead-valve, twin-cylinder, air-cooled engine, the station wagon engine was mounted horizontally under the floor at the rear to provide for a large, single rear-opening door. Producing 22 bhp, the 499-cc (originally 479-cc) unit was also used in the Bianchina, which had heralded Bianchi's postwar return to private-car manufacture. (I)

This was the first year that no American Motors product bore the Rambler name. The AMX introduced in 1968 utilized the same 290-cu in, V-8 engine as the larger Javelin and was a two-seater sports coupe with bucket seats and dual exhaust system. Intended to compete with the Chevrolet Camaro and Ford's Mustang, the Javelin and the AMX were introduced during a somewhat rocky period in the company's fortunes, and sales between 1967 and 1969 continued to fall. The AMX was finally discontinued in 1971. (USA)

Variations on a theme; Volkswagen's Beetle has changed little in outward appearance since Porsche produced the first prototypes at Stuttgart in 1936, and the Karmann Ghia derivatives also shown are virtually identical to those first introduced in the early fifties. The VW has, however, been constantly improved technically and by 1973 was offering a "1600" version of the same theme. (D)

Representing remarkable value in the United Kingdom in 1968, this 2.4-liter Jaguar 240 still looked good, notwithstanding the fact that the design was by then thirteen years old. Unveiled at Earls Court in the autumn of 1955, the first 2.4 heralded a new era for Jaguar, and, although the model was now nearing the end of its life, over 200,000 had by then found appreciative owners. (GB)

Another ageless Jaguar design, the immortal "E" type originally derived from the "C"- and "D"-type racing cars is shown here in 2 plus 2 Series Two guise in 1969, employing the 4.2-liter version of the famous overhead twin-cam engine. Customers for the 2 plus 2 also had the option of automatic transmission—an innovation missing from Jaguar's sporting range since the demise of the XK 150 in 1960. (GB)

Employing the 3,995-cc, 6-cylinder engine first introduced on the DB5 in 1964, this Aston Martin DB6 Mark II was announced late in 1969 for the 1970 season. Featuring a five-speed transmission and power steering, this model also gave customers the option of fuel injection. The 6-cylinder, twin-ohc engine was, however, destined to be replaced by a 5.4-liter V-8 of Aston Martin design derived from a racing engine intended for Lola. First announced in 1966, this eventually materialized in 1972, when Aston Martin was sold by the David Brown Group and the 6-cylinder engines were finally dropped. (GB)

Like Ford, General Motors also dabbled continuously with pollution and economy problems, and this lineup of experimental vehicles shows that they were keeping an open mind about the solution. Designed to provide short-range personal transport, their top speed was limited—in the range of 30–45 mph—and it was agreed that special roads would be needed to accommodate them, since it would not be safe to mix them with conventional traffic. Left to right are: the 511 gasoline-engined three-wheeler, the 512 gasoline-electric, the 512 electric, and the 512 gasoline-engined four-wheeler, all of which could park simultaneously in a space little larger than that required for a conventional car. (USA)

Based on the SX250 G.T. coupe designed by the David Ogle organization, the Reliant Scimitar was a far cry from the Sabre that had heralded Reliant's entry into sports-car production in 1962. Powered by the 2,553-cc Ford Zephyr 6-cylinder engine, the car featured fiber-glass bodywork, and in 1969 the coupe model was supplemented by a G.T. station wagon version (shown here). Demand was such that after 1970 Reliant concentrated on the latter model and the coupe was discontinued. (GB)

The C III research-and-development car announced by Mercedes-Benz in 1969 represented a most promising step in the saga of the Wankel engine. Employing a three-chamber version of the rotary unit, with a displacement of 36.6 cu in, the C III was comparable with a normal 3.6-liter engine. Mounted amidships and fed by means of direct injection via a mechanical 3-plunger pump, the unconventional power plant was capable of 330 bhp at 7,000 rpm and drove the vehicle from 0 to 62 mph in 5 seconds, with a maximum speed of 162 mph. Bodywork of fiberglass-reinforced synthetic material was bonded and riveted to a frame floor. By 1970 it had acquired a four-chamber engine producing 350 bhp and 190 mph, but a production car had not been offered by 1974. (D)

NOW

The Seventies

Already the products of the Seventies show an awareness of the changing needs—automobile manufacturers, headed by those in the United States, have conformed with most antipollution controls, and with speed and other safety measures that have become necessary with increasingly powerful vehicles and with increased numbers of cars on the roads. Design and construction bend toward safety today as never before (only ten years ago, whoever thought of putting the baby in a safety seat at the back of a car?), and antipollution measures have been taken by oil companies and automotive design engineers in response to new legal requirements, some of which are so stringent that some exhaust emissions are said to be cleaner than the air taken into the engine.

Other advances, more on the positive engineering side, have been made—the rotary engine, long tested in Germany and Japan, has overcome its initial sealing troubles, and, tried and tested in the NSU Sports Prinz and then put into the Ro 80 from the same company, now captures attention with its smooth performance.

Since the early Fifties, engine life has doubled, as lubricants and metals have been subjected to intense scrutiny and development. Two-liter "family" engines in many small European automobiles can develop up to 100 bhp, 100 mph, and have 100,000 miles of life. Tires, today so often radial, and with so much bigger surface, cling to the road twice as efficiently and last twice as long as they did ten years ago.

With the ever-lengthening superhighway system in Europe, long-distance motoring is approaching the American level, with a journey from Paris to St. Tropez, 600 miles away in the South of France, an easy day-trip. Scandinavian vacationers now argue knowledgeably about the state of the Athens-to-Thessalonika road in Greece.

Most changes have been evolutionary—the Austin Seven Mini of 1960 has evolved, smarter now and many times more sophisticated, into the present Mini, getting a safe 70 mph from the tiny 850-cc engine, and has accumulated a number of transverse-engined imitators on the way. Others seem to have changed outwardly hardly at all in the past decade, relying on detail and internal engineering to keep pace.

The experimenters and advocates of other methods of propulsion, their energies stimulated by the world oil shortage, have been busy. GM in America has long pioneered the re-emergence of steam, and their Pontiac steam-powered car is a good example of serious application, although as yet the clutchless, gearless, silent, nonpolluting 100-mph performance is offset by its bulky size and heavy thirst.

With the long search for a convenient form of electric power, one could be forgiven for expecting something more in this area, but the problems remain the heavy weight of batteries, the short range on a single charge, and slow speed—although commuter city cars may be a viable proposition.

The methane or LPG (liquid petroleum gas) engine has long been in limited use, and conversion kits are available in some countries, but the cost is still high, and storage difficulties arise. The Stirling engine, a hoary old system invented in 1816, that does not burn the fuel inside the cylinder but employs heated air to do the job, may, if made considerably more efficient, prove a marginal contestant to the internal-combustion engine.

However, the "nasty explosion engine" with the inefficient reciprocating pistons that shake and shudder, using a fuel that burns and smells, to say nothing of wasting most of its energy through the water and exhaust systems, is likely to remain for a while. Well, until the earth's depleted supply of oil runs out.

One of the top-drawer British products is this Aston Martin V-8, built to the same basic principles as the original in 1913—*to produce quality cars of good performance and appearance for discerning owner-driver with fast touring in mind.* The body line of the car has been determined by many factors. Racing experience, wind-tunnel statistics, safety data, and design principles relating to comfort and driving ease have all influenced the contours and interior of the V-8. Its power unit of 5,340 cc employs four overhead camshafts and four Weber carburetors and can take the car from rest to 60 in a rapid 6 seconds. (GB)

Smartest of the Ingolstadt line, this Audi 100 Coupe S is a 4-5-seater fastback powered by a 1,871-cc unit developing 115 bhp and a 0-60 acceleration of 9.7 seconds. As usual with this make, the quoted top and cruising speed are the same — 115 mph. (D)

Introduced in 1966 and re-styled in 1972, the Anadol was first designed by Reliant of Britain for the Turkish market and is now produced by Otosan Sanaytii AS at Istanbul. The new version of the 1,300-cc fiberglass-bodied family car is turned out at around 10,000 a year, still with the technical collaboration of the British company. (TR)

The largest and most deluxe car on American Motors (known for its smaller-car leanings) 1974 list was this aristocratic 195-bhp Ambassador sedan. Re-styled for looks and greater safety, the engine has no less than six emission-control features. (USA)

Also made by Reliant, this Bond Bug is a three-wheeler with an ancestry that goes back to the early 1950s, when its tiny engine swung right or left with the single front (steerable) wheel, the system adopted by Cugnot on the very first road vehicle in 1769! The Bug has a 700-cc 4-cylinder and a coil-spring suspension—and is taxed in Britain as a motorcycle. (GB)

A faster and more powerful version of the BMW 2-liter sports sedan is this 520i, with a fuel-injection, 1,990-cc, 130-bhp engine giving a top speed of 115 mph and acceleration from 0–60 in less than 11 seconds. Lessons learned from racing have been incorporated—cool air ducted onto the front disks, airflow panel under the car helps hold down the front wheels at high speed, and the hood has a built-in "weak-spot" for bending in case of frontal impact. And as BMW so aptly put it, the car is "larger inside than outside." (D)

Completely redesigned for 1974 was this Chrysler New Yorker, using the 440-cu in, V-8, 4-barrel carburetor engine. (USA)

The 1974 version of the 411 from the Bristol Motor Company housed a 6,556-cc engine and was claimed to be the "fastest true four-seater car." Of the handful of examples that come off the line every week, a high proportion go to the United States and, in accordance with regulations, use low-grade gasoline. "Very much a driver's car..." said Stirling Moss in a magazine test-feature. Top speed: 140 mph. (GB)

Low-lined and scalloped, this Cadillac Sedan de Ville is one of the latest offerings from the Detroit company. New features were the telescopic rear-bumper-ends which retreat into the fender extensions on impact. The V-8, 205-bhp unit remains the same as the previous year's model, but, once again, the accent is heavily on creature comforts such as deep pile carpeting, two-tone velour, quality floor pads, and so on, rightly diverting the buyer's interest from speed performance to leisurely luxury. (USA)

This is the larger of two models from Chrysler U.K., the 2-liter with the accent on automatics and European travel. It is made in France and distributed in Britain by Chrysler U.K. at a competitive price. With 90-mph cruising speed from its 4-cylinder, ohc, 100-bhp unit, it is a comfortable, fast ride, has a spacious interior and a number of standard items that are usually optional extras, including a tachometer. (GB)

Two unusual cars were seen on Chevrolet's "design and research" stands at exhibitions during 1973 and 1974—both experimental Corvettes with rotary engines, pointers to possible future changes in Corvette philosophy. This is the Four-Rotor, equipped with gull-wing doors for unobstructed entry. Low-line architecture (5 inches lower than the current production model) reduces drag without inducing unmanageable lift. Computerized digital readout gives all necessary working information from the instrument panel. (USA)

The legendary Corvette is called the "only sports car in America," with some justification. After twenty-two years on the highway and in motor sport, it has become a car typical of its country—fast-moving, sophisticated, highly-tuned, incisive. Passing through some fifty different forms, including experimental cars, the Chevrolet Corvette has stayed true to its original concept—a two-seater with the most advanced drive-lines and chassis possible using high-volume production components. Engine: 7,500-cc V-8 developing 275 bhp (optional). (USA)

First seen in September 1973, the Daimler Double-Six sedan (named after the first Double-Six introduced in 1927) has a V-12 unit of 5.3 liters, identical to the Jaguar's XJ12 engine, and an external appearance similar to the sister brand, with the exception of the traditional Daimler fluting on the radiator. (GB)

Latest in the Dutch range in 1974 was this DAF Marathon, with a 1,289-cc unit producing 63 bhp and employing the unique DAF Variomatic automatic gearing with an infinite number of ratios between 14.22 to 1 and 3.60 to 1. Maximum cruising and top speed is 145 km/h (90 mph). (NL)

The 4-cylinder, 602-cc Citroën Ami 8, typical of a modern utility car, has a folding back seat in the current style, more than doubling its luggage capacity to 16 cu ft. Its all-around independent hydropneumatic suspension and anti-roll bars front and rear give it a stable ride over almost every type of terrain. (F)

First seen in 1972, the Ferrari 365 GTB Daytona has a 4.4-liter V-12 of great energy and flexibility; breathing is by six Webers, and power output is a top-of-the-track 352 bhp. With that sort of performance one would expect, and get, a 0–6 figure of 5.4 seconds and a top speed of 180 mph. It was dropped in Britain in 1973 because of emission-control regulations, but manufacture in Italy continued. (I)

In 1974 Fiat listed some twenty-six different models or variants, from the 600-cc 126 to the 3¼-liter 130. This small clutch of 124's seen outside a London pub represents some of the middle range. On the left is the 1.5-liter 124 Special, developing 75 bhp; the center car is the 124 sedan (1,197 cc and 65 bhp); and at right is the Fiat 124 coupe with a 1,756-cc, twin-cam engine producing 118 bhp. (I)

This year Datsun of Japan brought its 6-cylinder, 2.6-liter version of the extremely sporting 240Z to Britain (introduced in Tokyo in 1973), calling it the 260Z. With a power-output of 162 bhp, 0–60 is reached in a bolting 8 seconds, and one has only to look at the rally results to judge its overall performance. An outright win in the car-breaking East African Safari Rally in 1973 proves the point. (J)

New to the prancing horse stable in 1974 was the Ferrari Berlinetta Boxer (or just "BB") with a V-12, 4,930 rear-mid engine developing a beguiling 380 bhp at 7,700 rpm, which, as the few who have had the experience will confirm, conveys one at some 188 mph when the road is available. (I)

The 1974 Mustang was shorter by 19 inches than the previous year's model — a change in the right direction — and 7 inches shorter than the original 1964 car. A claimed 20 mpg in normal city and suburban use is made, and Ford produces two versions, a notchback and the increasingly popular hatchback. A choice of a 4-cylinder, 2.3-liter (the first metric engine built in the USA) and a 2.8-liter engine is available. (USA)

The front-wheel-drive Honda Civic was elected No. 3 in the "Car of the Year" choice by journalists in 1973, the year of its introduction. A water-cooled, twin-choked, 4-cylinder, 1,169-cc engine performs well and, conforming to the policy of most Japanese companies, the Civic has a number of standard fittings that would not be expected on a small car. (J)

The development of the 16-valve, single-overhead-camshaft engine was another chapter in this Triumph's history of technical innovation — and is the most important feature of the Dolomite Sprint. Capacity: 1,998 cc, with a surprisingly high output of 127 bhp — an increase of 40 percent. (GB)

Another from AMC is the new-look Gremlin, a subcompact that helped set a trend toward smaller personal vehicles in America, although, with its 6-cylinder, 4,200-cc engine, it would be classed as a large car in Europe. Its upswept rear-end was a bold departure from the norm, heartily liked or disliked by all who saw it. (USA)

The Hillman Hunter, Grand Luxe version, with a lively 5-bearing, 1,725-cc, 4-cylinder unit with alloy head and high-lift camshaft plus twin-outlet exhaust manifold. In case you also expect walnut veneer—it's got some. (GB)

This flight of sporting Fords at Britain's Brands Hatch racing circuit during a sedan-car championship illustrates how the small Ford takes a large part in motor sport in the United Kingdom. The Escort in its various forms (all nineteen of them!) is second only to the Ford Cortina in number on the roads of Britain, from the modest 1,098-cc sedan to the extremely sporting Mexico and the 2-liter Escort RS 2000. (GB)

Now building some of the most expensive and advanced cars in the world, Italian Ferruccio Lamborghini started to tune Fiats after the last war, graduating to building his own vehicles from war-surplus parts. This is the Espada 400 GT Mk3, an impressive name for an exciting car. The comparatively small (3,929-cc) front-located engine gives 350 bhp from its 12 cylinders in V formation and a top speed of considerably more than any normal driver can use. (I)

An old name brought back for a new design, the Lancia Beta was Vincenzo Lancia's first production car—and the company's latest in 1972. The first brand-new design since joining Fiat, this Lancia has a choice of three (transverse) engines, from 1,438 to 1,756 cc, all of them Fiat twin-cam derivatives. The stylish five-seater has a five-speed transmission, high flexibility, and sure-footed handling. (I)

The Jaguar E-type Series Three, introduced in 1971, continued virtually unchanged into 1974, with the 60-degree, V-12 engine of 5,343 cc, developed from Jaguar's original V-12 which was designed and built as a racing unit. The first E-type was seen in 1961, with a 3.8-liter engine; all-around independent suspension and all-around disk brakes have been featured since those days, while anti-dive front suspension and lucas transistorized ignition are later developments. (GB)

Now under the Citroën flag, Maserati first produced the Bora in 1972. The car is offered with a 4,719-cc unit with the astonishing performance figures that would be expected from this make—0–60 mph in 6.5 seconds and top speed of 160 mph—coupled with an average of 12 mpg. (I)

The 4¹/₂-liter Mercedes-Benz 450 was voted "Car of the Year" at the end of 1973 by a panel of forty-five European motoring journalists. The 4.5 range of four cars was unveiled at Geneva in 1973 and all had automatic transmission as standard. The "new engine," observed the company modestly of its V-8, 225-bhp unit, "does not significantly raise the top speed beyond the 131 mph level, but has greater effect in terms of strong acceleration throughout the speed range ..." This is the long-wheelbase 450 SEL. (D)

Designed by the company whose cars and drivers have captured more-or-less every sporting-world championship available, this Lotus Elite (the first Lotus model of this name was introduced in 1959) was built to take full advantage of the high cruising speed offered by today's European auto routes. This sleek piece of engineering is a genuine four-seater and complies with all European and American design and safety regulations—and those expected in the foreseeable future. Its 2-liter, twin-ohc, 4-cylinder engine produces 155 bhp, and the wedge-shaped car has a top speed of around 128 mph. (GB)

The stylish new Mazda R×4, introduced in 1973, was the largest rotary-engined car produced to date by this company and coincided with their half-millionth production rotary-power unit. Claimed as the first rotary-engined car in the world to be fitted with automatic transmission, R×4's two-rotor unit develops 130 bhp and is equivalent to a conventional 2¹/₄-liter engine—although it is 30 percent lighter and has 30 percent fewer moving parts. (J)

The Mercury Cougar XR-7, redesigned in 1973, has more styling than previously and enters the middle-size luxury-car market. As is becoming traditional in automotive advertising throughout the world, more emphasis is now placed on comfort, safety, and in-car entertainment than ever before, to the exclusion of eulogistic essays on speed and high performance. Engine: 5,752-cc V-8. (USA)

"Understated elegance" is the term used in the brochure, and a new sporting rear appearance is also emphasized by this Lincoln. The brand has close links with the office of president, and has also been classed as one of the largest production cars ever made. Its grandeur is undeniable, and its ultra-smooth, 7,537-cc, V-8 engine continues to complete the atmosphere of elegance, although perhaps not all that understated. (USA)

The twin-rotor engine designed by Wankel powers this German NSU Ro 80, first seen in 1967. Front-wheel drive and selective automatic transmission give a light positive steering and deep range of performance. Equivalent to a conventional 2-liter, the unit puts out 113 bhp at 5,500 rpm, but has a fairly high gasoline consumption. (D)

Shown first in London during 1973, this MGB GT V-8 houses a 5-bearing, 3.5-liter unit (as an option to the established 1.8-liter B-series 4-cylinder version) producing 137 bhp at 5,000 rpm. For many years the make has strongly appealed to a small cross-section of enthusiasts (in addition to selling well in and out of its country of origin) who enjoy what could be termed nostalgic driving; it was the make owned by those fortunate enough to be able to buy a medium-priced sports car between the wars. (GB)

The Morgan Motor Company has done the almost-impossible—kept going under its own power since 1910, in the face of overwhelming competition. Its products are directed to an exclusive band of motorists who want to own a somewhat spartan, if high-performance, car that makes few concessions to modern styling. Shown here is the Morgan Plus 8, a 3½-liter, 8-cylinder, twin-carburetored, very open sports car with a cruising speed of 125 mph and a zero to 70 mph time of 7.5 seconds—a performance not given to many vehicles. (GB)

The legendary Mini still attracts worldwide attention. This is the top model of the Mini range, the high-performance 1275 GT. The transverse-engined Minis come in a dozen guises, from the modest 850-cc to the car pictured, and after 14 years of development it has been brought to a high level of reliability. Its road-holding and handling have long set the standard by which others are judged. Well over 3 million had been made by 1974. (GB)

In the intermediate range is the Oldsmobile Cutlass (this is the "S" Colonnade hardtop coupe) in its various forms, with the coupe versions coming high in popularity, probably for their individual, sporting image. The 350-cu in V-8 unit produces a useful 160 bhp installed but, in line with the present style, the accent inside is on luxury, not spartan speed. (USA)

The Morris Marina range was introduced in 1971 and offered in 1.3 and 1.8 liters, with or without twin-carburetors. A typical "fleet" car, the Marina sold some 300,000 within its first two years and is one of the top-selling cars in Britain. (GB)

In 1974 British Leyland offered the Rover 2200 as a replacement for the 10-year-old Rover 2000. Available in single- or twin-carburetor forms, the Rover engine was bored out to give 10 percent more capacity, which, with larger exhaust valves and SU HIF6 carbs, give it a smoother and smarter performance—a much-needed uplift. (GB)

Evocative of the sunny South of France, the Rolls-Royce Corniche was first produced in March 1971 and sold in addition to the Silver Shadow. The *dernier cir* in luxury, the distinguished vehicle seen here in Bosky Grove has long lost the town-carriage-and-dignity image and can show most other vehicles a clean pair of back wheels without apparent effort. The 6,750-cc, V-8 engine, independent suspension, disk brakes all around, height control, and numberless other refinements combine to give a car of unsurpassed comfort, smoothness, and silence—at any speed. (GB)

The Plymouth full-size car wheelbase (this is the Fury) was extended to 121.5 inches in 1974, with the 400-cu in, V-8, 2-barrel carburetor engine as standard. (USA)

Established safety pioneers, Saab have made their "99" one of the most advanced models of the Seventies—right down to the headlight wipers. Front-wheel-driven, the 99 has a safety body consisting of cage plus welded steel beams with reinforced side and front pillars, and impact-absorbing bumpers. Its 2-liter unit puts out some 95 bhp. (S)

From Pontiac, this V-8, 7½-liter, 250-bhp Firebird Transam showing the current fashion in front-end styling. Most powerful of the Firebirds from this stable, the Transam was extensively re-styled this year, although keeping some of its distinctive features, such as the twin ports. The two scoops under the front bumpers are new. (USA)

Two new general body trends became evident in the Seventies—the boxlike profile, sharp-edged and clean-cut; and, almost the reverse, the egg-shape of the British Leyland Allegro and the Alfasud. Here the square-profile Opel Record (1.7-liter or 1.9-liter-engined) shows a front end well in the mode of the day. Larger glass areas were also a growing feature, pioneered by BMW in the Sixties. (D)

The Toyota Automatic Loom Works made its first, somewhat experimental, Chevrolet-based car in 1935, after Kiichiro, son of the family, had visited British motor manufacturers during 1930, and in 1937 the Toyota Motor Co. was formed. Now, about forty years later, the Toyota range is one of the most sophisticated in the middle-market. This Celica 1600 ST (Sports Tourer) was first put on the road in 1972 and continues to increase in popularity both in Europe and America. A choice of a four- or five-speed transmission gives the car a sporty and flexible character, and its 105-mph top speed is enough for most conditions. (J)

A favorite in Britain and America as a sporting vehicle is this Triumph TR6, last of a line of lively TRs (the TR2 was first produced in 1953 from the Coventry factory). Its 2½-liter, 6-cylinder, fuel-injection power unit gives a top speed of 112 mph and an 0–60 time of 10.1 seconds. (GB)

The 1974 version of many a motoring enthusiast's dream car. Introduced in 1964, when it appeared with a new body, the Porsche Type 911 is still going strong, grown now from 2 liters to a 6-cylinder, 2,687-cc, and still one of the fastest and safest road cars in the normal driving range. This is the 2-liter car. (D)

One of the least expensive cars to be bought in Britain, the Skoda is small and, typical of eastern European productions, firmly based on economy of running costs. Using low-grade gasoline, its 1,107-cc engine develops 53 bhp and will take the car from 0–60 in an unspectacular 19 seconds. However, this is no pared-down "utility" vehicle—with four doors, forward-tilting rear seats, wall-to-wall carpets, twin-circuit braking systems, front disks, four-speed wipers, etc., the car is admirably kitted for its price. (CS)

Vauxhall's fast medium-size car is the XV 4/90, a well-designed vehicle with sporting tendencies, but one that for some curious reason has been overlooked by many British drivers who enjoy prudent but positive driving. Overdrive is optional, and its 2¼-liter, single-overhead-camshaft power unit will take the car up to 100 mph and to 60 in 12.5 seconds, a performance equal to several higher-priced products in the same field. (GB)

The Scirocco is another attempt by VW to widen the range and break free, at least in part, from the eternal Beetle. This one, similar in some ways to the Passat, has its 1,471-cc, 4-cylinder engine installed laterally, unlike the Passat, which is conventionally fitted. Three versions are built, including a 50-hp "economy" 1,093-cc car and a higher-compression 1.5-liter TS developing 80 bhp. The picture shows the 70-hp standard model. (D)

A luxury variation on a theme by Austin and Morris, the Wolseley is by now merely badge-engineered. However, this Wolseley Six has the east-west mounted 2¼-liter, 6-cylinder, overhead-camshaft (108-bhp) unit with a decidedly "torquey" character and a smooth, easy-holding ride with a considerable degree of interior comfort. (GB)

Introduced in May 1973, the Volkswagen Passat was a medium-range car based on a new concept for VW, with front-wheel drive, inclined single-overhead-camshaft, 4-cylinder engine and 55, 75, or 85 bhp. A lively car and useful in modern traffic conditions. (D)

A series of changes in the 1974 Volvo included a four-stage safety steering column, a heated driving seat (one could be forgiven a raised eyebrow at this one!) and, for this 164E, an electrically controlled fuel-injection system and 175 bhp from a 3-liter engine. (S)

Another from Eastern Europe, the 991-cc Wartburg Knight from the German Democratic Republic is a two-stroke—with a performance above the expected, at a maximum of 87 mph. Rugged in construction, it shares some of the spartan qualities of other European small cars—the Citroën Dyane, the small Renaults, and the Russian Moskvitch. (D)

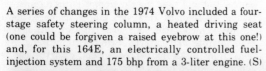

The 1.6- and 1.8-liter Alfettas from the Milan stable were joined in 1975 by the GT version. Housing a 118-bhp 1.8 unit with a rear-mounted 5-speed transmission, it is a handsome small car with distinct sporting tendencies. This Alfa Romeo product is in the classic tradition of the brand. (I)

The Audi 80, a smaller version of the 100, was given a 1,558-cc unit for 1976, with the exception of the basic model which retained the 1,296-cc engine. Developing 85 bhp and running on low-octane fuel, the 80 is an economy car of the middle (European) range that brings with it the quality of the famous Audi NSU combine. (D)

In the current fashion of being either an "Easter egg" or a "wedge," the new Austin/Morris 18/22 range, the Princess, is designed as the latter — an aerodynamic wedge that you either like or hate. However, British Leyland, now state-owned, describe the range as the biggest event since the previous biggest event in automotive matters, the Mini. With transverse engine, front-wheel drive, and hydragas suspension, the Princess owes much to the Mini tradition. Two engines are offered: a 1,798-cc 4-cylinder and a 2,227-cc six. The car has a number of refinements, including dual-circuit power-assisted brakes, and a surprisingly high standard of luxury trim for a medium-priced vehicle. (GB)

A completely new, smaller Cadillac was announced in 1975 by Cadillac Motor Car Division, GM's top-of-the-tree luxury United States car makers. The Cadillac Seville, with an overall length of 17 feet, is 27 inches shorter than the full-size Sedan de Ville, 8 inches narrower, and 9 cwt lighter—common sense designing for the late seventies. Powered by a healthy 5.7-liter V-8 with electronic fuel injection, and developing 180 net bhp, this latest addition to the classic Caddy line still represents the ultimate in United States luxury and style. (USA)

In its first year in the Buick line the subcompact Buick Skyhawk has given good account of itself, taking more than eight percent of the total Buick sales volume for the first half of the year. The key feature of the Skyhawk is the Buick V-6 engine, a unit that manages to combine economy, performance, and reliability. During 1976 the model offered a 5-speed overdrive manual transmission, in line with the world's urgent attempt to save fuel. (USA)

A genuine Chrysler Europe venture is the 1976 Alpine. A transverse front-mounted engine of either 1,294 or 1,442 cc supplies front-wheel power for a 5-door hatchback in the current style. Aimed at the upper-middle European market and sold in both France and Britain, this car is fast becoming a best-seller. Forty-seven expert judges from 15 countries in Europe voted the Chrysler Alpine (or its French equivalent, the Simca 1307/8) Car of the Year for 1976. (GB, F)

General Motors' T-car saga began way back in the sixties when Opel of Germany set out to develop a replacement for its 1-liter Kadett. It rapidly grew into an international GM project. Now as Brazil's, Chevrolet's, and Vauxhall's Chevette, Opel's Kadett, Japan's and Holden's Isuzu Gemini, the stubby minicar (engine sizes vary from 1 liter to 1.8 liters) has proved a sound GM move and a popular buy in much of the world's market. Shown is the 1976 Chevrolet Chevette Hatchback Coupe. (USA)

Another venture into the smaller-car bracket is this Chevrolet Monza Towne Coupe, with a 4.3 V-8 unit. This model has handsome, clean lines with a sensible minimum of metalwork. (USA)

Top of the Citröen tree, the CX 2200 appeared as the 1976 leader for the company. It had proved to be the European leader in its 2,000 (1,985 cc) form and was voted Car of the Year in 1975. In line with Citröen's policy, the CX range has an advanced design, although not so radically different from the ID and DS as they were from their predecessors in the mid-Fifties. CX 2200 Pallas and Safari versions (2,175 cc) were introduced in the Spring of 1976. (F)

The classically styled Cordoba, Chrysler's intermediate 2-door hardtop, nearly trebled its sales forecast during 1975, its introductory year. Little changed for 1976 except for its rather weighty grille, changed instrument cluster, and a new high-efficiency catalytic converter. It may be a comfort to know that all 1976 Chrysler-Plymouth cars are designed to roll over a full 360 degrees without any fuel leakage! (USA)

A proven sporting success—winning the East African Rally is no sinecure—Mitsubishi's Colt Gallant has recently invaded import markets in several areas. In 1,600-cc and 2-liter form this compact car produced 100 and 115 bhp at just over 6,000 rpm respectively—and in its newly offered GTO Sports Coupe form it puts out a full 125 bhp. The Gallant 1600 is the car adopted by Chrysler U.S. for their American small-car operation in place of the British Avenger. (J)

The 1976 Dodge Aspen represents current thinking—directing major sales efforts to buyers forced by the economic climate to purchase smaller-cars. It has a 225-cu in standard power plant, with larger units optional. A combination of aerodynamics, body design, and an all-new isolated transverse-torsion-bar front-suspension system makes the Aspen one of the smoothest and quietest riding cars ever produced by Chrysler, yet the handling is considerably more positive than past Dodge compacts. (The coupe is pictured.) (USA)

This Gemini from General Motors Holden of Australia clearly shows its ancestry, but its solidly conventional looks cloak a lively performance from its lightweight 1,584-cc ohc unit made specifically for the Gemini. This small car is heavily corrosion-protected, thoroughly ventilated for its climate, and offers full air conditioning. Three models—the sedan, the SL sedan, and a coupe—complete the range. Shown is the coupe, with power-boosted disk brakes, fully reclining bucket seats with integral headrests, and a sleek sportive appearance. (Aus)

More hatchback from Fiat. The 1976 128 3P joins the line of rear-opening cars that so many manufacturers have opted for in the mid-seventies. A successor to the 128 Coupe, this little model from Turin is usefully short at 12 feet, 6 inches; its 1,290-cc engine has a light thirst and a remarkably high 73 bhp. Disk brakes, 4-speed transmission, an "indeformable" passenger compartment, and sophisticated suspension come with the package. (I)

Ford covered their market with a total of 8 car lines and 32 models in 1976. This is the flagship called the Thunderbird. The original 1954 T-Bird was a genuine attempt to produce what Ford called a "personalized car"—in effect a sports car—and became a collector's item shortly after its demise. The 1976 model is not a direct ancestor, although the name may suggest it. Standard power is a 460-cu in engine, now recalibrated for improved fuel economy, coupled with automatic transmission. (USA)

Cobra II, the sporting version of the Mustang, is a name evocative of high performance and famous road-circuit races ever since Carol Shelby mounted a Ford V-8 engine in a British sports car. Racing versions of that Cobra swept to the World Manufacturers GT Championship of 1965. The Cobra 11 has a standard unit of 2.3 liters with 4-speed manual transmission, but 2.8 V-6 and 302-cu in V-8 engines are optional.

Ford of Britain's new Escort range was joined in 1976 by this Mexico. A high-performance sedan for enthusiasts, it is powered by a 1,600-cc single ohc engine. The rest of the vehicle—suspension, transmission, and body shell—is identical to the Escort RS 1800s that were driven to the first two places in Britain's RAC International Rally 1975. This tight, sporting model has special competition seats, additional instruments, and the fashionable "beard" air dam under the front end to prevent front lift at speed. Maximum speed is around 106 mph. (GB)

The long-awaited successor to the Jaguar E-type arrived during 1976. The XJ-S, the most exclusive and expensive Jaguar ever produced, sets new standards of engineering and comfort for the up-market purchaser. Its 5.3-liter fuel-injection V-12 power pack can take the coupe from 0 to 60 mph in just 6.8 seconds, and the sleek aerodynamic styling helps return a figure of 15—18 mpg. Aimed primarily at the North American market, the XJ-S is claimed to be the ultimate in luxury motoring for the really discerning driver. (GB)

The most sportive model of a range that now includes sedan coupe and spider (open sports 2-seater), the 2-liter Lancia Beta Monte Carlo has a transverse mid-engine rear-wheel drive layout similar to the World Championship—winning Stratos. (I)

Exciting, mid-engined, and aerodynamically near-perfect, the new British Lotus Esprit is a 2-liter 2-seater with Italian styling. Successor to the Europa Twin-Cam, its 156-bhp twin-ohc unit is reputed to give a 0–60 acceleration figure of 6–8 seconds, which puts the car among the world's most fleet-footed. Set in a backbone-and-space-frame skeleton, the engine, which has passed United States emission tests, drives through a Maserati (Citroën) transmission. (GB)

The Lincoln Continental, still the flagship of the fleet of Ford's Lincoln-Mercury Division, offers no radically new innovation for 1976, in line with policy, but certain standard equipment has become optional. A "search" stereo radio is available as is a quadrasonic tape player. Or would you care for a Cartier-signed digital clock? America's "Car of State" has them all for the asking. Illustrated is a Continental Mark IV. (USA)

Says Lincoln-Mercury of its 1976 lineup: "No changes have been made for the sake of change this year. All expertise and effort has gone into refining the product lineup." Welcome news, and long may it continue. So the Mercury Monarch has just this one addition to its range—the Grand Monarch Ghia. A luxury version, it features 4-wheeled disks, aluminum-spoked wheels, power windows and steering, and an optional-to-standard 250-IV 6-cylinder engine. (USA)

Mercedes-Benz continue their sporting image with the 350SL. A 2-seater with a reputation for speed plus safety, this one could be called the antithesis of the extreme sports car in its sophistication and silence. However, its performance is certainly in the upper sports bracket, with a top speed of 127 mph. The 350 SL has power-assisted disks all around, removable steel hardtop roof, and fully disappearing soft top. Agility with stability are its two great virtues. (D)

The Bobcat, the subcompact from Lincoln Mercury, was introduced in the United States in March 1975 and has proved a popular move. Offered as the Runabout—a 3-door hatchback—or the Villager station wagon, the Bobcat has as its standard power pack a 2,300-cc 4-cylinder unit and 4-speed manual transmission. The "MPG," an economical version of the Bobcat introduced in 1976, is shown. (USA)

Oldsmobile made a number of significant fuel-economy improvements in all their 34-model lineup for 1976, mainly through higher efficiency of the 260-cu in V-8 power unit, a lighter axle, a manual 5-speed overdrive transmission, and a 2.41 to 1 axle ratio. Highlights of the 4-seater sports coupe, Star-fire, are the soft plastic front-end panel, energy-absorbing front bumper, and rear hatchback. A Star-fire GT option, introduced in mid-1975, is equipped with tachometer, rally wheels, and special trim. (USA)

A sports coupe with high performance and good tight handling, the Opel Manta for 1976 has a new aero-dynamic shape very much in the contemporary mode. The previous version had been praised for its good looks, and the new model confirms the design talent of the German company. In five versions, the Manta has a 1.6-liter unit as standard, with a 1.9-liter engine optional. (Illustrated is the Manta Deluxe Coupe) (D)

Panther Westwinds is a small specialist maker with a plant near the old Brooklands circuit in England. The Panther sports roadster (J72) and Panther de Ville are two similarly audacious "replica" designs in wood and steel and chrome evoking memories of Bugatti, Hispano Suiza, and other 1928 exotica. A 6- or 12-cylinder Jaguar unit is housed in a mock-classic body that gives the impression of just warming up to beat the Orient Express from London to Istanbul. The Panther packs a punch, however, and will take an unwary driver up into the illegal velocity bracket all too quickly. (GB)

For 1976 Peugeot produced a car at the top end of its range—the 604, aimed at the luxury market and challenging the domination of Mercedes-Benz and Jaguar. Designed as the official French "ministerial" car, the 2.7-liter twin-cam engine powers a vehicle resplendent with *comfort sensuel* for a nation known for its somewhat Spartan transportation. (F)

With a wheelbase of just 122.5 inches, the Plymouth Volare is designed to appeal to the cost- and fuel-conscious public of 1976. This wagon, the smallest Plymouth offering of the year, has a deceptively large cargo capacity of 72 cu ft. In days of economy of design and models it is surprising to note that the Volare is offered in fastback coupe and sedan form and to find that another subcompact, the Arrow, was also put on the market later in the year. (USA)

Turbo-charging and K-Jetronic—the combination of exhaust-driven supercharging and continuous direct fuel injection—must add up to the most modern engine investment yet, and the Porsche Turbo has both. Although new in concept, the Turbo is no leap in the dark. Flagship of the 911 range, the experience behind the car, with its well-known 3-liter 6-cylinder opposed-piston unit and construction techniques, the Turbo is pure Porsche—robust, reliable, enormously flexible, and entirely practical. (D)

Renault's star of the year was the new 30TS, powered by the "co-op" 2.7-liter V-6 light-alloy engine designed by Volvo/Peugeot/Renault. The front-wheel drive 30TS is aimed at the executive market and has a number of built-in safety devices new to the make. In line with current European fashion, it claims a top speed of over 110 mph—although the number of countries in which a vehicle is permitted to reach this speed must be rapidly diminishing. (F)

The Rolls-Royce Camargue—designed and built in Britain and styled by Pininfarina of Italy. Based on the platform and running gear of the 10-year-old Silver Shadow, the Camargue is the top end of the R-R range, which makes it around the price of a comfortable family house. The 6,750-cc V-8 unit has (for the United States and Japan) a slightly lowered compression ratio at 7.3:1, enabling the use of lead-free fuel. The main change is the emphasis, now on owner-driving; previously, the company's top car had been designed primarily as a chauffeur-conducted vehicle. Gone too, is the upright grille — on the Camargue it leans forward just 4 degrees from the vertical. (GB)

Somewhere between a sedan, a coupe, and a station wagon is this 3-door Saab 99L Combi, which, say the makers, combines the space of a 5-seater sedan and the tailgate and load capacity of a station wagon. With a British ancestry, the single-carb 2-liter 4-cylinder power unit gives 100 bhp and 100-plus mph. The construction is still typically Swedish—with slight heaviness owing to thorough steel reinforcing. Latest in the range is the 99GL, with twin carburetors and 108 bhp. (S)

Fresh for 1976 in Europe from Japan's Toyota was the 2000 Sedan, and from the United States point of view, right in line with current thinking, keeping the power unit down to 2 liters, while accommodating "five six-footers," as the company claims. The single ohc engine produces a healthy 116 bhp at 5,000 rpm, using a single 2-choke carburetor. Conventional as the 2000 is, its standard of finish is impeccable and, typically Japanese, the equipment inside leaves little to be desired. (J)

The world's automotive exotica is quickly dwindling to a handful of small specialist manufacturers to whom, for some mysterious reason, enormous production costs seem to have little deterrent effect. Such is De Tomaso Automobili of Modena, Italy, home of that other legendary carmaker, Enzo Ferrari. This Longchamps looks almost ordinary compared with the aerodynamic De Tomaso Pantera, but, as the brochure states, its specification includes a "Motore 8 cilindri a V di 90°; cilindrata totale 5763 cc, con potenza 330 CV." (I)

As suppliers of small and medium sports cars, from MG Midget to Jaguar E-type, to the North American market, British Leyland continued in the tradition during 1976 with the Triumph TR7. A complete departure from previous styling, the TR7 complies with all current and anticipated emission laws. A true 2-seater, it has eschewed the "shoe-horn" 2+2 form and has, consequently, comfort and space for driver and passenger. High performance is provided by a 2-liter electronic fuel-injection single ohc unit fitted (in the United States) with twin Stromberg 175 CDSEV carburetors. (GB)

With major manufacturers clubbing together to produce a "co-operative" engine for their common use, it is no surprise to see General Motors planning a small car for construction in several countries. Based on GM's "T" car floor plan, and owing much to the Vauxhall Viva 1300, the hatchback Chevette from Luton is shorter than either, giving the car a totally new look for very small styling changes other than at the front end. Its 1,256-cc engine can give up to 50 mpg when driven with care. (GB)

Heralding the department of the Volkswagen Beetle after over a generation of production (prototypes were seen as early as 1936), the 895-cc VW Polo has a transverse front-mounted engine, is a 4-seater (almost), and is simple to drive and pleasant to handle. (D)

Volvo of Sweden has been known as one of the most conservative European auto manufacturers, but, with the 240 and 260 series, a major step was taken into the future. The latest, the 264 GL, has the advanced 2,664-cc V-6 all-alloy engine designed by a cooperative of Peugeot, Renault, and Volvo, and built in France. A completely new safety innovation is "Day Notice" lights—in effect, higher intensity parking lights that are active whenever the car is moving, to give warning to pedestrians that the car is in motion. Rear seat belts are also installed; Volvo maintains that the main danger to front occupants in a head-on crash are the rear passengers. (S)

Nothing much has been heard from AC since the Ford V-8 7-liter 428 series. Their ME 3000, in production for the home market by the end of 1976, is available for export in 1977. Based on the 1972 Bohanna Stables designed by Peter Bohanna and Robin Stables, the ME 3000 (as its designation suggests) is powered by a Ford V-6 3-liter engine mounted transversely amidships. The bodywork is of a double-skinned, fire-resistant fiberglass—a departure for AC except on their invalid cars—bringing the weight to about 1,800 lbs, and 135 mph is forecast. A Broadspeed turbo-charged version will be optional. (GB)

Christchurch, in the agricultural south of England, is about as unlikely a place for automobile manufacture as Redonda Beach, California, but the Albany is no ordinary car. One of the most attractive replica veteran cars on the market, the Model A relies on a Triumph Spitfire 1,500 ST engine governed to 40 mph for safety reasons, and, unlike its Edwardian ancestors, boasts the refinement of a self-starter and radio. (GB)

The 1977 AMC Pacer—now available as a station wagon—represents advanced thinking and incorporates a number of unusual features. Not the least of these is the asymmetrical doors, the passenger door being 4 inches wider than that on the driver's side. Powered by the AMC 232 CID six, both the sedan and the wagon offer the 258 CID six as an option, and, interestingly, the wagon utilizes compressed-gas cylinders to aid the operation of the tailgate. Sign of the times is the option of interior trim in Levi's denim! (USA)

Winner of six "Car of the Year" awards, the Audi 80 range suffered the disadvantage of being launched on the British market right at the start of the oil crisis in 1973. It weathered the storm successfully. In GTE gas-injection form it is one of the fastest (if not *the* fastest) accelerating 1,600-cc production sedan cars and was restyled for the 1977 year. Smallest in the range is the 1,300-cc 80L seen here in '77 styling, which, like its larger sisters, incorporates the self-stabilizing steering system pioneered by the firm. (D)

The flagship of the Audi fleet is the new 100LS announced for the 1977 year. Aimed at the executive market, this 2-liter sedan employs the same overhead-camshaft 115-bhp engine as the Porsche 924 and combines a top speed of 111 mph with fuel economy of 30 mpg overall. A 5-cylinder 2.2-liter version with Bosch K-Jetronic fuel injection is promised later in 1977 and, unlike those developed by Ford and Rover, will be the first 5-cylinder gasoline engine to achieve general production. (D)

One of the BMW's "3" series range, the 320 is an 109-mph 2-liter, two-door sedan that accelerates from 0 to 60 mph in a creditable 10.2 seconds. Now available as the 320i with a gas-injection engine, a top speed of 113 mph is possible. (D)

Redesigned for the 1977 model year, the BMW "5" range sports a new grille and hood line and realigned rear lamp clusters. Both of the 6-cylinder models, the 525 and the 528, have redesigned combustion chambers and altered carburetion, boosting output by 5 bhp. A new "piston" support of the rear-axle damper contributes to a much quieter car, and instrument visibility is enhanced by a new steering wheel. (D)

Replacing the 3.0 CS in the BMW 600 series is the new 3.3-liter 633 CSi, the world's first production car to boast a pre-drive safety check. By pressing a button on the instrument panel, seven lamps light if there is no fault in engine oil level, radiator water level, brake fluid, windshield washer, rear lights, stop lights, and brake-pad thickness. The all-steel two-door bodies are built by Karmann for BMW, and the model is available with manual transmission with limited slip differential, or with ZF automatic transmission. With a 6-cylinder engine of 3,210 cc inherited from the 3.0 CS, the gas-injection 633 CSi is capable of 133 mph. (D)

Chevrolet's 1977 Monza Spyder is a two-door hatch-back coupe with a low profile and a sporting image. With a small "beard" in front and a larger spoiler at the rear, it projects the image of a competition ancestry. Supplied with a 5-liter V-8 unit or a much smaller 4-cylinder 2.3-liter power pack, this car is versatile, handsome, and functional. (USA)

Dubbed the most successful car ever to bear the Chrysler nameplate, the Cordoba continued for the 1977 season distinguished by new front and rear styling, including a chrome-plated grill of formal design, rather more rectangular opera windows, and the option of the successful "T-bar" roof that appears on other Chrysler products. Fitted with the 400-cu in V-8 and the revolutionary "Lean Burn" electronic system, the Cordoba is also available with a 318-cu in unit, while customers in California and other high-altitude areas had to content themselves with the 360-cu in version. (USA)

The new 1977 luxury model of the Chrysler Alpine, the GLS, is one of the first all-British assembled Alpines since French-assembled cars ceased to be imported in mid-summer 1976. Identical mechanically to the 1,442-cc Alpine S, the GLS also features built-in head restraints, tinted glass, electric window lifters, and headlight washer-wipers. (GB)

Capable of a maximum speed of about 100 mph, the Chrysler Avenger 1600 Super is a thoroughly conventional automobile that has changed little in basic specification over the past two years, although performance has improved. Its ohv engine with chain-driven camshaft still relies on one Stromberg 150 CD 3 car-buretor and develops maximum power at 5,000 rpm. Coil-spring suspension all around results in a somewhat lively ride over all but the smoothest surfaces, but generally the car is without vices and behaves as one would expect at this stage of development. (GB)

The first child directly attributable to Citroën's marriage to Peugeot (upon whose 104 it is based) the LN hails from Citroën's Aulnay factory where it is produced alongside the CX. Designed to "strengthen Citroën's position at the bottom end of the market", it is difficult to see the logic of this, with the legendary 2CV, Ami and Dyane models already dominating that sphere. Even though fitted with the most powerful 32-bhp model of the Citroën flattwin engine it will have its work cut out to compete with VW's Polo or the Fiat 127. (F)

Available also with the standard "1600" as well as the more powerful "Astron80" 2-liter engine, the Celeste retains the 92-in wheelbase and general mechanical layout of the Colt Lancer, although the fastback body is completely new. Fitted with a five-speed transmission (direct on fourth), the Celeste 2000 is capable of 110 mph on low-grade fuel, but at the expense of a rather harsh ride. This is largely because of the employment of semi-elliptic springs at the rear—an anachronistic feature that contrasts with the twin counter-rotating balance shafts that contribute to the smooth running of the engine. (J)

Not a beach buggy, but a genuine all-terrain amphibious car, the Argocat is built by Crayford Auto Developments of Kent, England. Available in either six- or eight-wheeled form and with the choice of American Tecumseh two-stroke single-cylinder or Japanese Chapparal four-stroke single-cylinder engines, it incorporates a compact differential gear system (low, high, neutral, and reverse) with an automatic torque converter. Finding favor with the police and the military as well as with farmers, the Argocat is also available as a Snowmobile. A special feature is the non-rust body of polyethylene—virtually indestructible under the most arduous conditions. (GB)

Combining the well-proved and reliable front-wheel-drive layout of the Cherry 120A Coupe with a new, larger three-door body shell, Datsun's 1977 Cherry F.11 Coupe utilizes the transverse-mounted 1,171-cc engine adapted from the old 120Y Sunny unit (of which more than 4½ million have been produced) and all around independent suspension, incorporating coil springs and rear-mounted McPherson struts. (J)

Complementing Dodge's successful compact Aspen range at the top-of-the-line for 1977 is the Royal Monaco. Offered also in brougham form, it acquired a smaller sister in the mid-sized Monaco, the latter being distinguished by its vertically stacked headlights.

With a close eye on Federal emission controls and legislation, the 1977 Dodge lineup features increased availability of the Chrysler Electronic Spark Advance "Lean Burn" engine, with 400-cu in- and 360-cu in-V-8s supplementing the existing 400. (USA)

Now established as America's best-selling subcompact, the Ford Pinto entered 1977 with a sportier appearance than earlier models, and stiffer rear suspension provided it with more positive road handling. Standard power team is the economical 2.3-liter overhead-camshaft 4-cylinder unit with manual four-speed-transmission. A 2.8-liter engine is available to all versions except the Pony. (USA)

During the pioneer days of the automobile, motor manufacturers blatently copied the Mercedes shape. Today's makers could well take their slide rules to this 1977 Ford, Mark 4 in the Cortina lineage. Born in 1962, this model has been the most popular car in Great Britain almost from its launching, and it continues to top the charts. With its new clean and ageless look it should stay there for some time, and with a 17-model option embracing four power packs from 1,300 cc to an overhead-camshaft 2000 cc, it covers mid-range European requirements ideally. (GB)

NOW

It must have been a source of some satisfaction to designer Alec Issigonis when Ford GB announced their front-wheel-drive Fiesta baby car in July 1976. The transverse engine layout follows his successful policy with the BMC Mini and its successors. In fact, the Fiesta is a brave step by Ford and combines three schools of thought—one Anglo-German, one America, and one from Ghia of Turin. Truly European, its production is a joint effort shared by factories in Valencia, Dagenham, Saarlouis (Belgium), and Cologne, and all except Cologne will play a part in its final assembly. (GB)

Celebrating the 70th anniversary of the founding of the house of Lancia, a new high-powered luxury sedan was launched on the international market. Designed by Pininfarina, the body displays advanced styling, and an even more spacious interior is achieved by the use of front-wheel drive. The use of a 2,484-cc flat four engine—an area in which Lancia has plenty of experience—adds to the compactness of the design, and twin overhead camshafts allied to an overall advanced specification result in a top speed of 120 mph. The Gamma is available in sedan and two-door coupe forms. (I)

A successful year brought a fistful of new-look Lincoln models in 1977. The Continental Mark V follows the prestigious IV, and the division's redesigned intermediates all carry the Cougar motif in 1977. As well as extensive re-styling, Lincoln-Mercury fitted the DuraSpark system in 1977—a sophisticated electronic second-generation ignition that gives higher plug voltage during the starting and running cycles—and improved catalytic converters. Shown here is the 1977 Cougar Brougham, powered by the standard 302-cu in V-8 engine (351 in California). (USA)

Ironically, the last of the GM family to introduce a version of the T-car, which was originally based on an Opel body design, Opel's Kadett City utilizes the Opel 4-cylinder engine and four-speed transmission and is available with GM automatic transmission. The City has an 1,196-cc engine, but a smaller 993-cc unit is available. The larger-engined model, with compression stepped up to 9-1 (and known as the Strasbourg), offers automatic as an option. In its fastest form the City achieves 87 mph. (D)

First announced in 1970, the Opel's Ascona was given a longer wheelbase and newly developed suspension for 1977. It was also announced for the first time in right-hand-drive form for the UK market. Available in two- and four-door sedan form, the Ascona offers a choice of three engines—the 1.6-liter in 60-bhp or 75-bhp form and the well-tried Opel 1.9-liter unit with an output of 90 bhp. With the latter, the Ascona can achieve 104 mph. Automatic transmission is available as an option on all three variants. (D)

Latest in the Renault family of "fives" is the 5 GTL, a three-door fwd sedan that embodies fold-away rear seating for rapid conversion to an estate car. Derived from the R.5, and retaining all the fundamental qualities of that car, it employs a 4-cylinder, light-alloy head engine of 1,289 cc developed from those used in the 5 TS, 12, and 15 TL and can return a thrifty 60 mpg. With city driving in mind, deep polyester bumper shields are employed and are extended along both flanks of the car. Impacts of up to 4 mph can be absorbed without damage. (F)

Functional elegance stamps the 1977 Plymouth Gran Fury Brougham, shown here in two-door hardtop form. Automatic transmission, power steering, and power-assisted front-disc brakes are included in the package, and customers have the choice of both the 400- and 440-cu in V-8 fitted with the Chrysler electronic "Lean Burn" system, giving improved acceleration and response. Available also as a four-door sedan and in Suburban station wagon form, the 1977 lineup dropped the Custom model from the range. (USA)

Aimed at the European "middle-car" range, the 1977 Renault 14 embodies a transversely mounted 1.2-liter fwd power unit capable of nearly 90 mph, departing from traditional Renault layout. Compact, and with an overall length of only 13 ft 2 in, it has five doors and five seats (with fully adjusting rear seating) which will make it popular with the European family man. (F)

Coming at a time when British Leyland badly needed a potent weapon in the prestige market, the Rover 3500 is the success story of the year. It offers 125 mph, five doors, five gears (with genuine true overdrive on fifth) five seats, and a 3½-liter engine of thoroughly sporting demeanor and astonishing fuel frugality. The result of a five-year gestation period, the steel monocoque body bears a frontal resemblance to the Ferrari Daytona. (GB)

Powered by Renault's well-proved 90-hp, 4-cylinder, 1,647-cc engine and incorporating fwd all-independent suspension and an inbuilt safety specification derived from the Renault basic research vehicle, the 20/TL is a spacious five-seater designed to fill the gap between the 2.7-liter V-6 30TS and the 16 TX. Offered with 4-speed manual or three-speed automatic transmission, it has a top speed of 102.5 mph and commendable fuel consumption of from 25 to 31 mpg. (F)

Originally set up in 1953, and concentrating upon Fiat designs, SEAT of Spain have now developed an individuality of their own, and even include a Mercedes-engined model in their range. The 1200 Sport shown here boasts an 1,197-cc east-west configuration engine giving front wheel drive and 67 bhp at 5,600 rpm. Suspension is independent by McPherson strut, and the car is capable of a respectable 100 mph maximum. (E)

Claimed as "The estate car with (almost) everything," Toyota's 1977 Crown Custom Estate is a new version of the Crown with seven-seat accommodation and technical specifications almost identical with the 2.6-liter Crown Super Sedan, plus top-hinged tailgate. At just over 15 ft long, this estate car is a spacious vehicle by any standard, with a maximum lowered-seat cargo area of 27 sq ft. (J)

Smallest of the range of Toyota models is the 1000, available as a two-door sedan and in the estate version shown here. The latter model overcame some earlier criticisms of lack of space which the sedan attracted. The 993-cc front-mounted (rear-drive) inclined four-power unit is extremely economical and runs happily on low-grade gasoline. Suspension is unsophisticated, with rear semi-elliptics allied to McPherson struts at the front, but, like most Japanese cars, the 1000 offers a high level of initial equipment, including radio, reversing light, reclining seats, and inertia-reel seat belts. (J)

This rear view of the 1977 British TVR 3000M shows the unconventional rear end, redesigned to give improved airflow. A new air intake involving reshaping the front end has decreased air resistance, and the intake also acts as a spoiler apron, giving the low-lying sports car more ground adhesion at speed. Its 2,994-cc unit will take the car up to 120 mph, and the 0 to 60 acceleration figure of 7.7 sec is rapid enough to satisfy the expert sporting driver. (GB)

Styled by Guigario, like most of the current Volkswagen range, the Golf is the complete antipathy of the old Beetle, with its front wheel drive and water-cooled engine. Available with a choice of 1,100-cc or 1,600-cc transverse mounted units, buyers can also opt for three or five doors. A high-lifting tailgate and folding rear seats convert it quickly into a versatile estate; the transmission is filled with oil and sealed for life; and the chassis, steering rack, and door locks require no lubrication. All this, 35 mpg and a top speed of 100 mph (on the 1,600-cc LS variant) makes the Golf a worthy successor to the Beetle. (D)

The direct result of the marriage between the car-making interests of DAF and Volvo, the Volvo 66 is basically a DAF 66 with re-styled front end and an uprated specification in line with Volvo's more exacting standards. While the Variomatic drive is retained, the old centrifugal clutch is supplemented by a vacuum servo-operated unit, and Volvo's by now well-known rubber-covered bumpers are fitted. Produced in 1,100 and 1,300 form, the car gives Volvo a valuable foot in the common market and a badly needed economy car in their range. (H)

Introduced at the 1975 Earls Court Show, the Cavalier was designed to strengthen Vauxhall's representation in the slot between their Magnum and the VX range. Available in two- and four-door sedan form, or as a coupe (the latter with 1,897-cc cam-in-head ohv engine), the standard 1977 Cavalier wears a 1,584-cc ohv engine and four-speed transmission, although GM automatic transmission is an available option with both engines. (GB)

Designed to fill the "mid range" between the 66 and the 240 series, the 1977 Volvo 343 DL places a strong accent on safety while still providing a spacious three-door, five-seater sedan with very little less passenger area than the 240. Fitted with trans-axle automatic transmission, the top speed is 90 mph and the 1,397-cc engine, with chain-driven camshaft and carburetor built into the engine block, returns a commendable 32 to 35 mpg. (S)

Based on the earlier 15 TL, the Renault 15 GTL shares its predecessor's body shell and mechanics, but boasts a considerably altered frontal appearance and a simplified facia that does away with some of the Gallic idiosyncracies previously encountered. The 1,298-cc 60-bhp engine is shared with the 12TS and enjoys an enviable reputation for longevity and toughness, despite having been developed from the old 845-cc Dauphine unit. (F)

With a top speed of 140 mph and acceleration in the order of 0 to 60 mph in 7.4 seconds, the 450 SEL is the most powerful and expensive car in the 1977 Mercedes-Benz range. Fitted with an overhead camshaft 6.9-liter V-8 engine said to be virtually maintenance-free for the first 50,000 miles of its life (apart from oil changes) and three-speed torque converter automatic transmission allied to Mercedes-designed power steering, the 450 SEL maintains the high standard of luxury that customers expect from this company. (D)